Texas Ranger Tales II

by
Mike Cox

Republic of Texas Press

Library of Congress Cataloging-in-Publication Data

Cox, Mike.
  Texas ranger tales II / by Mike Cox.
     p. cm.
  Includes bibliographical references and index.
  ISBN 1-55622-640-3 (pbk.)
  1. Texas Rangers—History Anecdotes. 2. Texas Rangers Biography
  Anecdotes. 3. Frontier and pioneer life—Texas Anecdotes.
  4. Texas—History—1846-1950 Anecdotes. 5. Texas—History—1951-
  Anecdotes. I. Title.
  F391.C783   1999
  976.4—dc21   99-27602
                                                         CIP

Republic of Texas Press is an imprint of Wordware Publishing, Inc.
No part of this book may be reproduced in any form or by
any means without permission in writing from
Wordware Publishing, Inc.

Printed in the United States of America

ISBN 1-55622-640-3 (pbk)   1-55622-740-X (hbk)
10 9 8 7 6 5 4 3 2 1   10 9 8 7 6 5 4 3 2 1
9904

All inquiries for volume purchases of this book should be addressed to
Wordware Publishing, Inc., at 2320 Los Rios Boulevard, Plano, Texas
75074. Telephone inquiries may be made by calling:

(972) 423-0090

Contents

Foreword

by **Elmer Kelton**

As a spokesman for the Department of Public Safety, Mike Cox is in a particularly advantageous position to seek out stories of the legendary Texas Rangers. In this second volume he tells more tales about the lawmen who have worked, struggled, and sometimes died to bring order to Texas, from the state's earliest times to the recent past. Where possible he has separated fact from fable, though often that is difficult to do with subjects who so often in their own time appeared much larger than life.

In this book we meet men like John Salmon "Rip" Ford, farmer, surveyor, physician, newspaperman, and civil servant as well as Ranger and Civil War commander of Texas Confederate troops. Ford served without complaint wherever duty called him, whether behind a desk in some stuffy government office or in the saddle on long and dangerous treks far out on the Indian frontier. He led troops to victory in the final battle of the Civil War. Unknown to him and those who rode with him on the Gulf Coast, the war had already been declared over.

We meet hard-fighting Bigfoot Wallace, about whom it was said that it would be hard to tell a lie because the truth was so amazing. Indeed, many tall tales were told about him, some instigated by him, but his record needed no embellishment. He was a veteran of many a desperate Indian fight and participated in the notorious drawing of black and white beans in a Mexican prison to determine which captives would live and which would die, yet he managed to reach the ripe old age of eighty-one still able to go on an occasional toot and get himself thrown into jail.

There is the unlikely yet true story of the ranger "Horse Marines" who disobeyed orders and captured two supply ships off the Gulf Coast, diverting to needy Texas rebel forces a quantity of food, arms, and ammunition intended for Santa Anna's invading Mexican army.

From more recent times, Cox tells about such well-remembered Rangers as Tom Hickman, sometime cowboy and rodeo hand who enjoyed performing in the limelight but could hold down his end of a gunfight, as he once demonstrated in foiling a Clarksville bank robbery. When the smoke cleared, two robbers lay dead on the street.

Rounding out the book are miscellaneous Ranger anecdotes such as the one about Captain John Hays' Rangers, who climbed high up in a bee tree to take its store of honey and spotted twenty-five Comanches getting ready to charge. And the time Bigfoot Wallace unknowingly ate a skunk. And the time a veteran Ranger showed a rookie a thing or two about modern cooking by baking their dinner on the engine block of his automobile while they traveled down the road.

And the story about the Ranger captain who prayed just before his company attacked a bandit band: "Lord, if you'll just stick around for a few minutes, you'll see the goll-dangdest fight you ever witnessed. And Lord, if you can't see fit to help us, just please don't help them."

All in all, this is a grand collection of stories and characters, most of them little known until now. Mike Cox knows how to spin a good yarn.

"Texas Ranger Kitties Do!"
An
Introduction

This is a book of short, true stories about the Texas Rangers, but I'll start this introduction with a short, true story about my daughter, Hallie. There is a connection.

When Hallie was four years old we were in Amarillo visiting my father and his wife, Bill and Nina Cox. Linda and I were in the guest bedroom with Hallie when she stepped into a pair of my Western-style boots and wobbled up the hall into the living room. The size-10 boots came up to her hips, but she was able to shuffle across the carpet in them. Approaching my father, Hallie began meowing like a cat. Meowing was one of her favorite things to do in her mid-fours.

"Hallie," her grandpa said, "I don't think kitties wear cowboy boots."

At that, Hallie stopped meowing, narrowed her eyes, and spread her booted feet defiantly.

"Texas Ranger kitties do!" she said firmly.

Hallie's remark cannot be taken as typical of a child not yet in kindergarten. She knows, of course, that I work for the Texas Department of Public Safety—which includes the Rangers. And she often hears me talking about today's Rangers and those of yesterday. She understands that I write stories about the Rangers, but the term "media relations," which is what my day job is about and what brings me into contact with the modern Rangers, is still a bit abstract for her. Even so, her "Texas Ranger kitty" line certainly shows that she has already picked up on the mystique those two words—Texas Ranger—seem to have for people.

The Rangers observed their 175th anniversary in 1998. They are approaching their third century of protecting the people of Texas. The Ranger reputation, thanks to their real-life accomplishments and their fictional exploits in novels like *Lonesome Dove* and on television shows like

Walker, Texas Ranger, is worldwide. Hallie was right. *Texas Ranger kitties do!*

When *Texas Ranger Tales* was published in 1997, I had no idea I would do a second volume. Neither, I'm sure, did Republic of Texas Press. But then a wonderful thing began happening: Lots and lots of people bought the book. And then the second-largest writer's organization in the United States, the 1,600-member Austin Writer's League, honored the book with its annual Violet Crown Award as the best work of nonfiction for that year.

That much-appreciated recognition and plenty of eager readers would be reason enough to undertake a second volume, but there were other factors: I like to tell stories, and there is no shortage of Texas Ranger tales to tell.

Texas Rangers Tales II has twenty-two nonfiction stories on the Rangers, from the days of the Republic of Texas to modern times. I selected these stories because they are interesting and new. The book contains a fair amount of material—and images—never before published. Scouting for this information has been a wonderful adventure. But I am no Lone Ranger writer.

My name appears as author, but two other people helped immeasurably with my research and writing: Betty Wilke Cox, my mother, and Linda Aronovsky Cox, my wife. My mother is a great researcher and editor. Like a seasoned horseback Ranger, once she starts cutting for sign she's usually going to find what she's looking for. And though I've been writing professionally for more than thirty years, I'm still learning things from my mother when it comes to writing and editing.

Linda played a big part in editing the first book. The same goes for this one. She also helped with the research. Linda dug up the account, for instance, of Bill Blevins' Ranger adventures. She discovered his wonderful recollections—never before published—on the Internet among scores of Depression-era Works Progress Administration interviews now available online. Linda also found valuable information on the Spanish flu epidemic of 1918. In addition to helping research and edit the book, she kept the Cox family Ranger camp running and did most of the Hallie wranglin' while I was clicking the computer keyboard.

Finally, I have decided to commission all those who helped with *Texas Ranger Tales II* as Cox's Rangers. The muster roll of this elite group of friends and researchers includes: Donaly Brice, Texas State Library; Suzanne Campbell, West Texas History Center, Angelo State University; Felton Cochran, proprietor of the Cactus Book Shop in San Angelo, one of the most interesting bookstores in Texas; Mrs. Alex Early, Fort Worth Public Library; Ralph Elder, Center for American History at the University of Texas, without whom, it's not much of an exaggeration to say, no piece of Texana would ever be written; Marta Estrada and Terri M. Grant, Border Heritage Center, El Paso Public Library; Ken Hopkins, manager, Genealogy/Local History, Fort Worth Public Library; and Larry Hodge of Mason, who did not contribute specifically to the research of this book but allows me to hunt on the El Vente Ranch in South Texas while I'm unwinding from book writing.

Also, Byron Johnson, who as director of the Texas Ranger Hall of Fame and Museum in Waco has revitalized the facility; Gary McKee, fellow book lover, wrecked-ship junky, and able researcher; Tela Mange, Assistant Chief of Media Relations for the Department of Public Safety, who kept things under control when I took off some time to finish this book and who reminded me that "Texas is a big state"; Rick Miller, county attorney of Bell County and fellow member of the National Association for Outlaw and Lawmen History (NOLA); John Reeves, great-grandson of Ranger Captain J. H. Rogers; Carol Roark, manager, Texas/Dallas History and Archives, Dallas Public Library; Margaret Rose, Corpus Christi Public Library; Sloan Rodgers of Austin, enthusiastic researcher and Bigfoot Wallace's one-man fan club; Anna Salazar, Hondo Public Library; Christina Stopka, librarian/archivist at the Moody Texas Ranger Memorial Library; Leslie-Rahye Strickland, curator, Bell County Museum, Belton; Sally Victor, Larry Hodge's wife, who helped provide some material on Ranger John Dunn; Dr. Harold J. Weiss Jr.

of Leander, a retired history professor who has done much research on the Rangers; Dr. Ralph W. Widener Jr. of Dallas, who gladly shared his extensive research on John Salmon "Rip" Ford; Cheri Wolfe, archivist, Texas and Southwestern Cattle Raisers Association; and Ann Woods, Local History Collection, Cooke County Library, Gainesville.

Now, in true Ranger tradition, the tough part: Sorry, folks, but you have to furnish your own guns and horses.

Mike Cox
Austin, Texas

Isaac Burton and
His Horse Marines

Twenty Rangers did not single-handedly save the newborn Republic of Texas that summer after General Antonio Lopez de Santa Anna's defeat at San Jacinto, but their bold and unconventional action not only added to the further misery of the retreating Mexican army, it helped to feed and equip a contentious but ragtag Texian military.

After Santa Anna's escape on April 21, 1836 and his capture the following day, the rest of the Mexican army—at first uncertain of their leader's fate—retreated. No doubt fearing summary execution despite Sam Houston's assurances that he would not be harmed, Santa Anna wrote orders to his second in command, Italian-born General Vicente Filisola, to withdraw from Texas. On May 14 the captive Mexican general and interim Texas president David G. Burnet formalized the policy in what came to be called the Treaty of Velasco.

Santa Anna ordered Filisola to proceed to San Antonio, but after conferring with his staff, the general moved instead toward Victoria. His men were hungry. Fleeing east after the fall of the Alamo in March, the Texans—soldiers and civilians alike—had stripped the province of supplies. No pigs or cows remained for Filisola's soldiers to seize and butcher, no ears of ripened corn to strip from their stalks. But Filisola believed the foraging would be better along the Victoria road. Then too, he expected supplies and reprovisioning to come by sea.

The general made his decisions based on reality. The congress in Mexico City, outraged by news of Santa Anna's debacle, ordered a continuation of the war. If Filisola could not do it, they would name a commander who could.

Houston, laid up with a bullet hole in his ankle suffered during the rout of Santa Anna, turned his command over to thirty-two-year-old Secretary of War Thomas J. Rusk. The newly commissioned brigadier general marched westward with roughly 350 men and by late May set up headquarters at the old Spanish presidio of La Bahia, outside Goliad. Rusk knew Filisola's army must be nearby. But under the terms of the Treaty of Velasco, Rusk could come no closer than five leagues—about thirteen miles—of the retreating Mexicans. Still, prudence demanded that he remain aware of Filisola's movements. The Mexican army had violated assurances before, namely in the massacre two months earlier of Colonel James Fannin's men at Goliad.

On May 29 Rusk ordered Isaac Burton, commander of a twenty-man Ranger company, to scout the flat coastal plain from the Guadalupe River to Mission Bay near Refugio. Four days later, at Refugio, the Rangers learned from one of their scouts that a suspicious vessel had been seen in Copano Bay.

Burton and his men rode the twenty miles to Copano, a port on the mid-Texas coast dating to Spanish colonial times. It never amounted to much as a settlement, but it overlooked one of the deeper bays in Texas, and it was the nearest point on the Gulf of Mexico to the key towns of Goliad and San Antonio. The Rangers made a cold camp, unwilling to expose their position.

Before daybreak on Friday, June 3, Burton ordered his men to conceal themselves and their horses in the brush on the bluff above the bay. In the distance they could see a two-masted, coastwise schooner riding at anchor. Ominously, she flew no flag. But she was close enough to shore for one of the sharp-eyed Rangers to make out her name: *Watchman*. Though the name indicated American registry, Burton was suspicious. At 8 A.M. the major sent two of his men—unarmed—to signal the ship as if they were in distress.

When the vessel ran up an American flag the Rangers did not respond. Then she pulled down the Stars and Stripes and hoisted the Mexican flag. Seeing that, the two Rangers beckoned the captain to send a boat ashore.

Quickly and quietly, the Rangers captured the five occupants of the boat—the captain and four sailors. Leaving four men behind to guard the prisoners, Burton ordered the rest of his company into the boat and they put out for the schooner.

As soon as the boat came alongside the ship, the Rangers scrambled aboard and took it without resistence.[1]

The Ranger captain sent a rider to Goliad with a hastily written communique to General Rusk reporting the successful seizure. Sometime later that day Rusk scratched out a reply to Burton. The general's reaction to the incident was less than effusive. He enclosed a copy of the armistice, as he called the document signed by Santa Anna and Burnet, noting, "You will see by this article that hostilities are to cease." The general also reminded Burton that the Mexicans still held at least forty Texan prisoners. "You will [therefore] return the provisions on board the Vessel and permit her to proceed as she may choose under directions of those who had the charge of her." Rusk then ordered the captain to return to headquarters as soon as possible, "keeping a good look out as the rear division of the Mexican Army are within nine miles of this place proceeding on towards Mattamoras [sic]."

Rusk can be excused for being a bit curt in his response to Burton. As he penned the letter, his men were busy collecting the charred, scattered remains of Fannin's executed command. The day after Burton captured the *Watchman*, Rusk presided over a military funeral for the slain Texans. He became so emotional he could not finish his speech.

Though Burton's reply to Rusk seems not to have survived, the Ranger either ignored the order to release the schooner or succeeded in changing the general's mind.

Ten days later, on June 13, Rusk wrote Burnet a long letter in which he noted in passing, "You will no doubt hear of the capture made by Capt. Burton. I had sent him out simply on a scouting expedition when he ran foul of the ship. You have inclosed [sic] copies of the letters and order which I transmitted to him upon the subject, he has not yet returned from Copano."

The Ranger's insubordination—if that's what it was—was a minor thing compared with the myriad other problems that Rusk and other officials of the interim government faced. The Republic's Ranging Corps and their comrades-in-arms among the regulars were not the most disciplined of fighting forces. In fact, some elements of the army bordered on mutiny after they learned that Santa Anna would be released from captivity as per the terms of the treaty signed by Burnet. In September Rusk wrote to the president asking for reference books on the subject of courts-martial. He needed to read up on "correct legal principles" to enable him to carry out Sam Houston's order to try a lieutenant colonel in the army for "high treason & Sedition."

Meanwhile, Burton intended for some of his Rangers to stay behind with the company's horses while the rest of the men escorted the schooner to Velasco. Unfavorable winds, however, prevented them from leaving the bay for two weeks. During the imposed wait, with little else to do but guard their prize, it is not wildly imaginative to assume that Burton and his Rangers sampled some of the captured ship's stores, possibly including the captain's liquor.

Twelve of the men rode out to continue scouting the coast.

On the evening of June 17 the Rangers—now only eight in number—sighted sails in the distance. Two other schooners approached the bar outside the bay.

"Lie low and keep dark," Burton ordered his Rangers. The next morning Burton directed the captain of the *Watchman* to raise the Mexican colors above the seized schooner. The Ranger then instructed him to signal the captains of the other two vessels "a politic and earnest invitation" to come aboard and "take a glass of grog." The captains soon lowered boats and made for the *Watchman*. Once the men were on board, Burton informed them that they were his prisoners "except" (as a contemporary newspaper later reported the event) "on their parole of honor not to disobey his orders until the vessels and cargoes were conveyed to Velasco." The captains agreed to those terms. The newspaper account did not mention whether the captives got their promised grog.

When the *Commanche* (in contemporary accounts, the word was spelled with two "m"s) and *Fanny Butler* made it across the bar and sailed close to the *Watchman*, Burton and his Rangers rowed out and boarded both schooners. Again, the seizures were accomplished with only threatened force. Like the *Watchman*, both vessels were laden with supplies intended for the Mexican army.

With his Rangers divided among the three schooners, Burton's captured flotilla—American vessels chartered by the Mexican government—set sail on June 19 to the northeast for Velasco, a busy port at the mouth of the Brazos River and the current seat of Texas government. From there, the vessels were escorted to Galveston for condemnation proceedings. Admiralty Judge Ben C. Franklin ordered the cargoes of the three schooners forfeited to the Republic of Texas but released the vessels to their American owners.

Isaac Burton and his Rangers captured three schooners laden with supplies for the Mexican army. (Author's collection)

Burton's seizure was a windfall for the financially strapped young Republic. The cargo—which included barrels of pickled pork, beef jerky, 30 containers of rice, 90 barrels of beans, and 400 barrels of bread as well as gunpowder, ammunition, bayonets, and muskets—was valued at $25,000. By way of comparison, all the Mexican property seized by Houston's army at San Jacinto sold for only $11,184.87. Not only were the supplies captured by Burton prevented from reaching the Mexican army, they fed and armed Texas troops.

Matagorda merchant and militia member Ira Ingram noted the significance of the seizure in a letter to William Parker on June 30:

> [The] vessels were freighted with supplies for the enemy. He [the Mexican command] expected to meet them at Copano on his return. But they have been transferred to us. His subsistence, to enable him to open a campaign, has now to be replaced by other shipments from New Orleans packed from Matamoras, hauled on carts and waggons [sic], or driven to the frontier, on the foot.

President Burnet, also understanding that Burton had dealt the Mexican army a severe logistical blow, seems to have taken no offense at the Ranger's impertinence in detaining the ships against Rusk's orders, if indeed that had been the case. When Burnet got a letter from some of Burton's men complaining about lack of supplies (it can easily be conjectured that the Rangers felt they should have been entitled to some of the arms they had helped capture), the president wrote them a conciliatory letter, but one clearly supportive of Burton:

> The Government and the people of Texas know how to appreciate the generous and chivalric motives which prompted you to abandon the comfort of homes, abounding in the good things of life, to peril your lives in defence [sic] of our liberties; and we only regret that we have not the means of contributing more largely to your comforts.
>
> Major Burton has the reputation of a brave man, an enterprising officer and a gentleman, and his inability to equip you according to his alleged promise, is probably to be attributed to the general destitution of the country.

The president went on to tell the men, "If you have been disappointed, in your expectations in the Ranging Corps, you are free to attach yourselves to such other portion of the Army as you may prefer.... Your engagement to Major Burton will be considered absolved by your incorporation with the main Army."

The man who oversaw the capture of three ships without firing a shot was born Isaac Watts Burton in 1805 at Cherokee Corner in Clarke County, Georgia. He was raised and educated in the Augusta area. Receiving an unsolicited appointment to the United States Military Academy in 1822, he attended classes until February 1823 and formally withdrew the following May 25. The future Ranger's brief West Point career ended, he later wrote, "Not...for want of capacity, but from utter want of application and perfect recklessness of consequences."

Leaving New York, Burton returned to Georgia where, he recalled, he "followed or prosecuted...various modes or schemes for a living in none of which however have I been either eminently successful or peculiarly unfortunate so that little of interest or importance could with due regard to veracity be recorded." His writing style gives away one of the "various modes" he "followed or prosecuted"—the study and practice of law. Commas and periods, however, apparently were not as important to him as finding just the right word.

He had come to Texas in January 1832, following a blue-eyed belle whose parents had decided to move west. That September, as required of Texas colonists by Mexico, Burton had converted to Catholicism. He also married the sweetheart he had trailed to Texas, "and with all the formalities was made a useful member of society. Nor have I yet thought that I erred in so doing unless it be from the consciousness that I have a helpmate worthy of a far better man than I now am or am likely to be."

On August 2, 1832, Burton participated in the Battle of Nacogdoches, the first armed clash between Anglos and Mexicans in the province of Coahuila and Texas. Three years later, with Texas on the eve of open rebellion against Mexico, the General Council of the provisional government of Texas appointed Burton as captain of a ranging company on November 29, 1835. His first assignment, detailed in orders from Sam Houston's acting adjutant general dated December 19, was to set up a recruiting station at Sabine. He was to submit weekly reports to Major R. M. Williamson, commander of the Ranging Corps.

By the spring of 1836 Burton was serving in Texas' regular army, such as it was. As a private in redheaded Henry Karnes' cavalry company, Burton fought at San Jacinto. At some point after the battle—the date has not been ascertained—Burton again was given command of a Ranger company. Correspondence from the Republic period variously referred to him as captain or major. In function, as commander of a company, he did the work usually expected of a captain. But the president of the Republic had referred to him as a major. By late summer, he apparently had been promoted to colonel.

No matter his official rank, Burton soon acquired a lasting and colorful nickname for his men—the Horse Marines. Unfortunately, the designation was not entirely accurate. The word "marine" implied that the men involved in the incident were regular military. In fact, they were not part of Texas' regular military establishment. They wore no uniforms. They were Rangers, a paramilitary force paid from government funds. A better, though admittedly less catchy, choice would have been "Marine Rangers." But thanks to a Kentuckian who wrote a letter to his hometown newspaper describing the capture of the three schooners, Burton's Rangers are firmly anchored in Texas history as "Horse Marines."

The sobriquet is attributed to Edward J. Wilson, a Kentucky colonel who came to Texas as commander of the Lexington Ladies' Legion. Its members were all male, of course, but it was a memorable name. Colonel Wilson reported the exploits of Burton and his Rangers in a letter the *Kentucky Gazette* published on July 28, 1836:

> On yesterday [news came] of the capture of three Mexican vessels by a troop of horses—these you will call 'Horse Marines' I suppose.... It may be well enough to explain how this wonderful circumstance happened. The vessels entertained no doubt of that place being in the possessions of the Mexicans. The first one sailed up, and cabled [signaled], without discovering her mistake. The troops went aboard

and seized her. The next day they saw two other vessels coming; they hoisted the Mexican flag on board the vessel they had taken. The coming vessels seeing this, came up carelessly, and cabled, when they in turn were visited by this company of Horse Marines—a new kind of troops, you will say—and the last two shared the same fate as the first.

Perhaps on the strength of the fame he gained in the bloodless seizure of the three Mexican vessels, Burton placed his name on the ballot in the September 5, 1836 general election, seeking to represent the Nacogdoches area in the Republic's First Congress as one of its fourteen senators. He lost in a contested election to Robert A. Irion. Though Irion won the seat, in a Senate lottery to determine the length of each member's term he was one of the new lawmakers to draw a one-year term. Less than a month after his opponent took his seat in the Senate, the newly elected president Sam Houston, on November 10, 1836, appointed Burton to serve as a commissioner to negotiate a treaty with the Indians.

When Irion's term expired a year later, Burton prevailed at the polls in the next election. He served in the Second, Third, and Fourth Congresses, from September 25, 1837 to February 5, 1840.

As senator, Burton played a role in selecting a site for the Republic's capital. He was one of five commissioners appointed by President Mirabeau B. Lamar in January 1839 to choose a location for the seat of government. Though Burton initially argued that the capital should be on the more populated Brazos River, the commissioners eventually unanimously agreed on a village on the Colorado River called Waterloo. Soon after, the name was changed to Austin.

Burton was an ally of Lamar in his political battles against former President Houston and his supporters. The senator, like Lamar, shared little of Houston's tolerance for Indians; Burton was hawkish in his outlook. He voted against a bill sympathetic to Cherokee land claims in East Texas and was one of only three senators to oppose a bill outlawing dueling in Texas.

Between congressional sessions, Burton practiced law in Nacogdoches. With Charles D. Ferris as a partner, he also published the *(Nacogdoches) Texas Chronicle*.

Burton moved to Crockett, in Houston County, in 1841. He died there in January 1843, only thirty-eight years old.[2]

The story of his most notable exploit as a Ranger did not gain wide circulation until 1855, when Henderson Yoakum's two-volume *History of Texas* was published. The book contained a 235-word description of the seizure of the three supply ships, which has served as the primary source for most of its subsequent retellings.

One of those stories appeared in the *San Antonio Light* a century after the celebrated seizure of the schooners. "'The Horse Marines' had made Texas Ranger history on the briny deep," the newspaper writer concluded. "Think of them [the Rangers] as hard-riding, automobile-pushing landlubbers if you will, but remember they took three ships."

Using the term "briny deep" stretched it a bit, but Burton and his men[3] did more than add to the Ranger legend. Arguably, they had helped save Texas from a renewed Mexican campaign aimed at nullifying the effect of San Jacinto.

Seizure of the three vessels was the only known occasion Rangers operated as marines. (Drawing by Roger Moore)

...... ✪ ......

Notes

1 Octavia Rogan's 1938 account of the incident says Burton hid his men in the brush and went alone to the beach. Pretending he needed help, he fired his pistol into the air to signal the schooner. When the schooner's boat neared the shore, she said, someone in the landing party spotted the rifles of the concealed Rangers. The ensign ordered the boat back to the *Watchman*, but Burton threw his lariat over the dingy's prow and pulled it ashore. Burton then had five of his men change clothes with the sailors. The other Rangers got in the boat, posing as hungry castaways. When the Texans climbed aboard the schooner, Burton asked for food. The Rangers captured the vessel when the captain turned to order something for the "castaways" to eat. Though the version seems a bit movie-like, one of the sources Rogan listed was a descendant of Burton. The story may have some elements of truth, particularly the castaway ruse. Roping the boat, however, seems a bit exaggerated.

2 Burton is buried in the old section of Glenwood Cemetery in Crockett. In 1936, during the Texas Centennial, a gray granite historical marker was erected at the site. The day of the month he died is not on the marker and does not appear in any known biographical sketch.

3 In addition to Burton, the seven Rangers who accomplished the second round of seizures were listed in the *Telegraph and Texas Register* as Andrew J. Grey, William Fitzmorris [?], Willie or Willis [?] [last name illegible], Samuel Smith, [first name not published] Barnes, Chester Blackwell [?] and James Boylen.

Sources

Carroll, Bess. "Horse Marines: Texas Rangers Capture Three Mexican Vessels." *San Antonio Light*, June 2, 1936.

Cox, Mike. *Historic Austin: An Illustrated History*. San Antonio: Historical Publishing Network, 1998, pp. 12-13.

Dixon, Sam Houston and Louis Wiltz Kemp. *The Heroes of San Jacinto*. Houston: Anson Jones Press, 1932, pp. 309-311.

Houston County Historical Commission. *History of Houston County, Texas 1687-1979*. Crockett: 1979, pp. 221-222.

Huson, Hobart. *El Copano: Ancient Port of Bexar and La Bahia.* Refugio: *The Refugio Timely Remarks*, 1935.

Jenkins, John H., ed. *The Papers of the Texas Revolution 1835-1836.* Austin: Presidial Press, 1973, pp. 135-136, 258, 374, 511, 513-514.

Pierce, Gerald S. *Texas Under Arms: The Camps, Posts, Forts, & Military Towns of the Republic of Texas 1836-1846.* Austin: The Encino Press, 1969, pp. 37-38, 57-58.

Rogan, Octavia F. "Major Isaac Watts Burton of the Horse Marines, Charter Member, Grand Lodge of Texas." *Texas Grand Lodge Magazine*, March 1938, pp. 125-126.

Spaw, Patsy McDonald. *The Texas Senate*, Vol. 1. College Station: Texas A&M University Press, 1991.

Telegraph and Texas Register. Houston, August 2, 1836.

Texas House of Representatives. *Biographical Directory of the Texan Conventions and Congresses, 1832-1845.* Austin: Book Exchange, 1941.

Yoakum, Henderson L. *History of Texas from Its First Settlement in 1685 to Its Annexation to the United States in 1846*, Vol. II. New York: 1855, pp. 181-182.

It Would Never Do To Run

When thirty-four-year-old "Wildcat" Z. N. Morrell said he was going to Texas that spring of 1836, his fellow Tennesseans openly called him a fool. They predicted he would not get far beyond the Sabine River before he and his wife and two children were killed by the Mexican army or the Indians.

The Baptist preacher, however, opted to place his trust in God—and his doctor. His physician told him if he stayed in Tennessee he would probably die of consumption. Even relocation to a different clime likely would only delay the inevitable, his doctor said. Morrell—a friend of Sam Houston and David Crockett—figured he would just as soon die in Texas.

"Seldom in life had I turned back," he later wrote. "We traveled on."

Within a few months, a group of Texas Rangers would be mighty glad Morrell made the choice he did.

He came alone to Texas in the fall of 1835, planning to meet Crockett for a bear hunt at a place called the Falls of the Brazos. The falls, at a point on the river where a ten-foot drop-off occurred, was one of Texas' better known landmarks. The river was shallow there and easy to cross. Too, it marked the confluence of several Indian trails. Though well beyond the established frontier of Texas, a few settlers had built cabins in the vicinity of the falls as early as 1834. They called their community, which was a part of Sterling Robertson's colony, Sarahville de Viesca. For protection against Indians the colonists had built a log stockade surrounding several cabins and called it Fort Viesca. In December 1835, after Benjamin Milam died in the Battle of Bexar at San Antonio, the fort and community were renamed in his honor.

Morrell liked what he saw at the falls. After some exploratory travel elsewhere in the province, he went back to Tennessee and, in April 1836, returned with his family to Texas.

Not long after he got to Texas, Morrell learned of his friend Houston's victory over General Antonio Lopez de Santa Anna on April 21. After sparing the captured Mexican dictator's life against the wishes of most of the men in his army, Houston did not have to be particularly persuasive in getting Santa Anna to order his other forces to return to Mexico.

With Texas safe from Mexico at least for the time being, Morrell returned to the settlement at the Falls of the Brazos, arriving in the fall of 1836. He found that Fort Milam had been occupied by Rangers that summer to protect the settlers from Indians.

Acting Secretary of War Frederick A. Sawyer's order to Colonel Robert M. Coleman to raise three companies of mounted men "for the Special purpose of protecting frontier inhabitants" had made it plain what the provisional government of Texas wanted: "You will at all times bear in mind the purpose for which you are detached, the complete protection of the inhabitants will not, it is hoped, be disappointed."

Paid $25 a month, these Rangers had to provide their own horses, weapons, equipment, and clothing. The Republic furnished them ammunition when it was available and, occasionally, beef. Most of the time the Rangers lived off the land, their meat coming from wild game, primarily deer and turkey. After twelve months service to the Republic they were entitled to a land bounty of 1,280 acres.

One of the men who enlisted in the Rangers under this Congressional Act was twenty-three-year-old George Bernard Erath, who signed up on October 1, 1836. As a lieutenant under Captain Thomas H. Barron, Erath was sent to Fort Milam at the Falls of the Brazos.

Born in Vienna, Austria, on January 1, 1813, Erath had come to Texas in 1833 via New Orleans and Cincinnati, Ohio. He worked as a surveyor, but in 1835 he became a Ranger, soon demonstrating he could sight a rifle as accurately as a transit. On March 1, 1836, he enlisted in a more traditional military unit for service during the revolution, taking part in the Battle of San Jacinto. After the war he went back into another Ranger company, though he continued doing survey work as well.

Early in January 1837, Morrell later recalled, the commander at Fort Milam came to him with worrisome news. An inventory of supplies showed that the Rangers had fewer than five rounds of ammunition per man. Worse, the government of the new republic had no funding for replacement. Even if money were available, lead and powder were in short supply everywhere in Texas.

Ammunition was scarce, but not Indians. Nearly 15,000 Indians were believed to inhabit Texas at that time. People of European descent living in Texas still outnumbered the Indians, but the ratio was only two to one. Newly elected President Houston had tried to reach out to the Comanches, the fiercest of the tribes found in the republic, but Anglo movements up the Brazos and Colorado Rivers had begun to cause friction. Four months before Erath joined the Rangers, Comanches attacked Isaac Parker's family fort near the headwaters of the Navasota River, only thirty-five miles from the Falls of the Brazos. The Indians killed five men and kidnapped five people—two women and three children.

(Author's collection)

Morrell summarized the situation: "We were of course in imminent peril."

It is not clear from Morrell's memoir whether the Rangers suggested a way he could help, or whether it was his own idea.

"This was *our country*, and *our fight*," Morrell continued with his story. "Although it was painful under the circumstances to leave my loved ones, exposed as they would be, my sense of duty to the land of my adoption required that I should go alone to the town of Washington [-on-the-Brazos]…in search of powder and lead, at my own charges."

Armed with his Bible, Morrell saddled up and began moving down a well-worn trail along the Brazos. He traveled thirty miles—a hard day's ride—without seeing another human.

At Nashville, the first settlement downstream from the falls, he found "six or eight families" and gathered them together for a sermon.

After spending the night with one of the families, Morrell continued his journey down the Brazos. Shortly before sundown, he reached Washington-on-the-Brazos, then one of the principal towns of the republic. Again, he rounded up the faithful, preaching the first Baptist sermon ever heard there.

In the morning, Morrell set out to find the powder and lead needed by the Rangers. Checking every store in town—which did not take long—he located only one keg of lead. No merchant had any gunpowder for sale.

"As much lead as was thought to be safe was put into my saddle-bags," he wrote. "Several bars were bent, a string run through them, and balanced on the horn of the saddle."

Morrell mounted his horse and took the trail to Independence, hoping to find gunpowder there. But in that community, as in Washington-on-the-Brazos, no one had any gunpowder in stock. "It looked more like dependence then than independence," he wrote of Independence with tongue in cheek.

Leaving Independence, he headed back upriver. Swimming his lead-laden horse across a swollen creek to take up the trail to Jackson's trading post, located about eight miles from Nashville, Morrell arrived at the store late in the day.

Tired and as hungry as the wolves that prowled the Brazos River bottoms, the preacher asked the proprietor of the remote trading post if he had any gunpowder. A load had recently arrived by wagon from Columbia, Morrell learned, but all the powder had already been spoken for.

In his recollections, Morrell did not spell out his exact words, but he must have fallen back on the oratorical skills that served him well behind the pulpit. The preacher, "shivering then in my cold, wet clothing," described the perilous conditions upriver and his long ride in search of powder and ball.

"After some threats made on both sides of the question," Morrell wrote, the proprietor and his other customers agreed that Morrell could buy six canisters of powder for the Rangers.

His mission accomplished, Morrell did not linger. Back at Fort Milam with the much-needed ammunition late on the fourth day of his trip, the preacher had covered 240 miles. The Rangers were elated. Morrell must have been exhausted.

"There was no danger of starvation with plenty of ammunition," he wrote, "and hopes were entertained that the Indians could now be held in check."

But on January 4, not long after Morrell's return, a Ranger sergeant hurried in from a scout to report that he had found a dozen sets of Indian tracks about as many miles from the fort. The tracks told the story plainly: The Indians were headed "down the country" toward the settlements.

Morrell had solved the Rangers' ammunition problem, but the men also were short of horseflesh. Erath's superior, a Lieutenant Curtis, suggested he take a party of Rangers out on foot in pursuit of the Indians. Erath knew better than that.

Delayed by rain and discussions of strategy, Erath and ten Rangers finally rode out of the fort about 9 o'clock on the morning of January 6. Also along were three volunteers, including two brothers "not fifteen years old," and four other men headed for "the settlements" who said they would tag along with the Rangers as long as they stayed on the main trail down river.

Only four of the Rangers had been in a fight before, but the others were ready to give it a try. Erath was somewhat concerned about their weaponry, but there was nothing he could do about it. Though all of the Rangers carried long arms, one had a smoothbore musket and another just a shotgun. Only three of the Rangers, including Erath, had a pistol. The lieutenant did take some comfort in knowing that all his men were good shots.

"We went on a few hours longer before he struck the Indian trail," Erath would write. "And behold! instead of a dozen the signs showed a hundred, all on foot."

At first the trail was easy enough to follow. It led to a freshly abandoned campsite, a cluster of shelters made of grass laid over sticks. Each of the eight or ten huts could accommodate as many Indians, the Ranger lieutenant judged.

Though the tracks were plain, the Rangers could not tell what tribe they were trailing. They could be "wild Indians," Erath speculated, or Indians from farther east, possibly Caddo. "An Indian, or an old hunter, could have told by the cut of the moccasin soles to what tribe they belonged," he recalled, "but we did not have the art, and were perplexed on the subject."

Twenty-three miles out of Fort Milam, the Rangers lost the trail, but not for long. Riding on in the general direction Erath believed the Indians to be traveling, the Rangers soon heard the Indians calling to each other in a creek bottom. The voices sounded no more than a half mile distant.

Not wanting the Indians to hear him, Erath pulled his Rangers back another half mile, sending two men forward as scouts. They found the Indians camped on high ground at a bend of Elm Creek, not far from present-day Rosebud in Cameron County, and slipped back to the main body of Rangers to report to Erath.

After dark it snowed. The Rangers spent a frigid night wrapped in their blankets. They could not start a fire for fear of alerting the Indians. As daylight approached on the morning of January 7, the Rangers left their horses tied and crept to within rifle range of the Indian camp. Erath counted at least one hundred Indians, and the warriors were all well armed. As the Ranger watched the Indians tending to their morning cook fires, a dog trotted up and began sniffing in the direction of the Rangers. Expecting to be detected at any moment, Erath decided to attack.

The Rangers attacked as the Indians sat around their morning campfires.
(Author's collection)

Though outnumbered, the thirteen Texans picked targets
—Erath told them to try not to double up on any one
brave—and cut loose with their long arms. Stepping aside
from the cloud of smoke, Erath saw that the volley had
killed or wounded several Indians. As the Rangers and volunteers struggled to reload, the uninjured warriors began
returning fire.

If all the Rangers had pistols, Erath realized, they could
have rushed closer and continued to press the surprise attack.
As it was, the Indians quickly understood that they had
numerical superiority and moved to outflank the Rangers.
Soon Ranger David Clark and Frank Childress, one of the
civilians, were hit.

With lead cutting through the branches of the trees, Erath
told the Rangers to fall back and split into two groups. As the
men followed orders, the Indians charged. The lieutenant
fired at the first Indian he could get a bead on, standing his

19

ground to protect the Ranger retreat. About thirty feet away he saw another Indian. The Indian looked fiercely at the Ranger while vigorously working to reload his rifle.

Seeing this, Erath knew there was no room for precision in his own reloading. Taking no time for careful measurement, the Ranger stuck his powder horn nipple down his barrel and stopped pouring when he thought the load was about right. Just as Erath rammed in a ball, the Indian finished loading his rifle and leveled it at the Ranger.

Quickly shouldering his gun, Erath managed to fire at the same time as the Indian.

The two adversaries each went down, but only one of them was dead. Erath had put a bit too much powder into his rifle, though fortunately not enough to blow it up. The kick of the discharge had knocked him over.

"George, are you hurt?" one of the retreating Rangers yelled.

"No, I ish not hurt," the Austrian-born Ranger replied. "My gun knocks down before and behind." Or so wrote the Reverend Morrell, thirty-five years later.

Safe for the moment, Erath soon was in trouble again. Each time he tried to climb out of the creekbed he slipped on the icy bank. Finally, two of his men came to his rescue and pulled him up on the other side.

Erath fired at the same time the Indian did. (Author's collection)

The Ranger told his men to continue falling back in squads. Executing a classic tactic of the muzzle loader era, one squad fired and fell back to reload while another squad came forward to start the cycle over again. This slowed the Indian attack, but they kept coming.

Suddenly the Indians charged again. Screaming and brandishing their weapons as they ran, they broke through the Ranger line and cut off Erath and his sergeant, who scrambled for safety in a nearby ravine. There they found Ranger Clark, clearly mortally wounded. When Clark saw that the gunlock on the sergeant's rifle had been ruined by an Indian ball, with another round having bent his ramrod and a third shattering his powder horn, he offered his rifle and gear, but the sergeant would not take it. Erath did not write in his memoir what he and the sergeant said to Clark. Perhaps they assured him that they would come back for him. Maybe, realizing he was dying, he insisted on giving them a message for his family and friends. Whatever transpired, it could not have taken long, because the Indians were moving closer. Running in separate directions, the two Rangers managed to rejoin the other Rangers.

As abruptly as it began, the Indian attack abated. When the Rangers heard screaming they knew why. The Indians had found Clark. Soon after Clark's cries died out, the Rangers heard a new sound, a chorus of low, eerie wailing. The Indians had begun to mourn their own dead. The Rangers ran back to their horses and made for another Ranger outpost on the Little River in what is now Bell County. Both sides had had enough fighting.

Morrell got the details of the fight firsthand. When the Rangers returned with reinforcements to the scene of the battle, they found that Clark had been scalped and his hands cut off. The body of Childress, one of the civilians, was sitting against a tree. He had died from a gunshot wound, escaping mutilation.

"But for this engagement," Morrell later wrote, "this large body of Indians would very soon have been in the settlements below, killing, burning and stealing; for they never came down in such large numbers in those days without desperate ends in view.... Now I felt a thousand times paid for my long ride to Washington, amid so much exposure and anxiety. This work was done with the ammunition that I procured on that trip."

Painting of Erath in his later years. (Author's collection)

Erath left the Rangers not long after the Elm Creek fight to continue his career as a surveyor. He laid out the town sites of Caldwell, Waco, and Stephenville and served in the Congress of the Republic of Texas and later, after statehood, in the Texas Legislature. Erath and Erath County were named for him.

In 1886, blind and in failing health, Erath dictated his memoirs—including his adventures as a Ranger and his role in the Elm Creek fight—to his daughter. He died on May 13, 1891, and is buried in Waco's Oakwood Cemetery.

A life-size bronze statue of Erath—a surveyor's tripod over his shoulder and a rifle in his hand—was donated to the City of Waco by a local bank in 1976. Dedicated on June 26 that year, the sculpture by artist Robert Summers has traveled almost as much as Erath did. First it was in Indian Spring Park, then it was moved to the Waco Convention Center. Later, it was moved to the Texas Ranger Hall of Fame and Museum in the Fort Fisher complex on the Brazos River at I-35.

Sources

Erath, George B. *The Memoirs of Major George B. Erath, 1813-1891 as Dictated to Lucy A. Erath*. Waco: Waco Heritage Society, 1956.

History of Falls County, Texas. Marlin, Texas: Old Settlers and Veteran's Association of Falls County, Texas, 1947.

Morrell, Z. N. *Flowers and Fruits From The Wilderness; or, Thirty-Six Years in Texas and Two Winters in Honduras*. Waco: Baylor University Press, 1976, reprint of 1872 and 1886 editions.

Pierce, Gerald S. *Texas Under Arms: The Camps, Posts, Forts, & Military Towns of the Republic of Texas, 1836-1846*. Austin: The Encino Press, 1969.

Waco Heritage & History. Vol. 7, No. 4, Winter 1976, pp. 1-8.

Wilkins, Frederick. *The Legend Begins: The Texas Rangers 1823-1845*. Austin: State House Press, 1996, pp. 32-36.

His Friends Called Him Foot

Fannie Bramlette and her sister Alice perched on the split rail fence jabbering like two excited mockingbirds, watching impatiently for their father.

Finally, the two girls spotted his small spring wagon, painted a stylish green, rolling around a bend in the rutted road that passed their Frio County ranch house. A big man the children knew only as "the captain" filled the seat beside

MacHenry Bramlette. The captain's white beard dipped over the front collar of his long blue military overcoat, a garment stripped of all insignia. His saddle horse, Kitty Sue, and his two hounds, Sowder and Rock, trailed behind the wagon. His rifle, Sweet Lips, lay close at hand in the bed of the wagon.

His full name was almost as long as his six foot two inch, 240-pound body, but for most of his life William Alexander Anderson Wallace was best known as Bigfoot Wallace. His friends called him Foot.

Plains Indians continued to threaten the lives and livestock of the settlers of Southwest Texas in the early 1870s. Bramlette had pulled an arrow from a neighbor whose place had been raided. Now he began worrying about Wallace. The old frontiersman lived alone on Chicon Creek. Whenever news spread of Indian raids in the vicinity, Bramlette rode over to check on Wallace, fearing he had been scalped for sure.

Early engraved image of Wallace. (Author's collection)

Not that Wallace was a doddering old-timer. He was still on the sunny side of sixty. But even his reputation as an Indian fighter would not save him if a raiding party caught him alone. Not wanting to wound an old man's pride, Bramlette pointed out how obliged he'd be to have another hand around to share the workload. Finally, he convinced Wallace to come and live with the family, at least until the Indian troubles ended. It turned out, however, that Wallace would live with the Bramlettes the rest of his life.

"We children always loved him dearly," Fannie Bramlette wrote years later, "and I think he was one of the kindest and most understanding men I ever knew."

A lifetime hunter, Wallace helped supply the Bramlettes with fresh meat. He also worked in their garden. Beyond that, he was something of a surrogate grandfather to the Bramlette children. As a natural storyteller with plenty of material to choose from, he kept the children entertained.

Wallace was born in Virginia on April 13, 1817. Within a couple of decades, the lure of adventure and free land drew many to the new republic west of the Sabine. But Wallace came to Texas in 1837 for one specific reason: revenge. He wanted sanguinary retribution for the death of his oldest brother, Sam, one of the 330 men under Colonel James Fannin executed by the Mexican army at Goliad. Wallace's cousin, William, and a more distant relative, Major B. C. Wallace, were shot down in the same massacre.

His father tried to talk him out of his grim mission, but the young Virginian swore that he intended to devote "the balance of my days killing Mexicans."

Wallace did not spend his entire life as an avenging angel, but he made a good start of it. More than once in the process he nearly got killed himself.

By the time Wallace reached Texas, the formal fighting with Mexico was over. He spent his first three years in the new republic obtaining the land bounty his brother had been entitled to for his military service, hunting the bountiful game he found, and trying to earn a living. Those interests took him to Bastrop, La Grange, San Antonio, and in 1839, Austin, the newly selected site of the Republic's capital.

The first human blood Wallace spilled on Texas soil was not an act of retribution but in the interest of survival. The incident occurred west of Austin when Wallace tracked down a notorious Waco Indian known for his towering height and the size-fourteen moccasin prints he left behind. The brave had an Indian name, but to the early settlers of Travis County he was known as "Bigfoot." Encountering the Waco near Mount Bonnell, Wallace wounded him with a rifle shot. Though the Indian escaped with his life, he lost his nickname. William Alexander Anderson Wallace became Bigfoot.

Wallace liked to say he lived in Texas five years—two of them after becoming a Texas Ranger—before he developed a taste for two of the young republic's more popular beverages: coffee and whiskey.

Sometime early in 1840 (no official paperwork providing an exact date is known to exist), two ranging companies, one in San Antonio and one in Victoria, were created to cope with a growing Indian problem. By midyear eleven companies were in the field operating under various authorizations. The men furnished their own weapons and mounts. The companies had inadequate funding and no centralized command structure, but they did not lack for work.

The captain of the San Antonio company was John Coffee Hays, a Tennessean born the same month and year as Wallace. Before taking up ranging, Hays had been working out of San Antonio as a surveyor. He knew the country, and though he had no formal military training, he quickly demonstrated that on some instinctive level he knew how to fight. Hays also knew how to pick fighters. One of the men he accepted into his company was Wallace.

Most of what is known about Wallace's service as a Ranger comes from the work of two writers who knew him. John Crittendon Duval published *The Adventures of Big-Foot Wallace* in 1870, and Andrew Jackson Sowell wrote a book about the old frontiersman shortly before Wallace died.

Except for the two books, details of Wallace's experiences with Hays and his men are as scarce as official paperwork listing the men who served under Hays. Though the specifics of their activities are hazy, their three-part mission remained clear: to protect the western frontier against hostile Indians, to safeguard the San Antonio area—and the roads leading to it—from Mexican outlaws and sometimes the Mexican military, and to curb cow-thieving Texans. The Rangers quickly developed a reputation for effectiveness.

When Hays and his men rode into Austin in 1841, their arrival made news. According to the *Austin City Gazette*:

> Capt. Hays, of the San Antonio Spy Company, arrived here on Monday morning last. He had pursued a party of Mexicans to within twenty miles of the Rio Grande, he however, avoided engaging them in consequence of the great disparity of numbers; the Mexicans numbering about three hundred men.

Hays and his Rangers were brave but not stupid. When it came to a fight they tried to set their own terms.

The article in the Austin newspaper went on to carp about the proliferation of cattle thieves in Texas:

> The trade between the Rio Grande and Bexar is represented as being broken up in consequence of the Mexican Guerrilla Bands intercepting all caravans they can lay hands on returning from Texas; while the Texian cow-thieves are playing the same game on all they can catch, either going or coming.
>
> Could not some plan be devised by which a dozen or two of these cow-boys could be caught and punished? *They* are doing far more mischief to the country than the Mexicans.

Actually, Hays' Rangers *were* doing something about cattle and horse thieves, no matter their ethnicity: Indian, Mexican, or Anglo. The Rangers practiced the so-called *ley de fuego* (law of fire) borrowed from Hispanic culture. Simply put, they operated as a one-stop judicial system. Those suspected of serious crimes against the Republic's citizens—if they were not killed outright in fighting with the Rangers—were summarily executed. Texas had a judicial system, but the drawing of exacting criminal complaints, indictment by grand jury, and the careful weighing of evidence by judge or jury were not always practiced on the frontier.

Wallace told Andrew Jackson Sowell of one such case of instant justice.

"On one occasion," as Sowell later wrote the story, "they captured a notorious [horse thief] named Antonio Corao. Four of the company were detailed to shoot him, namely: 'Bigfoot' Wallace, Chapman Woolfork, Sam Walker, and William Powell. The execution took place at the head of the San Antonio River, above town."

The old Ranger told Sowell that Corao was dispatched sometime between 1840 and 1841. If that time frame is correct, it would have precluded Walker's participation in the event since he did not come to Texas until 1842. There is no known documentation of Wallace's story, but why would Hays want to officially report an extralegal act? Considering the conditions that existed in Texas at the time, the story is plausible.

Some years later, Wallace later related, he was with a group of acquaintances at the old Southern Hotel in San Antonio when a man who was *muy borracho* came up to him.

Slurring his words, the drunk demanded to know: "Are you Bigfoot Wallace?"

"Yes," Wallace replied. "What do you want?"

"You helped kill Antonio Corao," the man said, crowding in on Wallace menacingly, "and he was a friend of mine."

"He was?" Wallace said, pulling a long knife he knew how to use very well. "I want to kill all his friends, too!"

Word of that kind of attitude on the part of the Rangers spreading across Texas and down into Mexico had a pacifying effect. Late in 1841 the Houston *Telegraph and Texas Register* noted:

> The spy company under Captain Hays has been very efficient.... So great has been the protection and security resulting from the active enterprise of this excellent officer that the settlements are extending on every side around the city [of San Antonio] and the country is assuming the appearance of peace and prosperity that characterized it previous to the Revolution.

The peace and prosperity were short-lived. Residents in San Antonio woke up on September 12, 1842—a Sunday morning—to find the community blanketed in an early autumn fog and surrounded by twelve hundred Mexican troops under General Adrian Woll. While Hays and his men were out on a scout, the Mexican force had marched on San Antonio along the same route used six years earlier by General Antonio Lopez de Santa Anna. Woll's soldiers recaptured San Antonio with ease. The Ranger captain lacked enough men to go up against the Mexicans. He pulled back to report what had happened.

Woll's occupation of San Antonio was more a demonstration of Mexico's ability and willingness to reclaim its lost lands than invasion. After nine days in San Antonio, Woll proclaimed that Texas was still a Mexican province and returned to Mexico.

Prior to the arrival of the Mexican force, Wallace and fellow Ranger Nathaniel Mallon (later sheriff of Bexar County) were dispatched to Austin for more powder, percussion caps, and lead. When the Rangers reached the new capital, a collection of log cabins and milled-wood government buildings on the edge of the frontier, they learned two residents had been killed by Indians less than two miles from town. Fearing a similar fate, no one had yet stepped forward to bring the men's bodies in for burial. Wallace and Mallon offered to handle the task. Bolstered by the attitude of the Rangers, a few volunteers went with them in the wagon.

After bringing the two bodies into Austin, the Rangers headed back for San Antonio via Seguin with the supplies they had picked up. At Seguin, a settlement on the Guadalupe River, they found Captain Hays, who was there awaiting reinforcements.

Hays' Rangers soon took part in the September 25, 1842 Battle of Salado Creek in Medina County, an indecisive engagement. Both the Texans and the Mexicans claimed victory. General Woll lost enough soldiers, however, to convince him that Texans did not share his government's view that Texas still was a part of Mexico.

For Wallace the battle was the beginning of a series of events that did not have much to do with being a Ranger but had a lot to do with luck—both good and bad.

Wallace left Hays' company to join the Somervell Expedition, a Texas invasion of Mexico in retaliation for Woll's incursion. But the effort never had the full support of the government and became more of a filibustering adventure than anything else. As such, it was the beginning of an extended misadventure for Wallace. When General Alexander Somervell disbanded the Texas troops at the border, Wallace joined another group determined to wreak havoc and seize property in Mexico. They soon were captured by the Mexican army, and every tenth man was ordered executed. The men fated to stand before a firing squad were selected by a lottery. Men who drew white beans from a clay pot lived. A black bean meant death. Wallace drew a white bean, but he and the other Texans were kept in Perote Prison at Veracruz until 1844.

Once more back in Texas, Wallace rejoined Hays' Rangers on December 30, 1844. As is the case with most early-day Rangers, the holdings of the State Archives in Austin shed little light on Wallace's service.

Not long after he took up rangering again, Wallace survived what he later said was the hardest fight of his life, worse than anything he had experienced in Mexico.

"Jack Hays ordered the Rangers out after the Indians had made a raid on the settlements in the east," later related F. E. Harris, who as a young man in the 1890s heard many of Wallace's stories of his days in the Rangers. "They pursued the redskins, who were Comanches, up into the Concho country."

Wallace was one of forty Rangers who soon found themselves in a fight with hundreds of Indians, Harris said.

"At Paint Rock," he continued, "they were surrounded and a fight lasting two or three days took place. When it started Wallace said he made a scout and came back to camp reporting that the odds were against them. He said they fought the whole Comanche tribe, and finally beat them."

The Rangers killed dozens of Indians but miraculously had only one man wounded. They fought so hard the Comanches lost their will and decided to leave well enough alone.

"Wallace told me about this fight under a live oak tree in John Thomas' yard at Big Foot [Texas] in July 1892," Harris said. "I know [Wallace participated] for I got a letter from another survivor of the fight who told me that Wallace was ...there."

Surviving records show that Wallace re-enlisted three times, serving under Hays until September 28, 1845. Hays' muster rolls for 1840, the year Wallace said he first joined the legendary Ranger captain, are missing, the result of one of several early fires, a theft, or some other circumstance. While historian Frederick Wilkins wrote that he believed "there is some doubt about his [Wallace's] claims to have been with Hays as an official member of [the 1840] company," absence of evidence is not necessarily evidence of absence. Barring the discovery of "new" old documents in some collector's or distant descendant's estate, Texas probably never will know when Wallace's service transcended from voluntary to official and to what extent, if any, some of his recollections constituted hearsay.

Wallace's record as a Ranger during the Mexican War is better documented. He went straight from Hays' company to the 1st Regiment of Texas Mounted Volunteers as a first sergeant under Captain Richard A. Gillespie. On June 29, 1846, he was elected first lieutenant, which placed him second in command. He was discharged from the regiment on September 29, 1846.

Four years later, though the American victory in the Mexican War had for the time being eliminated most problems with Mexico, Wallace went back to work as an Indian-fighting Ranger. In 1850 he was captain of a Ranger company of eighty-six men stationed near Fort Inge in Southwest Texas. When Wallace was appointed to raise the company, the *Texas State Gazette* in Austin called him "an energetic and experienced old ranger." He was only thirty-three, and most of his Rangers were in their twenties. But the newspaper was dead right in calling the captain energetic and experienced.

As usual, the Ranger company was created to deal with a pressing problem. Hostile Indians along the frontier posed a grave danger to settlers. Wallace's company was one of four mustered into service to scout for Indians along and below the Nueces River and above the Rio Grande. Though funded by the state, the Rangers were under the command of the U.S. military.

In the early summer of 1850, Captain William J. Hardee, commander of Fort Inge, was ordered to undertake a major campaign against the Indians. The operation would be a joint federal-state effort.

Hardee sent Wallace to scout down the Nueces River while regular cavalry worked along the Frio River. The bluecoats encountered Indians first, skirmishing with a small band on July 11. Wallace, meanwhile, rode from the Nueces toward Corpus Christi to check a report of an Indian attack in that vicinity. Finding no trace of hostiles, the Ranger captain received orders from Hardee to move back up the Nueces to Espantosa Lake in present-day Dimmit County. This time Wallace found Indians.

"Captain Wallace...met with a considerable body of Indians on the left bank of the Nueces," Hardee later reported, making a wild fight sound routine. "They attacked him, and in the encounter Wallace reports to have killed seven Indians, wounded nine, and to have three of his own command wounded. None of the other parties met with Indians."

The fight took place at a feature called the Black Hills, about sixteen miles from present-day Cotulla, in late July. As their horses picked their way upriver, Wallace and the nineteen Rangers he had with him struggled with an enemy as merciless as Comanches: thirst. Their canteens hung empty on their saddles. Just then they wanted water a lot more than they wanted Indians. Every time they approached a known water hole, they found it bone dry.

Wallace told his men he was sure they could find water along Todos Santos Creek, which emptied into the Nueces in the Black Hills area. The Ranger captain was right. There was water. Unfortunately for the parched Rangers, a band of eighty Comanches had already staked out the water hole. They were not inclined to offer hospitality.

"Dismount, men," Wallace ordered. "Secure your horses. Quick!"

The Indians mounted their ponies and began riding toward the Rangers, but they stopped and pulled back when they saw rifles pointed in their direction. Wallace guessed they had expected the Rangers to flee in the face of such overwhelming numbers. When the Indians realized the Rangers intended to make a stand, it made them more contemplative. Wallace could see their leader, gesturing wildly among the braves for them to attack. The Comanches did not seem to share the chief's enthusiasm for an immediate advance on the Rangers.

The chief charged alone toward the Rangers until he realized his warriors were not following him.

As Sowell got the story from Wallace:

> The chief again harangued his warriors and came to the charge, not even looking back to see if they were coming. This time the brave old chief came within gun shot, and seeing some of the rangers about to fire, dexterously threw himself on the opposite of his horse.

Three rifles cracked about the same time and the horse fell dead in his tracks. The chief quickly regained his feet, not being hit himself, and looked for his braves to see if they were coming to his assistance.

With a heavy muzzle-loading rifle that had once belonged to Jim Bowie, Wallace dropped the chief with a shot that went through both of his hips. When the Indian hit the ground, he let loose with "two loud peculiar whoops," which the other Indians answered. This time, they charged.

"For a time," Sowell wrote, "things were mixed." After a short but intense fight, the Indians pulled back, leaving several dead. The thirsty Rangers rushed to the water hole to get a drink. To their horror, they found it full of maggot-covered cowhides. The Indians had camped there to make lariats. They must have had another source of drinking water.

The captain and ten men advanced to the next water hole. Two wounded Rangers stayed behind along with one Ranger who was suffering from a fever and six others on the verge of heat exhaustion. Sure enough, the hole held water. But the Indians held the water hole.

Returning to the site of the first skirmish, as Sowell later related it, Wallace told his men that he "was going to have a drink of water if he had to fight Indians all day for it."

With some of the acutely thirsty men, Wallace went back to the water hole and the Comanches.

"A battle commenced at once," Sowell wrote, "but a close charge led by Wallace and [Edward Dixon] Westfall drove the Comanches away."

Wallace did not give chase. He and his men threw themselves down and lapped water alongside their horses. After filling their canteens, they rode back to the other Rangers and gave them water.

In the morning Wallace and his men collected all the blankets, shields, bows, and arrows they could find and, along with some horses and mules they had captured, returned to Fort Inge.

In his report to headquarters, Hardee briefly acknowledged Wallace's participation in the campaign:

"The volunteers, with few exceptions, evinced much energy and intelligence, and obeyed my orders."

Wallace's company was discharged on May 4, 1851, but reorganized the following day for another six months. The captain's departure from the state payroll marked his last service as a Texas Ranger, though as a private citizen and while working as a stagecoach driver along the San Antonio-El Paso route, he would do more Indian fighting.

An incident near the end of his long life shows that the people of Texas, at least in the final years of the nineteenth century, did not much care whether Bigfoot Wallace had fought in the name of duty, necessity, or money.

"His bearing and address is that of a man who has carried the enthusiasm of youth into old age," a writer who called himself "Brazos" wrote of Wallace in 1898. "His eyes kindle with a martial fire as he moves restlessly about, never happier than when engaged in telling stories of old wars and desperate hand-to-hand encounters with savage Comanches."

Those who knew him best, however, understood that Wallace had not lived to a ripe old age by taking unnecessary chances, even though he never backed off from a fight.

"Hell, Wallace would get behind a tree as quick as any of us," former Ranger Sam McCombs remembered.

Over the years Wallace lost most of his hearing but never his verve. After moving in with the Bramlettes, he was content to stay in Frio County most of the time but occasionally took to the road to visit old friends or attend a reunion. One such trip brought him to Seguin, where he teamed up with Robert Hall, an old comrade from his ranging days. When word got out that the two Texas heroes were in town, a delegation of local citizens showed up at their hotel with a band. They asked Hall to come outside and make a speech.

Big Foot Wallace never missed a chance to attend an old-timer's reunion. (Photo by L.A. Wilke from author's collection)

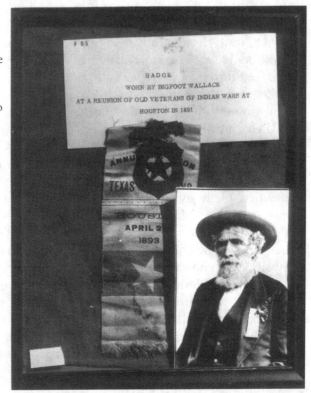

"I can't make a speech," Hall replied, "but, boys, if you will play me something quick and devilish I will dance a jig."

When the band broke out into "his Satanic Majesty's nocturnal revelry," as the *St. Louis Globe-Democrat* later reported, "these two old warriors danced on the pavement like boys, and the people of old Seguin hurrahed and told them that they owned the town."

Though he didn't mind a little dancing or whiskey, in his later years Wallace had taken up reading the Bible.

"I never saw him in church but twice in my life," F. E. Harris said of Wallace.

However, the old Ranger did attend the first night of a two-day revival in Frio County. But after Wallace got word that the preacher had said, "I'd rather baptize Bigfoot Wallace than Grover Cleveland," he didn't come back for the second night.

By 1898 Wallace was living in the home of Fannie Bramlette, now a married woman with a family of her own. Another guest, though only on a temporary basis, was George Holcombe. He had been publisher of the nearby *Devine News* but had sold that newspaper and planned to move to Luling to take over the newspaper there. He also had published Sowell's book on Wallace. While staying with Fannie (Mrs. W. W. Cochran), Holcombe folded the folios and prepared the book for binding.

Christmas passed and the last year of the nineteenth century began. The old Ranger, who had celebrated his eighty-first birthday the previous spring with whiskey-laced eggnog, was not as lively as usual. He had a mild fever and a cold. But on January 6 he told Fannie he was feeling better. He sat outside her house for a spell, leaning his chair against the wall. When he came in, he visited with Holcombe and his old friend, MacHenry Bramlette, late into the night.

The next morning, Bramlette, Holcombe, and Wallace were talking as Wallace sat on his bed putting on his shoes. Suddenly, Fannie, who was in her kitchen, heard her father's voice: "Foot, Foot! What's the matter?" When she rushed into the room, her father and Holcombe were gently laying the old man back on the bed.

"He's gone," Holcombe said.

Wallace was buried in the Longview Cemetery in Frio County the following day. A month later his casket was disinterred and taken to Austin for burial in the State Cemetery with full military honors.

A small museum in the tiny Frio County community named in his honor is the only Texas memorial to Wallace other than his gravestone. The marker bears a short epitaph for a tall man: "Here Lies He Who Spent His Manhood Defending the Homes of Texas. Brave, Honest, and Faithful."

Early postcard image of Wallace Museum at Big Foot, Texas in Frio County. (Author's collection)

On January 7, 1999, a century after the old Ranger's death, readers of the *Austin American-Statesman's* obituary page may have been a bit startled to see a vintage photograph that looked out of place in a late twentieth-century newspaper. "Capt. W. A. A. 'Bigfoot' Wallace," read the caption under the one by two column-inch image, "Frontiersman and Early Austinite/April 3, 1817–January 7, 1899/Buried–State Cemetery Austin, Texas." The notice was paid for by a young admirer of Bigfoot, Sloan Rodgers of Austin. "I just thought he deserved some recognition," Rodgers said of the memorial.

Texas tale teller J. Frank Dobie summed up Wallace's life best: "He was a mellow and convivial man.... Without directing events, he was there when they happened."

Sources

"Brazos." (Author unknown). *Life of Robert Hall: Indian Fighter and Veteran of Three Great Wars*. Austin: State House Press, 1992, reprint of 1898 edition, pp. 6, 107-121.

Duval, John Crittenden. *The Adventures of Big-Foot Wallace, the Texas Ranger and Hunter*. Macon, Georgia: Burke, 1870.

Farris, Frances Bramlette. Edited with an Introduction by C. L. Sonnichsen. *From Rattlesnakes to Road Agents: Rough Times on the Frio*. Fort Worth: Texas Christian University Press, 1985, pp. 34-49.

_____. "The Domestication of Big Foot Wallace." *Southwest Review*, Winter 1944.

Rodgers, Sloan. Interview with the author, January 31, 1999.

Smith, Thomas Tyree. *Fort Inge: Sharps, Spurs, and Sabers on the Texas Frontier 1849-1869*. Austin: Eakin Press, 1993, pp. 40-44, 49-50, 189-190.

Sowell, A. J. *Life of "Big Foot" Wallace The Great Ranger Captain*. Introduction by Mike Cox. Austin: State House Press, 1989, reprint of 1899 edition.

Thompson, Fred. "William Alexander Anderson Wallace." *Austin American-Statesman*, June 13, 1937.

Vestal, Stanley. *Bigfoot Wallace: A Biography*. Boston: Houghton-Mifflin, 1942.

Wilkins, Frederick. *The Legend Begins: The Texas Rangers 1823-1845*. Austin: State House Press, 1996, p. 74.

"Rip" (Rest in Peace) Ford

They sat in a smoke-filled room in San Antonio's Menger Hotel, a young man whose artwork would capture the spirit of the Old West and an old man who had known the sting of what he called "dogwood switches"—Indian arrows.

"I found him a very old man, with a wealth of snow-white hair and beard—bent, but not withered," Frederick Remington later described John Salmon "Rip" Ford. "As he sunk on his stiffened limbs into the arm-chair, we disposed ourselves quietly and almost reverentially, while we lighted cigars."

The thirty-four-year-old Yale-educated artist and writer, introduced to Ford by a mutual friend, began trying to get the octogenarian to start talking, hoping to "loosen the history of a wild past from one of the very few tongues which can still wag on the days when the Texans, the Comanches, and the Mexicans chased one another over the plains of Texas, and shot and stabbed to find who should inherit the land."

The question of inheritance had long been settled by the time Remington met Ford in the first part of 1896. Ford, Remington soon realized, had a big hand in doing the settling.

Remington's interview with Ford appeared in an article he wrote for the following December's issue of *Harper's Magazine*, "How the Law Got Into the Chaparral." Though the artist could turn a passable descriptive phrase, the magazine piece demonstrated that Remington's greatest talent lay in his drawings, not his word pictures. He bungled facts, place names, and other proper nouns (referring, for instance, to the Clear Fork of the Brazos as the "Deer" Fork). Worst of all, he failed to provide context.

Anyone reading Remington's article would have thought Ford a mere aged Texas Ranger with just enough wind left to spin a few yarns about his days on the frontier. While that was true enough, Ford had done much more with his long life than fight Indians, though that certainly brought him fame.

"As far as I can determine," Dallas historian Dr. Ralph Widener Jr. would write of Ford more than a century after Remington had his turn:

> he was...one of the most talented Rangers *ever*: doctor, lawyer, editor, publisher, member of Congress of the Republic of Texas, member Texas Senate and House of Representatives, mayor of Austin and Brownsville...Indian fighter, Texas Ranger, commanded U.S. forces and Confederate forces, helped map out the first road from Austin to El Paso for those men and women going west to the goldfields of California, surveyor.

Born in South Carolina on May 26, 1815, Ford grew up in Tennessee, where his family had moved when he was two. Ford's father ran a plantation, but the young John Salmon was not interested in farming. By sixteen, the well-read teenager was certified to teach school. Three years later he began studying medicine under the tutelage of a doctor in Shelbyville, Tennessee and soon gained a reputation for his successful treatment of smallpox patients. He married a local woman, and a year later he was the father of twins, a boy and a girl.

The wooded hills of Tennessee were a long way from Texas, but news of Texas' struggle for independence from Mexico eventually reached there. Many Tennesseans saddled up to join the fight. Their letters home inspired others, one of whom was Ford. He was training a company of volunteers intent on joining the Texas cause when word reached Tennessee of Sam Houston's defeat of General Antonio Lopez de Santa Anna at San Jacinto on April 21, 1836. Though the fighting was over, Ford still came to Texas, a decision that would cost him his marriage.

The twenty-one-year-old Tennessean settled in San Augustine in East Texas, where he continued practicing medicine. There, Ford met another young man from Tennessee, John Coffee Hays. Neither man had made it to Texas in time to take part in its revolution, but when the need arose, they offered their services as volunteer Indian fighters. Both men proved adept at it.

Earliest known portrait of "Rip" Ford.
(Author's collection)

While continuing to minister to the medical needs of people in and around San Augustine—Ford earned $50 for the surgical removal of a piece of bone from a ten-year-old boy's brain—the Tennessee transplant occasionally worked as a surveyor and began reading the law. In 1841 Ford was granted a law license by the Republic of Texas. Having two means of income soon paid off. He noted in a journal he kept on his legal practice that he received a dozen eggs and some peaches for his successful defense of a man accused of stealing a saddle.

Three years later, with the possibility of annexation to the United States standing as the Republic's overriding political issue, Ford ran for Congress. Receiving more votes than his two opponents combined, Ford was elected as a representative from San Augustine County. This was his second try at gaining public office. Former President Sam Houston had beat him in 1840 the first time he had run for Congress.

As a Congressman, Ford was a staunch advocate for Texas' admission to the Union. His principal argument would shape his thinking for years to come: Texas' frontier had to be protected, and statehood was the best way to accomplish that.

If Texas failed to protect her frontier, he wrote in a letter to the *San Augustine Red-Lander*:

> The Colorado would soon be its limit; the next recess would bring us to the Brazos; the third would not stop short of the Trinity. Thus we would be driven—step by step, from one portion to another, until we could not make a single foot print upon the soil of Texas without incurring molestation. By protecting the frontier...we would keep danger at a distance; we would give an impetus to immigration; we would develop the resources of the country, and would reap a rich harvest.

Ford concluded, "protection and allegiance are reciprocal terms. I care not if a man were placed on the banks of the Rio Grande, and the sands were crumbling beneath his feet, if he claimed to be a citizen of Texas, and demeaned himself as such, I would go for protecting him."

On June 17, 1845, it was Ford who introduced in the Republic's Congress a joint resolution that Texas accept the U.S. Congress' offer to annex Texas if she would adopt a state constitution guaranteeing a republican form of government.

The Texas lawmaking body approved Ford's resolution as well as President Anson Jones' call for a constitutional convention. Ford, not chosen as a delegate to the convention that met at Washington-on-the-Brazos in midsummer, covered the proceedings for a newspaper, the beginning of yet another of his many careers.

In October 1845, newly remarried, Ford and a partner purchased the *Texas National Register,* which had been published in Washington-on-the-Brazos, and moved the newspaper to the capital in Austin. Early in 1846 he changed the name of the sheet to the *Texas Democrat.*

Ford was pro-Houston in his politics, which did not make him hugely popular in Austin, a city that had, only a few years before, resisted at the point of arms the president's bid to remove the government's papers from the capital. "A proposition was made to throw the press and type into the Colorado River," Ford later wrote, "[but] it met with no encouragement. Luckily, the editor indicated great partiality for the place and made all right with the citizens."

His newspaper earned him a little money, and at the age of thirty, Ford was a happy man. But pneumonia took the life of his new wife in August 1846, less than a year after they had married. Grief and circumstances soon combined to steer Ford toward his next career: rangering.

When war broke out with Mexico—an inevitable event once annexation occurred—the United States called for volunteers. Ford's old friend Jack Hays, who had distinguished himself as a Ranger during the days of Texas' independence as a republic, was commissioned to raise seven companies of Rangers for federal service in the war.

With nothing to lose but his sadness at the loss of his wife and firmly believing what he had written about the notion of protection and allegiance, Ford signed up for Ranger duty. His service with Hays along the border and in Mexico steeled him as a fighter and earned him the nickname he would have for the rest of his long life: Rip. As adjutant of Hays' regiment, it was Ford's hard duty to send official word of a Ranger's death to his family back in the states. He politely included the sentiment "Rest in Peace" at the beginning of each message, later shortening it to R.I.P.

When Remington interviewed Ford a half-century after the Mexican War, the old Ranger offered a few anecdotes relating to the conflict, but it was another campaign that clearly burned the brightest in Ford's memory. Ford fought many fights, but his greatest moment as a Texas Ranger came in

1858 when he led a hundred men against an Indian nation, taking on the Comanches nearly five hundred miles beyond the frontier in what became known as the Battle of Antelope Hills.

In his previous campaigns, both during and after the Mexican War, Ford had been a Ranger in function, but he and his colleagues were in reality part of a federal force. As irregulars, they did not wear uniforms, but their arms, provisions, and payroll were federally funded. They were Rangers from Texas, but they were not *Texas* Rangers, a point often overlooked in their histories.

Ford's service in 1858, however, was made possible by a $70,000 state legislative appropriation. Not that state officials did not at first try to get the federal government to pick up the tab in handling the Comanche problem. Governor Hardin R. Runnels appealed to the U.S. military for help, and the Texas-based command agreed, but Washington took no action.

Portrait of Governor Hardin R. Runnels, who commissioned Ford as Senior Ranger Captain. (Author's collection)

In 1857 the Indian situation in Texas was so bad it cost Sam Houston—who was running for governor after returning to Texas from the U.S. Senate—his only electoral defeat. The candidate who beat him was Runnels. In his inaugural address, the new governor asked the legislature to do something immediately to provide protection to the frontier. Senator George B. Erath, a former Ranger, helped push through a bill entitled "An act for the better protection of the frontier." Runnels signed it into law on January 27, 1858.

The following day the governor offered Ford a commission as senior captain of a force of one hundred Rangers. Ford accepted it. "It is an excellent appointment," the *Austin State Gazette* said in an editorial on January 30. "He is an old Indian fighter, and we predict that he will rid the frontier of all annoyance in the first campaign."

The "old Indian fighter" was only forty-three. An early photograph of Ford, discovered more than a century after his death, shows a tall man with big ears and thick dark hair over a high forehead. Napoleon style, he had one gloved hand stuck inside his long buckskin coat. His other hand held a black stovepipe hat. Hanging on his belt was a revolver in a leather holster with a snap cover. He was not smiling for the camera, and he did not look much like an old man.

As distinctive in appearance was the Indian chief Ford and his Rangers would face in battle. No camera ever captured his image, but Po-bish-e-quash-o—whites called him Iron Jacket —must have presented a striking visage. His gaze would have been fierce and defiant, reflecting his belief and that of his followers that he was invincible to arrow or bullet. In battle he wore a coat of Spanish mail, a burnished cuirass removed from a dead European soldier by one of Po-bish-e-quash-o's forebears. The body armor gave him powerful medicine. In battle against other Indians, Iron Jacket pursed his lips and made a show of blowing toward the enemies as if to ward off their arrows.

Ford would be leading his Rangers deep into Comancheria, as their territory on the plains was called, but he had no trouble getting volunteers. The senior captain picked only the best, even mustering out some Rangers already in the field under an earlier legislative act. One member of the expedition who would not be on the state's payroll was Will Ford, the senior captain's father.

A turn-of-the-century drawing of Iron Jacket. (Author's collection)

Weaponry was not as easy a proposition as manpower. The U.S. Army turned down a request for Colt revolvers, since the Rangers were not in federal service. But when the Rangers rode out of Austin one morning near the end of February, most of them were carrying two six-shooters and a rifle. A newspaper reported that the force was capable of firing 1,500 shots before anyone would need to stop and reload. By frontier standards, the Rangers had awesome firepower.

But their ammunition had to stay dry. Each Ranger was issued a leather pannier that Ford called a *cayaque*. The case, which held ammunition and a blanket, was considered waterproof. Following the Rangers were sixteen mule-drawn wagons loaded with other supplies.

The Rangers marched up the Colorado from Austin, then along an upper tributary of the river, Pecan Bayou. By February 27 Ford and his men were camped along the bayou at Chandler, the village that would become Brownwood. His force augmented by more men riding in from San Antonio, Ford stayed in the area long enough for his scouts to assure him there were no hostile Indians between his Rangers and the settlements. He left a small detachment to protect the settlers at Chandler and moved northwest beyond the frontier.

On the Clear Fork of the Brazos, near an Indian reservation set up by the state in 1854, Ford established a base of operations he named Camp Runnels in honor of the governor. Shrewdly, the captain recruited a force of friendly Indians from the reservation, mostly Tonkawas, to join him in the expedition. Then he began drilling his men, training his Rangers to shoot from horseback or afoot. Though he had no formal military training, Ford was an avid reader with a large personal library of books dealing with military tactics.

As the Rangers honed their fighting skills, Indian scouts sent out by Ford to gather intelligence brought back word that they could find no Comanche camps in Texas. But they had learned that the Comanches were concentrated in great numbers along the Canadian River, across the Red River in Indian Territory. Ford had no authority to leave Texas, but on April 22 he left Camp Runnels and headed north. Seven days later he crossed the Red River.

The Rangers and their Indian allies moved slower now, taking time to replenish their meat supply with buffalo. Too, the terrain was tough going for the wagons. The Texans were moving northwest, along the base of the Wichita Mountains. On May 8 Ford's scouts struck a wide, fresh Indian trail. Following the trail, they came to a recently abandoned campsite. Judging from the number of fire rings they found, the scouts estimated they were close on the heels of up to four hundred Indians. When a scout recovered two arrows from a wounded buffalo, Ford had confirmation that the Indians he trailed were indeed Comanches.

On May 11 one of Ford's scouts saw from a distance a lone Comanche hunting buffalo. Watching as the Indian led away a horse piled with fresh meat, the scout learned the way to the Comanche camp.

Fearing another hunter might spot his Rangers, Ford readied his attack. He left his father and two Rangers behind with the muleskinners to guard the wagons and pack animals, ordered his men to check their weapons and gear, and moved out. Reaching the deep ruts of the wagon trail from Fort Smith, Arkansas, to Santa Fe, Ford suddenly saw movement in the distance. Ordering the Rangers and partisan Indians to take cover in nearby ravines, Ford alighted from his horse and walked with Shaply P. Ross, a veteran Indian fighter and leader of the reservation Indians, to higher ground. Focusing his spyglass, the captain confirmed what he suspected—at least three hundred Comanches moving in the distant valley of the Canadian. Amazingly, perhaps because they were over-confident so deep in their own territory, the Indians did not realize they were being trailed. When the Indians rode out of sight, Ford reformed his ranks, ordered his men to keep to the low ground, and resumed his slow stalk.

With the sun getting low, Ford stopped his column to make camp, planning to close ground between the Rangers and the hostiles under cover of darkness. He would charge the Comanches at dawn. But to do that he needed his chief scout and interpreter, Keechi. When the Indian did not return to camp, Ford settled his men in for the night.

At daylight the scout returned to report that the Comanches were camped on high ground on the other side of the wide, shallow river. Ford ordered his men to saddle up and move out. At seven o'clock they came to an outlying camp of five lodges. The partisan Indians attacked. Most of the occupants were killed or captured, but two Comanches managed to mount their horses and race toward the main camp to warn of the approaching invaders.

The Texans and their allies ran their horses three miles before reaching a point where they could see the Comanche village. Halting briefly, they counted scores of white tepees spread out along the river. Smoke rose from dozens of camp-fires. From their vantage point, Ford and his men could see the two fleeing Comanches splashing across the river. Unwittingly, the two warriors had shown Ford the best crossing.

Soon the Rangers, with the friendly Indians on their front and to their right flank, were galloping across the river toward the sprawling village. Ford had the Indians take the lead in hopes that the Comanches would think the Tonkawas were the only foe they faced. When the friendly Indians engaged the Comanches, Ford would move in with his Rangers and their repeating weapons.

As Ford waited for his Indians to close in on the camp, a solitary figure rode forth. Iron Jacket would walk his pony a short distance, then stop and ride in a circle, exhaling loudly. He was making medicine, and warriors who believed in the magic of the armor he wore followed him.

"The mail-clad and gorgeously-caparisoned Comanche chieftain moved in, seeming confident of being invulnerable," Ford later wrote. "About six rifle shots rang on the air: the chief's horse jumped about six feet straight up and fell. Another barrage followed, and the Comanche medicine man was no more."

Iron Jacket's unexpected death broke the Indian spirit. A confrontation between one hundred Texas Rangers and three hundred warriors of the most feared Plains tribe on the continent quickly turned into a rout.

The battle on the Canadian left at least seventy-six Comanches dead, though Ford believed the casualty count was higher, assuming that a number of wounded Indians probably died later. One Ranger died in the fighting, along with one of the Indian allies. Another Ranger suffered three lance wounds but recovered.

Eighteen Indian women and children were taken captive, including a young boy believed to have been Iron Jacket's son. The Rangers also rounded up three hundred Comanche horses. One of the captives told the Rangers that the Comanches had been preparing for an extensive raid into Texas. Bundles of dried meat found in the camp backed up the story.

"The battle of Antelope Hills...was probably one of the most splendid exhibitions of Indian warfare ever enacted on Texas soil," Adam R. Johnson, an old Indian fighter and former Confederate brigadier general, wrote in his 1904 book *The Partisan Rangers.* The battle was not exactly on Texas soil, but it had been brilliantly carried out by Ford and his Rangers.

Ford's 1858 Canadian River campaign did not solve the Indian problem in Texas for all time, but it had several enduring effects:

★ The campaign changed U.S. military thinking in regard to protecting the frontier. A defensive strategy would never be successful, the military finally realized. If the Indian threat were to be ended, offensive operations would be necessary. As Ford wrote in his report to Governor Runnels, "The Comanches can be followed, overtaken, and beaten, provided the pursuers will be laborious, vigilant, and are willing to undergo privations."

★ The events leading to Ford's campaign showed the people of Texas and their political leadership that the federal government could not always be counted on to provide adequate protection to the state. Texas needed a permanent Ranger force.

★ The title conferred on Ford—senior captain—became the traditional designation for the commander of the Texas Rangers.

Ford would ride as a Ranger once more, taking on the Mexican bandit Juan N. Cortina in 1859 along the Rio Grande border. During the Civil War, Ford commanded Confederate forces in South Texas and successfully engaged Federal troops in the Battle of Palmito Ranch in May 1865, the last battle of what Texans often called the War of Northern Aggression. Three years later he moved to Brownsville. He edited a newspaper there and later served as the city's mayor. Back in Austin by the mid-1870s, he was elected to the state senate in 1876 and held office until 1879. His last stint of public service was as superintendent of the state Deaf and Dumb School, which later became the Texas School for the Deaf.

After retiring from the state facility in 1883, Ford moved to San Antonio and began writing his memoir, a work filling nearly 1,300 handwritten pages. His prose, rich in detail, never placed emphasis on himself. "The writer will not endeavor to become the hero upon all extraordinary events and [will] let the book speak of himself alone," Ford wrote in a "Statement of Purpose" in 1885. He intended to publish his recollections, but they never saw print in his lifetime.

The old Ranger suffered a paralyzing stroke on October 1, 1897. He hung on for more than a month, dying at the age of eighty-two on November 3. He was buried in San Antonio's Confederate Cemetery with Masonic ceremony, eulogized as "the last of the Ranger chieftains, whose name for nearly a half century had been a household word in Texas."

Sources

Hughes, W. J. *Rebellious Ranger: Rip Ford and the Old Southwest.* Norman: University of Oklahoma Press, 1964.

Johnson, Adam R. "The Battle of Antelope Hills." *Frontier Times,* February 1924, pp. 12-14.

Oates, Stephen B., ed. *Rip Ford's Texas.* Austin: University of Texas Press, 1963.

Remington, Frederick. "How the Law Got Into the Chaparral." *Harper's New Monthly Magazine,* December 1896, pp. 60-69.

Widener, Ralph W. Jr. *John Salmon ("Rip") Ford.* Unpublished manuscript.

_____. Interview with the author, August 20, 1998.

What Goes Around Comes Around

As a young Ranger, Orville T. Word already had been in several scrapes with Indians, but the order just given him by Captain Buck Barry was the toughest he had ever faced.[1]

A couple of weeks earlier, Barry's Tonkawa scouts had ridden into camp with a lone Comanche taken prisoner on the upper reaches of the San Saba River.[2] Since his capture, the Indian not only hadn't tried to escape, he seemed to be getting quite fond of Ranger cooking.

Captain Barry did not believe it was the state's obligation to fatten up one of its enemies.

"I'm getting tired of feeding that Indian," the captain told Word one day. "Take him out and get shed of him."

In addition to being Word's captain, the seasoned Indian fighter was Word's uncle. The young Ranger eyed Barry for some clue to his thinking. "Get shed of him" could be taken two ways, and the captain offered no further explanation.

"All right," Word finally replied.

As the other Rangers looked on indifferently, Word looped a rope around the Comanche, saddled up, and headed out from camp with the Indian in tow. Word kept his horse at an easy walk, deep in reflection. Had his uncle meant for him to execute the prisoner? Or was it his intention merely for him to let the Comanche go? One unarmed Indian without his pony was not particularly dangerous.

Word knew what the Comanches did to innocent families on the western edge of settlement. Too, he knew the Bible well enough to recite the adage "An eye for an eye, a tooth for a tooth." On the other hand, the Comanche prisoner had not killed anyone that Word knew of. And he had not been unruly while in Ranger custody. Shooting him when he was not even putting up a fight seemed a bit harsh, even by frontier standards of justice.

About five miles out from the Ranger camp, Word finally had it worked out in his mind what his uncle must have meant. The Ranger pulled his big pistol from its scabbard and loosened the lasso around the Indian. The Comanche's eyes narrowed as he faced the muzzle.

"Hit the breeze," Word commanded, motioning for the Indian to take his leave.

Free of the rope, the Indian hesitated only a moment before he bolted away from the Ranger.

As the Indian fled, Word raised his pistol. Pointing it skywards, he pulled the trigger just as the Indian disappeared into the brush. Back in the Ranger camp, the boys heard a single shot.

When Word returned, his report was as ambiguous as his order from the captain had been. "He escaped," is all the young Ranger had to say about the matter. No one pressed for details. As the years piled up like drifting tumbleweeds, Word all but forgot the incident. Like many young men who served for a short time as a Ranger, he soon left the Rangers and turned his attention to earning a living and raising a family.

Twenty years after he spared the Comanche's life, Word was pushing a herd of cattle up the trail from Texas to Indian Territory. Near Fort Sill, he and his cowboys set up camp. As they did so, a crowd of reservation Indians built up around them.

Suddenly, one of the Indians, his face creased with age, charged toward Word. Before the former Ranger had time to react, the Indian was pumping his hand like a long-lost friend. Soon the Indian had his arms wrapped around the startled cowman. Finally managing to push him back, Word recognized the Indian as the Comanche whose life he had spared back in Bosque County. Clearly, the Indian remembered the experience better than he did.

As Word later told the story, the old Indian communicated to him that he was not a wealthy man. He had no horses, blankets, or other goods to give Word as tokens of his gratitude for not killing him back in Texas when he had the chance. Though his possessions were meager, the Comanche continued, there was one gift he could offer Word. Effusive in his language and gratitude, the Indian walked away leaving Word to ponder what was next. A knife? A blanket? Some trinket? The cowman had no idea what to expect.

An hour later, the beaming Indian returned. Walking obediently behind him were his six wives. Two of the women, the Comanche said, now belonged to Word as repayment for the decision he had made in Texas. The choice of which two was Word's, the Indian added.

Now Word was as taken aback as the Indian had been years before when the Ranger had drawn his pistol. True, he'd been on the dusty cattle trail for weeks, but the old women gathering gleefully around him were no sight for sore eyes. They had big smiles but few teeth. Their clothing was far from fancy, and, on top of everything else, they did not seem to have bathed recently.

Remembering his manners, Word protested the excessive generosity of such a gift as two women for one cowboy. His fellow cowpunchers enjoyed his dilemma immensely. Word told the Comanche that he was much obliged, but he positively could not accept his far-too-kind offer.

The old Indian, struggling to understand why Word seemed so reluctant to add to his family, offered the one-time Ranger even more assurances of his sincerity as one of the women tossed a live turtle on the cowboys' campfire. Not

(Drawing by Roger Moore)

long after it stopped moving, she raked it out of the coals and broke open its shell with a handy rock. Soon she was sucking down the half-cooked meat with obvious gusto.

The Comanche misread Word's horrified reaction as offense at not having been offered some of the delicacy. Mortified at this new affront to his Anglo friend, the Indian grabbed a rawhide horse hobble and lashed the woman for her social gaffe.

Word tried again to explain that the Indian did not owe him anything. As far as he was concerned, they were and always had been even.

The Comanche was growing frustrated. He spoke harshly in Comanche to his wives, ordering them to decide among themselves which two should offer comfort to the Texan. Saying things Word could not understand and didn't mind that he couldn't, the crooning Indian women advanced upon him. Their kisses and caresses, intended to convince him of the right choice to make, caused Word to light out as if the Comanches were after his scalp, not his affection.

Word made one circle around his chuck wagon, the six women barely arm's reach behind him. On the second pass, they caught up with him, forcing him up on the wagon. Desperate now, Word spotted the bullwhip that the outfit's cook used to get their mules moving, coiled like a snake on the springseat of the wagon. He picked up the whip and popped it right in front of the women. That cooled their ardor and sent them running.

Standing in the wagon, his face reddening at the laughter of the other cowhands and assorted Comanches who had drifted over to see what all the commotion was about, it crossed Word's mind that shooting the prisoner two decades earlier would have saved him a whole lot of trouble.

Though cracking the whip had ended the immediate crisis, Word never convinced the Indian he had saved that he expected no recompense for not killing him. A week later his outfit broke camp and he never saw the Indian—or his half dozen wives—again.[3]

······ ★ ······

Notes

[1] When Word related this story late in life, he made no mention of when it happened. James Buckner Barry (1821-1906) first came to Bosque County in 1855, a decade after his arrival in Texas. He commanded ranging companies raised in Bosque County at various times into the 1870s. The events described by Word probably happened in the second half of the 1850s or during the Civil War. One contemporary newspaper said of Barry: "He has been in more fights and killed more Indians with the same force than any other officer that was ever on the frontier."

[2] Rangers rarely took prisoners in the Indian fighting days. As T. R. Fehrenbach said of the Rangers in his classic book *Comanches: The Destruction of a People* (New York: Alfred A. Knopf, 1974), "They battled by raid and ambush...they took few prisoners. They did not make the potentially fatal mistake...of perceiving their enemies as men like themselves."

In 1934 former Frontier Battalion Ranger Caleb M. Grady related a story he heard shortly after joining Captain William Jeff Maltby's Company E in 1875. The Rangers wounded a Comanche and presented him to Major John B. Jones, commander of the Frontier Battalion. "Major, we have a pet for you," one of them said. "Not for me," Jones replied. "I want no prisoners." The Indian, who boasted in Spanish of all the Anglos he had killed, was kept for several days and then asked if he would like to go back to the reservation at Fort Sill. When he said yes, they gave him a slow horse and a head start, then rode him down and killed him. "Curly Hatcher scalped him and threw his body into a thicket, where it lay and dried up," Grady wrote.

[3] Word was raised in Hunt County, Texas, on Caddo Creek. Eventually he settled in West Texas, running a ranch between Sonora and Ozona. Around 1912 he told the story of the grateful Indian to newspaper publisher and grassroots historian J. Marvin Hunter, who retold it in his *Frontier Times* magazine thirty years later.

Sources

Gipson, Fred. "Too Much Gratitude." *Farm and Ranch Magazine*, undated clipping, p. 21.

Grady, C. M. "Fifty-eight Years in Texas." *Frontier Times*, June 1934, p. 385.

Greer, James K., ed. *Buck Barry: Texas Ranger and Frontiersman.* Waco: Friends of the Moody Texas Ranger Library, 1978.

Hunter, J. Marvin. "The Gratitude of an Indian." *Frontier Times*, Vol. 19, No. 12, September 1942, pp. 427-429.

Walnut Springs Signal, October 15, 1898.

Hard and Bloody Work

Wild hogs are not fastidious creatures.

When Captain Henry Joseph Richarz and his Medina County men dismounted at Fort Inge, the German-born Ranger could hardly believe the destruction wrought by feral pigs and, to a lesser extent, by loose livestock. Officers' quarters and barracks at the fort in Uvalde County—abandoned by the U.S. Army eighteen months earlier—were open to the elements and the hogs. Richarz saw that porcine marauders had rooted under the flooring and torn up anything the departing military and the human scavengers who followed had not bothered to carry off.

The Army had established the fort in 1849 on a prominence overlooking the Leona River. As Richarz wrote in his first report, the buildings—occupied continuously except during the Civil War—were "in a very dilapidated shape."

His Rangers, recruited to fight Indians, spent four days cleaning and repairing "as far as could be done." Though Richarz deemed it necessary to report the hog problem to Adjutant General James Davidson in Austin, before long untidy hogs would seem quite inconsequential to the captain. Richarz' report to headquarters soon stoically reported a deeply personal tragedy.

Like many German Texans, Richarz came to the United States because of political upheaval in his native land. Born on September 8, 1822, in Eltersberg, a town on the Rhine in Dusseldorf near Cologne, Richarz participated in the liberal revolt of 1848. He soon found it expedient to leave the country.

So did thousands of other Germans, and many of them chose to come to Texas. After a trans-Atlantic voyage, Richarz came to Texas via New Orleans. By 1846 he and his wife Josefa had a son. Seven years later the family was living on the edge of the frontier near Fort Lincoln in what is now Medina County.

58

Richarz clearly had no intention of ever again living in Germany. In San Antonio on June 16, 1852, he began the naturalization process. Soon he had the papers declaring himself a citizen of the United States.

Before long, the newly enfranchised American became a public servant as well. Richarz opened the first post office at D'Hanis, in Medina County, and continued as postmaster until the Civil War began. During the war he served in a Home Guard company in Medina County.

With most able-bodied men off fighting Yankees, the Home Guard's primary role was protecting settlers from Indians. When federal troops returned to Texas after the war, they faced the dual responsibility of dealing with the problems associated with Reconstruction along with frontier defense. Just as it had been before the war, the U.S. Army was stretched too thin to do the job adequately.

The law creating a Frontier Force of Ranger companies was the state's first postwar effort to protect its western frontier

H. J. Richarz. (Photo courtesy Texas State Library, Archives Division)

from Indians. When the Legislature authorized the creation of twenty Ranger companies in the summer of 1870, Richarz seemed the natural choice to head up one of the units. Soon he had a commission as captain of Company E. Most of his men were recruited in Medina County.

Four days after Richarz set up camp at old Fort Inge, the captain learned that a "sheepman" had been attacked by six Kickapoo Indians near the Nueces. The captain led twenty-four Rangers forty miles downriver cutting for sign, but heavy rains had washed out the Indians' trail. The only help the Rangers could offer was the professional service of their surgeon, Doctor S. E. Woodbridge, who extracted a bullet from the shoulder of the wounded man.

Richarz' scout took him near Fort Clark at Brackettville. Being in the area, he stopped by to check in with the post commander. The officer, Richarz reported, "afforded us with greatest kindness, and all necessities."

Almost two weeks after leaving Fort Inge, the Rangers returned. Waiting for the captain was a communiqué from the commander of Fort Duncan at Eagle Pass. Eight days earlier a party of Indians had raided two ranches farther up the Nueces near old Fort Ewell, an abandoned army post on the San Antonio-Laredo road in the then unorganized county of La Salle. The Indians escaped into Mexico. It was a common pattern.

Though Richarz knew that pursuing those raiders would be futile, he made sure to keep his best horses at Fort Inge. He was, as he reported, "ready for any emergency at an hour's notice." But the grazing around the old fort was poor, forcing Richarz to keep half of his company and thirty horses at a separate camp on the Nueces, about ten miles west of the fort.

While Richarz and his Rangers seemed to be working well with the military, the state-federal cooperation did not extend all the way up the chain of command. When the Ranger companies were organized, General J. J. Reynolds, commander of the Fifth Military District, assured the state that the Army would furnish the Rangers food and forage. But on October 7

Adjutant General E. D. Townsend wired Reynolds from Washington: The provisioning of Rangers was to stop.

Governor E. J. Davis, saying it would take more than a month for the state to furnish supplies to its Rangers, immediately appealed the decision. The adjutant general referred the matter to the secretary of war and President Ulysses S. Grant. The president told Townsend the answer was still no, and the adjutant general telegraphed Davis that "furnishing of rations to State troops, not authorized to be mustered into the service of the United States, cannot be sanctioned."

Texas officials did not like the news and made sure that the newspapers learned about it.

"Everything seems to conspire against the unfortunate people of the Texas frontier," the *Austin Daily Journal* wrote. "The United States government *don't* [newspaper's italics] protect them from the Indians and *won't let* the State government do it, in the only effective way."

The newly authorized Ranger force was supposed to be funded through the sale of bonds, but no one was buying the state's paper. The *Daily Journal* thought it knew why:

> The meanest scoundrel that walks the earth, is the Texan, who, in this emergency, when the lives of hundreds of families are at stake, is found circulating false statements for the purpose of injuring the credit of the State, and thereby preventing the Governor from procuring the money to keep this force in the field.... Let the people, regardless of party politics, put the brand of utter condemnation upon such men, for they are more Indian than the savages themselves.

Rangers "actively at work on the frontier" were "discouraged and disheartened," the newspaper asserted. But if politics in the capital bothered Richarz, it is not reflected in his reports to the adjutant general. The Ranger captain's only preoccupation seemed to be Indians.

From their village about twenty miles deep into Mexico, the Kickapoo brazenly sent word that they intended to come to Texas and fight the Rangers. Richarz accepted the challenge, scouting from Fort Inge down to the Rio Grande. "They did not cross the river to meet me," he reported.

Three days after returning from that scout, Richarz sent his lieutenant and twenty-three men out on another patrol. The Rangers were ordered to head up the Nueces from the fort, then loop back to the south, pass near Fort Clark, and go to the Rio Grande before returning to Fort Inge.

"The Indians in Mexico," Richarz reported, "are in league with border Mexicans and have undoubtedly been informed by the same of our movements."

While half of Richarz' Rangers worked their way south, some one hundred Kickapoo splashed across the river above Eagle Pass. The raiding party split into three groups. One attacked a ranch on Turkey Creek and captured three horses. As soon as the captain heard about the raid, he dispatched fourteen Rangers under Doctor Woodbridge and Corporal Alfred Echard[1] to pursue the Indians. When one of the men returned to Fort Inge with a lame horse, Richarz learned the Rangers, in a brief engagement with some of the Indians, had recovered the three stolen horses and two others. The Indians, meanwhile, killed three persons on Chapa Rosa Creek. The Ranger reported that the detachment was still hot on the trail of the main body of Indians.

The captain's opinion of the military along the border began to erode. Indians crossed into Texas within rifle shot of Fort Duncan, he complained to Austin.

"I am at a loss how to protect 200 miles of frontier and 10,000 miles of territory with my fifty men, if the United States Government allows these savages to hover on the banks of the Rio Grande watching my movements and crossing into Texas when they please," Richarz wrote.

Despite the frustration expressed in his report to headquarters, when the sun rose the next morning Richarz rode out of Fort Inge with fourteen Rangers and three volunteers to scout for Indians. Before the Rangers made camp that evening, riders from Fort Duncan brought a report that an estimated five hundred Indians—Comanches, Kiowas, Kickapoo, and Lipan Apaches—"are sweeping this part of the state in every direction."

The Rangers kept moving south, scouting for Indian sign. Twenty-five miles from the Rio Grande, Richarz encountered a party of army officers and a civilian. They told the captain, as he later reported, what happened when Doctor Woodbridge finally caught up with the Indians he had been chasing: "On an open prairie twelve miles from the Rio Grande [the Rangers] gallantly charged the Indians and ...stood their ground against seventy well armed savages, and defeated them, killing eight warriors and wounding about fifteen." The Rangers lost one man, Lorenz Biediger, in the fight. The remainder of the Indians escaped across the river into Mexico.

With no further reason to continue south, Richarz swung back toward the Nueces, intending to move back up the river.

Richarz sent a rider toward the Eagle Pass road in hopes he could bring back word of any recently reported Indian movements. The captain and his men were sitting around their fire the night of December 8 when the scout galloped into camp. The guide's news was as hard as any man could expect to hear. With professional detachment, Richarz noted in a report to headquarters that he had been informed "that another band of Indians had appeared near my post, at Fort Inge, in overwhelming numbers had attacked two of my rangers at the Blanco [creek], sixteen miles east of Fort Inge, and killed them. These ...are Walter Richarz (my son) and Joseph Riff."

Richarz immediately broke camp and rode through the night, reaching the fort before sunup. At the Ranger camp, the captain "found to my satisfaction that Lieutenant [Xavier] Wanz had started with the reserve force on hand in hot pursuit of the murderers of my son and Joseph Riff." All but three of his men left immediately to catch up with the lieutenant.

Though the death of his son hit him like a Comanche lance in the gut, Richarz was worried that Doctor Woodbridge and his men might be attacked on their way back to the fort by Indians seeking revenge for the loss he had inflicted on them. At daybreak, Richarz and his remaining three Rangers left the fort to join the doctor's detachment.

"But I met the Doctor coming back into the Post," Richarz reported, "and he had no loss other than [Biediger]. The Doctor was carrying the shield of one of the Comanche Chiefs killed in action, as a trophy."

The doctor also sported a bruise received when one of the Indians struck him on the forehead with a tomahawk. The blow unhorsed Woodbridge, but two Rangers galloped to his rescue and helped the momentarily stunned physician remount to continue the fight.

Richarz was hopeful that "the lesson given to the savages" by his Rangers would discourage further incursions into Texas, but he was not optimistic. He knew the only real solution to the problem, but he did not have the means or authority to carry it out. His December 9 report to Austin—written only three days after the death of his son—began: "Since my last report we have had hard and bloody work here." The captain then summarized the situation he and his Rangers faced and illustrated his frustrations:

> I would like to have some reinforcements, at any rate be authorized to fill my company to the number as first organized. My men and horses have not had any rest worth speaking of since my arrival here. The grass is getting worse every day. The tribes, protected by the Mexicans, have a secure base of operations two hundred fifty miles long....
>
> It is not reasonable to be expected that I can always successfully operate in every direction against half a thousand well armed savages with thirty-eight privates. I am not able to have two strong scouts out in different directions at the same time. Though we will not count numbers if we fight, I may lose too many men without having the satisfaction of destroying the enemy.
>
> If it were not for this cursed international law [barring armed Americans from riding into Mexico] I would know very well what to do to clean out these bloody savages on the other side of the Rio Grande.

In the vernacular of a good officer, Richarz nevertheless submitted his report "respectfully."

Five days later two of Richarz' scouts returned to Fort Inge with more bad news. The Indians believed to have killed his son had enough horses with them to change saddles almost hourly during their flight. The Rangers had no spare horses, and their mounts had gone without corn for nearly three weeks. They simply could not close the distance between themselves and the fresher mounts of the raiders. Reluctantly, Lieutenant Wanz ended the pursuit.

Throughout the first half of 1871 Richarz and his men continued to trail Indians. But with the Indians taking sanctuary in Mexico, the Rangers under his command never got a chance to face the hostiles in any major engagement. By summer the state had no funds to maintain its Ranger force. On June 15, 1871, Richarz and his company were mustered out of service. The state owed them back pay, and most of the captains had receipts for supplies and equipment they purchased out of their own pockets for their companies.

The bonds intended to fund the Rangers never sold well, but that was not the only problem. It eventually came to light that Adjutant General Davidson had been siphoning state funds. Estimates of how much money he skimmed for himself varied from $5,000 to more than $34,000. No one knew for sure how much money the general stole. And Davidson was not available to offer any details, having fled the state for Belgium.

The memory that he had lost a son in the service of a corrupt carpetbagger state government must have festered in Richarz like an embedded arrowhead not surgically removable.

After his Ranger service, Richarz was elected to the Texas House of Representatives in November 1880. He served in the 17th Legislature during a session noted for the passage of a bill setting the railroad passenger fare at three cents a mile.

The onset of a severe hearing disability, as the *Hondo Anvil Herald* reported, left him "incapacitated from further public service." Richarz may have had trouble understanding what people around him said, but his eyesight was undiminished

H. J. Richarz in his later years. (Photo courtesy Texas State Library, Archives Division)

by age. He could still read fine print, and though his only enemy was old age, he could still shoot.

"[He] never misses a rabbit or turkey at the distance of eighty yards with a rifle," former Ranger A. J. Sowell wrote of Richarz in 1900.

The old Ranger, Sowell continued, "spends a quiet life on the west bank of the Seco, a romantic spot near the foot of the hills, where he attends to his irrigated garden and orchard." His final years were spent with his daughter, Eda, and her husband, Louis Rudinger.

Richarz died at his daughter's residence on Seco Creek on May 21, 1910, at the age of eighty-seven. C. F. Luckenbach, an old friend, read Richarz's life history at his graveside.

"Every person in the community attended the funeral, in spite of the muddy roads," the *Hondo Anvil Herald* reported.

He is buried in the Richarz family plot in D'Hanis next to his son—a young Ranger who died in the line of duty, fighting Indians under his father's command.

······ ✪ ······

Notes

[1] Echard may have been the only Prussian cavalry lieutenant to serve as a Texas Ranger. He came to Texas on a twelve-month leave of absence granted by the Prussian War Department. As Richarz reported to headquarters, "As this country suited him very much he intended to invest his capital in some agricultural enterprise." When Echard learned that war had broken out with France, the German officer reported to the Prussian consul in Galveston that he intended to leave Texas and rejoin his regiment at Berlin. With news that the war seemed short-lived, however, Echard decided to join the Rangers "in order to do something suited to his taste and to know the country."

Later, he got a letter from his mother enclosing orders for him to report to his regiment in France. Richarz wrote Austin on December 21, 1870, requesting permission to furlough him from the Rangers so he could resume his career in the Prussian army.

Echard left Texas—and the Rangers—with regret. "He is one of my best men," Richarz wrote, "a soldier up to the mark."

Sources

Haas, H.E. "Captain Henry Joseph Richarz." *Hondo Anvil Herald*, May [?] 1910.

Pirkle, Jack. *Directory of Cemeteries in the Western Half of Medina County*. Hondo: n.p., 1993, p. 122.

"A Ranger Captain," *Voice of the Mexican Border*, November 1933, pp. 137-141.

"The Rangers," *Austin Daily Journal*, October 20, 1870.

Smith, Thomas Tyree. *Fort Inge: Sharps, Spurs, and Sabers on the Texas Frontier, 1849-1869*. Austin: Eakin Press, 1993, pp. 170-171, 220.

Sowell, A. J. *Early Settlers and Indian Fighters of Southwest Texas*. Austin: State House Press, 1986, facsimile reproduction of 1900 edition, pp. 202-205.

Stovall, Allan A. *Breaks of the Balcones: A Regional History*. Barksdale, Texas: n.p., 1967, p. 194.

"Xavier Wanz Came to Texas in 1845." *Frontier Times*, Vol. 7, No. 5, February 1930, p. 208.

The Cry of the Death Bird

Old-timers on the frontier called it the death bird. It flew at night, not to bring death but to warn of its approach.

Mere superstition, most would say. But not former Ranger Isaac Motes. As far as he was concerned, the death bird once saved his life.[1]

"Almost every western frontiersman of fifty years ago believed thoroughly in the existence of the death bird," Motes recalled in the early 1920s. "Especially was it believed to be the protector of officers of the law and women and children. Many old plainsmen will tell you of cases where the death bird was believed to have saved their lives, and woe to the man who heard its cry and heeded it not."

Settlers along Texas' western frontier in the early 1870s needed all the protection they could get. They dreaded each full moon, the most likely time of the month for an Indian raid. Violent death was no stranger along the border and along the edge of settlement.

In 1871 Motes[2] and several Rangers were camped near what later became the town of Albany in present-day Shackleford County in north central Texas. They learned that a large party of Comanches had jumped the reservation in Indian Territory. They were riding to West Texas to take horses, cattle, and scalps. Most of the Ranger company's men were in the area of Fort Worth, a young cow town on the Trinity River, more than a hundred miles away. The lieutenant in charge dispatched one of their scouts, an Indian they called Indian Jim[3], with orders to ride to Fort Worth and summon the rest of the Rangers.

The trip should have taken no more than three days. By the end of the third day after Indian Jim's departure, the Ranger lieutenant grew worried. At noon on the fourth day, the officer ordered Motes to take up Indian Jim's trail and bring the Rangers back from North Texas. He detailed another group of men to Fort Concho to alert a company of Rangers camped there.

"I traveled all that afternoon," Motes later recalled, "keeping as much as possible in the timber and on the ridges so as to avoid being ambushed by the Indians."

Motes was almost fifty miles from Fort Worth and riding over a stretch of rocky terrain when his horse suddenly went lame. That slowed him considerably. Worse, he had no hope of outrunning them if he encountered Indians.

Late that evening, Motes saw something off to his left in the distance. He thought it might be an Indian reconnoitering from a hilltop, but he had only a quick glimpse before whoever—or whatever—it was disappeared. Worried that a band of Indians might be skirting his flank, waiting for an opportunity to attack, the Ranger rode as hard as he dared on a sore-footed horse for cover in the timber along the Clear Fork of the Brazos.

Once he reached the trees, he felt better. He splashed across the river and began moving north, sticking to the shelter of the timber. About five hundred yards above where he had crossed the river, he came up on a narrow, high-banked valley to his right. He turned up the valley, walking his horse under a canopy of tree limbs and hanging vines until he found a good campsite.

"Here I staked out my horse and rubbed his leg for a while," Motes recalled. "Then I took the saddle, blanket, rifle, and six-shooter and laid down at the foot of a large postoak with wide spreading branches."

Motes had ridden most of the day under an overcast sky. The night was still and sultry. Soon, he heard far-off thunder. He untied his slicker from behind the cantle of his saddle and draped it over his shoulders, careful to shield his rifle and pistol from rain sure to come.

A flash of lightning and a loud crack of thunder jolted the Ranger awake around midnight. A thunderstorm was blowing in from the northwest. Motes felt edgy, "as though something else had helped to wake me."

That's when he heard an owl hooting. It sounded like the bird was about a hundred yards or so upriver.

The hooting of an owl in the night was believed by many to be a harbinger of death. (Author's collection)

"At first I paid no heed to it," Motes said, "but the next time I noted it more intently and thought it sounded unnatural. The third time I felt this more strongly."

A savvy frontiersman, Motes knew that Indians signaled to each other by imitating the howl of a wolf or the nocturnal call of the owl.

"Not more than a minute after I heard the owl the third time I heard another over to the east of me," he said. "I lay still, listening for a repetition of the sound, that I might tell if possible whether it were really an owl."

With each flash of lighting as the thunderstorm moved closer, the Ranger strained to see if any figures were moving toward him in the darkness.

"All at once," Motes wrote, "I heard the scream of the death bird overhead."

The owl must have been sitting on a limb near the top of the tree the Ranger had bedded down beneath. As it took flight, it let loose with a long wailing sound that sent goose bumps down the back of Motes' neck. But with the surge of adrenaline stimulated by the eerie sound came an idea. Moving quickly, he rolled his blanket and stuck it upright on his saddle against the tree, draping it with his slicker. In the darkness the improvised dummy might pass for a human form.

"I made sure that my six-shooter was safely in its belt, then hugging my rifle to my bosom, I rolled noiselessly away from the tree down the slight decline... in the opposite direction from which I had heard the first owl," he continued.

"Whenever a flash of lightning came I stopped and remained perfectly still until darkness came again."

He got about thirty yards from the tree and then positioned himself so he could see—and shoot—in both directions.

Suddenly, Motes was startled to hear his horse whinny. He'd ridden the horse six years, and it had never done such a dangerous thing at night in Indian country.

Easing his rifle to his shoulder, he waited for another flash of lighting, hoping to see what had spooked his horse. But when it came, the Ranger saw nothing. With the next flash, Motes glimpsed a silhouette beyond his horse. It was not a good enough target to shoot at, especially since pulling the trigger would immediately reveal his location. He waited for another flash.

"Then the flash came and simultaneously I heard the sharp twang of a bow string followed by the thud of an arrow as it struck my saddle under the tree," he wrote.

Before he had time to congratulate himself on the ruse that had spared his belly from an arrow—at least for the time being—Motes heard a sound that did not fit at all with what he expected: another snap of a bowstring, followed by a muted cry of pain somewhere out there in the black night. The groans grew weaker and weaker. Soon there was silence.

Motes knelt in the darkness, waiting for a target and wondering if one Indian had killed another by mistake. His horse gave another friendly whinny, and Motes recognized a familiar whistle—Indian Jim's signal.

Motes whistled back but got no answer.

"I then began to crawl in the direction [of the whistle] during periods of darkness," he wrote, "and finally reached him where he lay a little distance from my horse, just where I had seen the dark object."

The Ranger realized he had come close to shooting Indian Jim.

"After a close handclasp we lay still as death for more than an hour, waiting and watching for signs of hostile Indians," Motes said. "Then in low whispers he told me that he had reached the river late that night and had accidentally selected this place to camp, without knowing I was there."

The two spent the rest of the night hidden in the brush, fearful more Indians might be around. At first light, the two emerged from concealment and moved in the direction Motes had heard the moaning. It didn't take them long to find a dead Comanche, an arrow through his chest. Nearby, the shaft of another arrow protruded from the Ranger's make-shift dummy, its metal tip embedded in his saddle.

Motes had been right the day before when he thought he saw an Indian. The Comanche had trailed him to his camp. Perhaps the Indian, as unsure in the darkness as Motes had been, had called out in imitation of an owl. Bedded down within earshot, Indian Jim recognized the call and realized the Comanche was stalking someone. When the friendly Indian investigated, he found the hostile Indian, for some reason out alone, closing in on the Ranger, and he killed him.

The cry of the death bird—and the Ranger's alertness—had saved his scalp.

······ ✪ ······

Notes

[1] The notion that the owl is a bird of bad luck or death dates back a couple of centuries or more. According to *A Dictionary of Superstitions,* the superstition was that the screech owl, "a most abominable and unlucky bird, sends forth its hoarse and dismal voice, it is the omen of the approach of some terrible thing.... Its visits and wild shriekings foretell the death of someone in the neighborhood [and] it gained the name of the deathbird." The entry does not say that anyone thought the cry of the bird was lucky.

[2] Isaac Motes' name is not listed in the adjutant general's records at the Texas State Archives. Since the surviving records are incomplete, this does not necessarily mean that Motes never rode as a Ranger. He could have been a member of a volunteer company. His recollection of the death bird incident, which first appeared in the *El Paso Times* and was reprinted in J. Marvin Hunter's *Frontier Times,* is a little polished for an old Indian fighter. It may be that he told his story to someone with a flair for writing, who in turn dramatized it a bit and gave the Ranger a fictional name. On the other hand, the

story could be a piece of fiction, though that is not the way it was presented. A white man's rescue at the hands of a nonwhite servant or social inferior was a literary convention used by Rudyard Kipling, Mark Twain, and others. Before them, Chaucer and Shakespeare found the death bird to be a handy dramatic element.

3 Though Motes did not say so in his account of the incident, Indian Jim, if he existed, likely was a Tonkawa. As Robert Wooster wrote in *Soldiers, Sutlers and Settlers: Garrison Life on the Western Frontier* (College Station: Texas A&M University Press, 1987), "About two hundred Tonkawa scouts and their families lived near Fort Griffin [which was located near present-day Albany] during the 1870s." T. R. Fehrenbach, in his excellent study of the Comanches, noted that Texas Rangers had been using the "Tonks," as they were called, as scouts for more than thirty years by the 1870s.

Sources

Fehrenbach, T. R. *Comanches, the Destruction of a People*. New York: Alfred A. Knopf, 1974, p. 343.

Motes, Isaac. "The Cry of the Death Bird Served as a Warning." *Frontier Times*, Vol. 1, No. 1, October 1923, pp. 20-21.

Opie, Iona and Moira Tatem, eds. *A Dictionary of Superstitions*. Oxford (England) and New York: Oxford University Press, 1989, pp. 295-96.

The Mutiny of Company H

When Bland Chamberlain came to Corpus Christi recruiting men for a Ranger company, nineteen-year-old John Dunn[1]—folks called him Red after the color of his hair—just happened to be looking for a job. So was his younger brother Matt. If they could have a little adventure while they were at it, all the better.

Neither had paid much attention to the political wrangling in Austin that led to the formation of the Ranger company they were about to join. All they knew was that the legislature had called for a Frontier Force to protect Texas from Indians. The law creating the force, which went into effect on June 13, 1870, did not even mention the word "Ranger," but that is what the members of the Frontier Force would be: nonuniformed, mounted irregulars whose primary duty was to scout the frontier. What did interest the Dunn boys was the pay—$50 a month for privates. Of course, as Rangers always had done, it would be up to each of them to furnish horse, tack, revolver, and anything else they felt they would need to keep themselves safe or comfortable on the edge of settled Texas. The Dunn boys signed up.

Chamberlain had already recruited a number of men in San Antonio, and as Dunn soon realized, the captain had not done very well. Either he was not a good judge of men or else he had to accept whatever he could find to fill his company.

Of the sixty-man unit, only five were Texans—the Dunns, L. O'Dougherty, Wiley Nickolls, and William O. Nieland. Company H had eight Mexican-Americans; one Frenchman, who had served in Emperor Maximillian's army in Mexico; a man from Louisiana named Billie Cline—the bugler; a fellow from Mississippi, R.B. Oliver; and a man who had ridden with Quantrill's guerrillas during the Civil War, Gus Poole. As Dunn later recalled, "the rest of the company was fished out

74

of the slums in San Antonio by the first sergeant, John Morgan."

Though Captain Chamberlain and First Lieutenant H. Flynn commanded the newly created company, Sergeant Morgan ran it. He had worn yellow chevrons in the U.S. Army and, to Dunn's thinking, "was a regular brute." Dunn had heard that shortly after the Civil War, Morgan was in a Federal detachment at Gonzales. When one of the soldiers had some difficulty with a local doctor, the sergeant led a file of soldiers to the hotel where the physician stayed. As the doctor walked up the steps to the hotel, Morgan told him to stop. At the same time, the sergeant ordered his men to fire. They did and the doctor fell dead. Those may or may not have been the full circumstances of the incident, but that was the way Dunn got the story. Morgan tried to run the Ranger company like an army outfit, but most of the boys, including Red and Matt Dunn, did not take well to that much discipline.

Leaving Corpus Christi, the Ranger recruits rode to San Antonio where they were formally mustered into service on November 15, 1870. The new Rangers then moved to a camp on Salado Creek that served as a staging area for the newly created state force. Morgan scouted the bars in the Alamo City, looking for any ex-soldiers who had not gotten all the fighting out of their system during the Civil War. To Dunn's mind, the men the sergeant brought back to the Ranger camp were "some of the most dilapidated, diseased, moth-eaten specimens of humanity that I have ever seen. Some of them could not stay on a trotting horse without holding on to the 'timber knocker' as they called the pummel of the saddle."

As they sat in camp a few days later, a stranger rode up, tied his horse, approached a group of the Rangers, and began asking questions. Seeming to recognize the man, O'Dougherty came up and, as Dunn put it, "began abusing him." The stranger, whose name was Sullivan, said he was not looking for trouble, got back on his horse, and left.

Curious, the other Rangers asked O'Dougherty what the problem was. O'Dougherty said that they'd had a fight a couple of years before and that he had lost. They had both been drinking at the time, but he had not forgotten the beating at the hands of Sullivan.

A couple of days later O'Dougherty approached Dunn. "Let's go out and kill some squirrels," he said.

Dunn agreed that sounded like a good idea. They rode about two miles from camp and came to a small house shaded by live oaks. Soon Dunn realized his hunting partner was after bigger game than squirrels.

"This is where that fellow Sullivan lives, and I wanted you to stand by me," he said.

Dunn, true to his Irish genes, never minded a good fight. But he had no stake in whatever differences existed between his fellow Ranger and Sullivan. With blood in his eye, O'Dougherty paid no attention to Dunn's response. He rode up to the front door and "helloed the house." When a man named Brady came to the door, the Ranger asked for Sullivan. When he appeared, O'Dougherty asked him if he was interested in another round.

Sullivan said he was not anxious to fight, but if forced he would try to do his best.

"There is not going to be any fighting around here," Brady told the Rangers. Standing near him was one of his two daughters.

"Get my hat," he told her. "I'm going to San Antonio and have that company moved away from here."

But what the young girl handed her father was a rifle, not his hat. Maybe the daughter figured that if her father was going to be riding to town, he'd need his Spencer carbine. Her mother, however, realized the girl's action caused a dangerous escalation of the situation. She jumped in front of her husband, hoping to calm him down before things got out of hand. But it was too late. Over his wife's shoulder, Brady fired a shot at O'Dougherty. (In recounting the incident, Dunn never offered an explanation of why Brady was so quick to take up Sullivan's cause. Maybe they were related or perhaps there was a little drinking involved.)

The shot went wild, but O'Dougherty pulled his pistol and pointed it toward the woman and her terrified daughters.

"No damn woman is going to get between me and a man when I am fighting," the Ranger declared.

Just as O'Dougherty squeezed the trigger, Dunn reached out and knocked down the pistol. Instead of hitting one of the females, the bullet penetrated the Ranger's saddle.

About that time, another shot from Brady went high and cut a branch off a mesquite tree.

"It fell squarely over my shoulders and hung there," Dunn recalled. "I let it stay. I had no particular use for it, but it was more convenient to take along than to lose time taking it off. We suddenly decided that discretion was the better part of valor and took a hurried departure."

The other five rounds in Brady's carbine whined over the Rangers' heads as they galloped back to camp. That ended the only gunfight Dunn participated in while in the service of Texas as a member of Company H.

From the camp in Bexar County, Company H rode south to Zapata County on the Rio Grande where they scouted the border, looking for Indians and cattle thieves. Not surprisingly, given the personnel Captain Chamberlain had to work with, their record was not spectacular. When the activities of the Frontier Force were summarized in the 1875 Adjutant General's Report, the only entry for Company H was: "arrested several rustlers on February 25, 1871." The record shows the company was disbanded three days later, on February 28.

When Chamberlain was notified his company was to be mustered out of service for want of funding, he left the border for Austin. With its supply wagons trailing behind, the company made no more than ten or twelve miles a day. As the Rangers slowly moved north, Dunn noticed that Sergeant Morgan seemed increasingly ill at ease. Realizing he was not popular with the men, the sergeant had managed to convince himself that some of the Rangers planned to kill him before they reached the capital. Though he was known to take an occasional nip himself, the sergeant suddenly became opposed to drinking—at least on the part of the privates in Company H. Alcohol and gunpowder, mixed together, could be harmful to someone's health, the sergeant reasoned.

Morgan prevailed on the captain to issue orders that no one could leave camp and that no whiskey was allowed in camp. To enforce the order, a roll call would be conducted each evening on the march to Austin. Rangering had not been nearly as much fun as most of the men had thought it would be, and now they could not even have a toddy or two or three around the campfire after a hard day in the saddle.

When the company made camp on a creek south of Beeville, Sergeant Morgan gathered them for a roll call and read them the new prohibition order. As the muttering Rangers dispersed after the roll call, the company's second sergeant, Wiley Nickolls—one of the Texans—summoned the Dunn boys and told them to come with him.

"Thinking that perhaps we were detailed for some purpose," Dunn later recalled, "we went with him to town. When we arrived there, he bought four bottles of whiskey."

Back in camp, the second sergeant and his escort had to walk within about ten feet of Captain Chamberlain and First Sergeant Morgan, who were sitting on a blanket playing cards with some of the Mexican Rangers. The captain happened to look up from his hand about that time.

"What have you there, Nickolls?" he asked.

"Whiskey," the second sergeant replied.

"Were you not at roll call?"

"Yes," Nickolls answered. "I was there and heard the orders, but I pay for my own whiskey and I am going to drink it."

Glancing back down, the captain pondered the insubordination—and his cards.

"All right," he said finally. "But I shall hold you responsible for anything that may happen."

After the short conversation with the captain, Nickolls strolled over to a group of Rangers and handed them two bottles of whiskey. Seeing that, Sergeant Morgan felt it was time to take action. He assembled the ex-military members of the company—his loyalists—and approached the Rangers with the already diminished stock of whiskey.

Morgan, a big man, positioned himself behind Nickolls and hit him hard on the back of his neck. That sent him crashing into the side of one of the supply wagons. Seeing that, Poole struck Morgan with his gun, knocking him down on all fours. The sergeant thus positioned, Oliver decided to go for a ride. Jumping on Morgan, he sank his spurs into the sergeant's flanks. Just like a horse would respond in the same situation, Morgan started bucking.

"He finally tore loose from Oliver," Dunn recalled, "but dragged him several feet, as the latter's spurs had fastened in Morgan's clothes. When Morgan did get loose, he went through space like a shooting star going straight toward the creek and passing his four partners who had already emigrated."

With Morgan in full retreat, Poole hard on his heels and prodding him with his gun, Captain Chamberlain and his card-playing pals also headed for the brush along the creek.

As the level in the whiskey bottles dropped, the stakes got higher. Soon the two factions were sniping at each other, though only a few of the fleeing Rangers had managed to get out of camp with their guns. It was too dark for the men to shoot accurately enough to hit someone, but about 10 P.M. Ranger Cline, the bugler, improved the odds by setting one of the company's wagons ablaze. Despite the enhanced lighting no one was hit, though firing continued sporadically throughout the night.

Shortly before sunup a few cooler, if throbbing, heads prevailed and succeeded in talking Nickolls into saddling up and getting out of camp. Not long after Nickolls left, the company doctor rode into camp at a gallop under a white flag with a message from the captain: If the Rangers in camp allowed him and the men with him to have their guns back, he would write the incident off as mere shenanigans and not report it as a mutiny—a capital offense under most military codes.

Dunn and the others returned the weapons, and the captain, Sergeant Morgan, and their followers came back to camp after a night in the brush. Morgan ordered most of the Rangers to go find the horses that had run off during the night. As soon as they left, despite Captain Chamberlain's promise of amnesty, the sergeant ordered the arrest of Cline,

O'Dougherty, Oliver, Poole, and one other Ranger whose name Dunn did not remember.[2]

"They were all taken to a blacksmith shop and irons were riveted to their wrists and legs," Dunn wrote. "Morgan stated that they would be tried for mutiny."

At the time of the incident near Beeville, Lieutenant Flynn had been absent. When he later rejoined the company in camp on Onion Creek, south of Austin, he asked why the five Rangers were in irons. After hearing the story, he summoned Morgan.

"Take the irons off those boys quick and handle them gentle!" he said.

When the burly sergeant started to say something, Flynn told him to follow orders or he would slap a pair of irons on him. The sergeant had the irons removed. That apparently was the end of the matter.[3]

Company H approached the capital city on St. Patrick's Day, 1871.

"We were so ragged that the officers were ashamed to take us into the city," Dunn recalled.

The Rangers set up camp near a military academy. While it was a logical place for the Rangers to bivouac, Captain Chamberlain had not noticed that a brewery was located less than a hundred yards from the encampment.

This is how Dunn told what happened next:

> As we had no money, we pawned pistols and carbines and bought beer by the keg. In the meantime, some of the cadets from the Academy happened to stroll into our camp. We filled them up with beer and in a few minutes a large crowd of them arrived.
>
> Among them were two cadets from Gonzales County who had plenty of money. They sent a Negro to town to get several bottles of whiskey. Then the fun began. In a short time, the place looked like a battlefield, with the cadets stretched out in their nice white uniforms and the Rangers in their dirty rags. The Academy had to send an ambulance after their casualties that night.

Company H camped near this Austin military academy, and the Rangers proceeded to get drunk. (Photo courtesy Austin History Center, Austin Public Library)

On March 18 those who could stand marched to the limestone capitol at the head of Congress Avenue to be discharged. "Some of the boys were [still] so drunk that it took two sober ones to hold each of them up while waiting for the discharge," Dunn wrote.

The state could pay the Rangers only a part of what they were owed. The men late of Company H were told, however, that they would be issued commissions as officers in the State Police force, which was then being organized, and would be sent vouchers for the rest of their pay. Dunn and several other former Rangers rode back to South Texas, camping for a time at the Santa Gertrudis Ranch of Richard King. They worked for King, whose huge ranch would soon bear his name, for three months. The vouchers and commissions never arrived.

"When we saw how badly we had been duped," Dunn remembered, "we left Santa Gertrudis and scattered, hunting work. None of us ever met again."

Despite his experience in Company H, John Dunn rode with the Rangers twice. (Photo courtesy Corpus Christi Public Library)

······ ⭐ ······

Notes

[1] Dunn's Ranger service was only one chapter of his long and colorful life. His father, a native of Kildare in Ireland, had come to Corpus Christi with General Zachary Taylor's troops shortly before the Mexican War began in 1846. Born in Nueces County on January 18, 1851, John "Red" Dunn had driven cattle to Kansas, shoveled coal in the boiler room of a Mississippi River steamboat, worked in the beef packing houses at Rockport, Texas, and raised cattle. He received a pension for his Ranger service (despite his experiences in Company H, he enlisted in Captain Warren Wallace's Frontier Company of Nueces County on June 29, 1874), but the discovery of oil on his property in the 1930s, as the *Corpus Christi Caller* put it, "added materially to his wealth." For years, he had amassed historical artifacts, displaying his collection in what was known as Dunn's Museum in Corpus Christi. He died in Corpus Christi on November 3, 1940, after a brief illness and was buried in Rose Hill Cemetery there. He was preceded in death by his brother Matt (born February 2, 1852), who died on December 26, 1935.

[2] Dunn's memory for names was not bad, which reflects well on the veracity of his account of the boozy "mutiny" of Company H. The captain's first name, according to muster rolls in the Texas State Archives, was Bland, not "Blan" as Dunn spelled it in his memoir. First Sergeant Morgan is on the muster roll as J. B. Morgan, a private, but a company elected its officers after mustering. Dunn misspelled Wiley Nickolls' last name as Nickels and left the "e" off Gus Poole's name. All the other names he mentions in his book are in the records as Dunn spelled them except for William O. Nieland. No one by that or any variant of that spelling has been found on any Ranger muster rolls.

[3] Morgan left the Rangers and drifted down to Mexico, where he soon ended up in prison. In an escape attempt, he was shot to death. "It is a blessing that the soil of Texas was not contaminated by drinking his blood," Dunn later wrote.

Sources

Dunn, J. B. (John). *Perilous Trails of Texas*. Dallas: Southwest Press, 1932.

Ingmire, Frances T. *Texas Ranger Service Records, 1847-1900*. St. Louis: n.p., 1982.

"John B. Dunn, Texas Pioneer, Dies Peacefully at 89." *Corpus Christi Caller,* November 4, 1940.

The Lawrence Dunn-Ellen O'Riley Lineage. n.p., 1991.

I Took a Notion I
Wanted to Be a Ranger

Not all Texas Rangers became famous. Some men just did their jobs until something better came along—marriage, running for sheriff or going to work for one, hiring on as a cattle inspector for the Texas and Southwestern Cattle Raisers Association, or venturing into ranching or some other business.

After riding with the Rangers for three years, Billy Blevins left state service to run a saloon in a railroad boomtown. He found dispensing liquor more profitable that meting out justice on a fading frontier.

Born in DeKalb County, Alabama, on October 17, 1856, William C. Blevins Jr.—he went by Billy—lived a long, full life. As time was about to run out on him, an interviewer employed by the Federal Writers' Project of the Works Progress Administration sat Blevins down for a talk in 1937. The old-timer told some fine stories, and most of them were probably true.

Blevins' family came to Texas after the Civil War, settling north of Fort Worth in Tarrant County. Like most youngsters on the frontier, Blevins quickly learned to ride and shoot. In 1879, when he was twenty-three, it occurred to him that he could get paid for those skills.

"I took a notion I wanted to be a Ranger and along with J. [Pete] Clark of my community and brother of Sterling Clark that afterwards was sheriff of Tarrant County, I joined the Texas Rangers," Blevins began. "We signed on with the Northern Company under Captain G. W. Arrington."[1]

The "Northern Company" was actually called Company C, but its area of responsibility was the northernmost in the state—the high plains of the Panhandle. When Blevins enlisted the company had its headquarters at Camp Roberts in Blanco Canyon in what is now Crosby County. The site had been chosen for its good water, a scarce resource in that part of Texas.

"We builded [sic] our headquarters out of mud-block adobe with walls nearly two feet thick," he recalled. "There was no flooring but the buildings provided warm shelter."

Most of the time, Blevins and his fellow Rangers were off on scouts, living in the open.

"We had to carry drinking water and tried to carry a sufficient supply, but frequently we would run short and get mighty thirsty," he said. "Bathing took place when we came to a water hole and had time. As a rule the boys wore . . . their hair long. At times we did not have the appearance of gentlemen and would cause a child to run with fear that would suddenly meet one of us."

In addition to having long hair (which was black), Blevins had brown eyes, what his enlistment paper described as a "florid" complexion, and stood five feet eight inches.

By the time Blevins became a Ranger, hostile Indians in Texas were getting about as scarce as the buffalo the Plains tribes once had depended on for food and shelter. The surviving Comanches and Kiowa—about eight thousand of them—were relegated to an eight-million-acre reservation set aside by Washington in the western portion of Indian Territory. But old ways were hard to give up, and small groups of renegade Indians still occasionally rode into Texas to steal cattle or horses.

Captain Arrington's Rangers scouted for Indians and cattle rustlers.
(Author's collection)

And though peace with the Indians technically had reigned since the end of the U.S. military campaign in 1875 called the Red River War, Blevins and the other Rangers all had heard stories of atrocities committed in earlier years. Consequently, they had no use for Comanches.

"They had given so much trouble and had committed so many beastly acts against the white folks that we had no mercy on them," Blevins told the WPA interviewer. "It is now over with and I may tell the feeling most of us had towards the Comanches. We delighted in having a chance to shoot them and did so if there was a plausible excuse. We were not supposed to do so but did vent our feelings for revenge. I look back now and know we did wrong many times."

If the Rangers "did wrong many times," it was not reported to headquarters in Austin. The adjutant general's biannual report reflects numerous reports of Indians in the Panhandle and several scouts by Captain Arrington in pursuit of them, but the document notes the killing of only one Indian in an engagement in January 1879. The year before had been different. Ranger A. A. Ruzin was killed on August 10, 1878, in a fight with Indians. If Blevins was not present when the one Indian was killed in early 1879, he certainly had an opportunity to hear tales of Indian fighting from other Rangers around the campfire. On the other hand, he may have been performing a bit to meet the expectations of the government interviewer. That, or Captain Arrington had been a bit lax in his paperwork, neglecting to mention the killing of reservation Indians who ventured into Texas.

Blevins certainly seemed to be speaking from experience when he talked about fighting Comanches.

"The Comanche Indians were well-built men . . . and were real hossmen," he said. "If we run on to some Comanches out of bounds [of their reservation in Indian Territory], we would shoot his pony out from under him [and] when that hoss hit the ground that Indian never went into a spill but hit the ground running. I have seen many of them go off their hoss that way. . . . It was really a pretty sight to see the Comanche with his feathered headdress and red breechcloth leave a falling hoss."

At Doan's Store, a trading post where the Western Cattle Trail crossed the Red River, Blevins once got an opportunity to see how fast a Comanche could mount a horse.

Captain Arrington and a recently arrested prisoner were inside the store run by Corwin Doan while the other Rangers waited outside.

"While [they] were in the store we saw a number of Comanche Indians trailing in on their ponies," Blevins told his Depression-era interviewer.

> The bucks went inside while the squaw remained on the outside tending to the hosses. Several of us Rangers started to visit with the squaws....I had not seen a white woman for over a year at that time and an Indian squaw began to look mighty beautiful to me.
>
> One of the squaws said to me, "Squaw want 'baccy." I had a full plug of the kind we used; it was such that we could chew, smoke in a pipe, or roll in a cigarette. That squaw was about to get that whole plug of tobacco when suddenly them bucks came out of the store as if they were shot out of a cannon. Each one of them leaped to their horses from a distance of five or more feet without laying a hand on the ponies. Everyone landed in the proper place on his hoss. The hosses were on the go the instant the bucks hit their backs.

From the captain, Blevins learned what had precipitated the rapid departure of the Comanches.

"One of the bucks asked Doan who we were, and when he answered Rangers they never waited to take another breath," Blevins said. "I wondered why all of them were bending low over their pony's neck as they dragged off....They were expecting a shot in the back at any second....They all hit it back towards their reservation."

Another meeting between the Rangers and the Comanches could have led to shooting, but it would have been an accident.

One night the company camped in Hardeman County near the Pease River. Blevins was standing guard.

"Suddenly I heard a number of persons talking Comanche Indian," he related. "When I heard those voices in an undertone coming through the still air I thought [Quanah] Parker ...had surrounded us. I flattened on the ground prone and hollered 'Halt!' and ordered them to stay where they were. Then I went to praying."

Blevins had a dark vision of the entire Ranger company being wiped out by the famous half-blood chief and his braves, who only three years earlier had been fighting General Ranald MacKenzie's Fourth Cavalry.

"There was no question in my mind but that would take place," he said. "To hear Comanche Indians talking at the edge of your camp in the middle of the night could not be accounted for except that they were there to get us."

What happened next relaxed Blevins a little.

"I will stay here, you call Captain Arrington," someone said. "Quanah wants to talk to him."

Blevins scurried back to camp and awakened the captain.

"Tell him to come with his crowd holding their hands high and advance to the campfire," Arrington said. "[And] when they get there to build up the fire."

Arrington and the other Rangers got their guns and moved away from the fire into the darkness. The Indians, realizing that Arrington was only taking what he thought to be a sensible precaution, complied with the order.

"Quanah was a majestic-looking person standing there with his arms folded across his chest and in full Indian dress while his interpreter stated his request," Blevins said. "Quanah wanted Arrington to give him permission to go into Parker County for the purpose of transacting some business. The Captain had no right to grant such request and told him so....Quanah did not think much of that and left disappointed."

Though Quanah was widely respected in northwest Texas and never caused any more trouble after moving to the reservation, Plains Indians found it harder to break off old habits.

Notified that a party of Indians had left the reservation, killed a cowboy, and were "engaged in rustling...cattle by means of stampeding the herd and picking up the strays," Arrington's Rangers set out on their trail.

"We were camped in a gully near a dry creek bed, and this particular morning the Captain and a few of the boys left to see if they could pick up a trail while the balance of us remained in camp," Blevins said.

With no Indian fighting immediately at hand, Blevins asked Orderly Sergeant J. B. "Bud" Kimball if he and Ranger Pete Clark could go turkey hunting.

Kimball, known for his fluent use of profanity, gave the two Rangers permission to go off by themselves.

"If you damn fools get lost, shoot three times and the rest of us will come down and kill both of you," he said.

Blevins and Clark moved down the creek bed a mile or so and came up on a flock of wild turkeys. Each brought down a bird. On their way back to camp, the two Rangers saw more game but were content with their two turkeys.

"We kept on walking, and finally it seemed to me that we had gone far enough to have reached the camp," Blevins said. "We parlayed a bit and decided to go on because we were sure we had not passed the camp and we had stayed in the creek bed."

When the sun went down they still had not found the Ranger camp. One of them fired three rapid shots, the traditional Western signal for help. When no reply seemed forthcoming, they fired another three rounds. Knowing well that shots fired on a still night in open country could be heard for a long way, Blevins concluded that something bad had happened to his fellow Rangers. Just to be absolutely sure, they snapped off three more shots into the air.

This time they heard two shots fired in reply. But the shots were coming from the wrong direction.

"I said to Clark, 'That is not our crowd.... What we have done is give our location to a bunch of Comanches'," Blevins recalled.

He knew that other than Rangers, the only people with guns in that part of the state would be Indians. Clearly, Indians had heard their shots and were moving in their direction.

The two Rangers glanced quickly around for a defensible position. Seeing none, they stretched prone on the ground. Unstrapping their cartridge belts, they spread them at hand's reach. Minus two cartridges expended in killing the turkeys and nine shots fired to signal their location, they were short eleven rounds.

"We figured they would circle us and close in," Blevins said. "We waited for the short fight and our end."

Maybe the two Rangers said their prayers. But before they got too deep in making final spiritual amends, they heard footsteps coming their way. Then Blevins recognized the articulate cussing of Sergeant Kimball.

"Here we are if it's us you're looking for," Blevins yelled.

"What in hell? And this place is it!" the sergeant bellowed. "Do you [the WPA interviewer replaced expletives with asterisks] think we are looking for rheumatism?"

Then Captain Arrington stepped forward.

"Are you boys lost?"

"No," Blevins replied, "we are not lost, but the camp has been moved a tolerable distance. Give us a drink of water."

"Water!" the captain shot back. "Don't mention that word again. We've been without it tramping all over this [expletive] country looking for you two, so don't mention water."

Blevins said he understood.

"Let's get going," Blevins said. "Where is the camp?"

Arrington pointed to a distant butte still visible in the growing darkness. "It's a short way beyond that," he said.

"I don't think so," Blevins said, bordering on insubordination.

The captain insisted that he was right and they kept walking.

"When we reached it the whole party concluded that we were wrong," Blevins recalled. The searchers were now as lost as the men they had been looking for.

The captain decided they should spend the night where they were and continue looking for their camp after daylight.

Without blankets or water, they spent an uncomfortable night.

Blevins was the first to wake up in the morning.

"Let's get going," he said loud enough to wake everyone else. "I want some water."

Despite a poor night's sleep, the young Ranger was still fast enough to dodge Arrington's boot.

"Next time you say water," the captain said, "it will be lead coming your way."

The thirsty Rangers quickly got their bearings and found their camp, which had not been far away. Soon they were well watered down and roasting a couple of turkeys over their campfire. Blevins did not mention whether they ever found the renegade Indians they had set out to track.

By the midpoint of Blevins' Ranger service, by far the greatest danger he and his colleagues faced was not Indians slipping off their reservation but the outlaw's bullet. Trailing cattle rustlers led Blevins to the wildest shootout of his career.

"One time we were scouting...in Yellow [House] Canyon and jumped a bunch of rustlers," he recalled. "We tailed them to the sand dunes on the [New Mexico] line where their hosses gave out."

The rustlers forted up on top of one of the dunes, which was covered in scrub oak.

"We had received word that they did not intend to be taken and would fight it out to the last man," the old Ranger continued, remembering back over more than half a century. "We were expecting a good battle and was ready for it."

The Rangers were anticipating that good battle, however, at the sand hill where they could see the rustler's horses. When they walked up on that rise without incident, they realized the rustlers had pulled back to a distant knoll and hidden in the brush.

"As we approached the dune they were in, we were suddenly treated to a shower of lead," Blevins said.

He recalled that one of the outlaw's first bullets hit a Ranger named Jim Moore in the heart and dropped him dead off his horse.

Ranger Private J. H. Moore did serve under Arrington when Blevins was in the company, but Moore completed his enlistment in Company C in good health. However, on March 31, 1887, as a private in Company F, he was killed in a gunfight in East Texas long after Blevins' rangering days were over. Arrington's reports do not indicate that he lost any men in his company in the line of duty during Blevins' period of service. Blevins apparently was stretching the blanket a bit for dramatic effect or confusing some details of the gunfight he described with the battle in East Texas that killed Moore.

Cattle rustling was a definite problem on the High Plains at the time, and Blevins' description of the shooting that followed seems plausible.

"We surrounded the dune and pinned fire on the boys," he said. "In less than thirty minutes there was no return fire from the rustlers. We then closed in on them shooting.... When we reached the spot where they were, we found eight men all branded."

"Branded" seemed to have been a popular Ranger euphemism for "dead." Blevins used it often during the interview.

"Our job was completed so we took Moore's body and left," Blevins continued. "Inside of twenty minutes after we left the spot, we heard the wolves fighting over the bodies. That was about the hardest fight...I took part in with the Rangers."

Ranch owners and their cowhands were no easier on rustlers than the Rangers.

"We found many rustlers hung up to dry," Blevins said. "Nobody seemed to know how the rustlers happened to get hung to a limb. Someone would tell us: 'I hear there are some rustlers naturalized over yonder.' We would cut them down and turn the bodies over to the sheriff of the county. In some parts of the country limbs were scarce and in that case rustlers would be given a short course in citizenship.... When we located such bodies we would always find neat bullet holes."

A search for rustlers soon led to another gunfight. Blevins was guarding the horses one night while the other Rangers slept. About midnight, he heard a fusillade of shots coming from the camp.

Rustlers, Blevins figured, had slipped up on the Rangers and killed them in their sleep.

"I flattened on the ground and I mean I flattened so they could not sky-line me," Blevins recalled. "I layed there for what seemed an age and nothing happened."

Hearing nothing more coming from camp, Blevins decided to slip up and take a look. Crawling on his belly, his rifle ready, the Ranger saw Ranger Jack O'Mally sitting up with a gun in his hand. All the other Rangers were rolled up in their Navajo blankets.

"What happened?" Blevins whispered.

"We had an awful battle," O'Mally replied.

"I know that," Blevins said. "Did you fellows spy the rustlers in time?"

"Hell no," O'Mally answered. "A drove of hydrophobia [rabid] cats run into us. Look around out there and you can see them."

Blevins stood and surveyed the battlefield. At least twenty-five dead skunks were scattered around the camp.

Captain Arrington resigned from the Rangers in the summer of 1882 to run for sheriff of Wheeler County. Blevins ended his Ranger career about the same time. But while his old boss stayed on the high plains, Blevins moved southwest to Toyah, a wild and wooly town twenty-five miles from Pecos on the newly completed Texas and Pacific Railroad.

With his Ranger experience, he probably could have gotten a job as a deputy sheriff, but he opted for a new line of work: running a saloon. Blevins stayed in Reeves County for a couple of years, then followed the railroad back to an even rowdier boomtown, Colorado City. There, he owned and operated one of the twenty-eight saloons doing a flourishing business in the community of fifteen hundred.

"I run a saloon there for eight years," Blevins recalled. "It [Colorado City] was the cow center of that section and no Sunday school meeting town at that time."

In 1892 Blevins drifted back to his home range in North Texas. He lived for a time in Weatherford and then moved to Greenville, in Hunt County, where he joined the International Order of Odd Fellows. From Greenville he returned to Fort Worth where he held a variety of jobs over the years, from his old standby livelihood of bartending to repairing streetcars for the Fort Worth Street Railway. Later he founded the Malt and Liquor Dealers Association of Texas and spent time in Austin as a lobbyist. Despite his background in the alcoholic beverage industry, in 1921 he was accepted into membership at Fort Worth's First Baptist Church and baptized by the flamboyant Reverend J. Frank Norris. From 1923 to 1927 he was a deputy Tarrant County clerk. In 1932 he ran for county treasurer but lost.

Blevins went from rangering to bartending. At Toyah, he worked in a saloon similar to this restored Old West bar in the museum at Pecos. (Author's collection)

On November 16, 1938, while raking leaves in his backyard, the old Ranger suffered a heart attack and died a few minutes later. He would have turned eighty-two the next day.

Five days after his death he was buried in the Redman Lodge plot at Mount Olivet Cemetery in Fort Worth.

Blevins had always looked back on his rangering days with nothing but fondness.

"They were a brave lot of fellows those days," he told the WPA worker. "They were men that could take it and give it."

And have a little fun while they were at it.

······ ✪ ······

Notes

[1] Blevins told the WPA interviewer that he joined the Rangers in 1879. Unless some of Blevins' paperwork was lost in the 1881 capitol fire, adjutant general's records in the State Archives show Blevins and his friend J. W. "Pete" Clark enlisted on the same day—March 1, 1881. Blevins was discharged on November 24, 1881, with service of six months and three days.

Sources

"Blevins Funeral Is Set for Today," *Fort Worth Star-Telegram*, November 20, 1938.

Blevins, William. Interview by Sheldon F. Gauthier. Tarrant County, Texas, Federal Writers' Project, 1937 in American Life Histories: Manuscripts from the Federal Writers' Project, 1936-1940, Library of Congress.

Ingmire, Frances J. *Texas Ranger Service Records, 1847-1900*. St. Louis: n.p., 1982.

"Noted Indian Fighter of Pioneer Days Dies," *Fort Worth Star-Telegram*, November 17, 1938.

"Cap" Arrington

George Washington "Cap" Arrington and his twenty Rangers had been in the saddle for the better—or worse—part of several weeks that summer of 1879, riding from the Brazos to the farthest outpost of settlement in Texas.

As Arrington unfastened the cinch and lifted the saddle off his horse, the thirty-four-year-old captain of Company C, Frontier Battalion watched as a ruddy-faced man rode toward him. The moment the man opened his mouth, Arrington knew by his brogue that he was Irish. A second or two later, the Ranger sized him up as a "shoulder-hitter," or thug.

In "a very loud and gruff voice," the visitor asked Arrington if he was the man in charge. The Ranger captain replied that he was.

"Colonel Davidson wants to see you," the Irishman said. "He says you are going to attack the Indians."

Observing that the U.S. Army certainly seemed to know a lot about his business, Arrington said he might call on the officer the next day.

The Irishman wheeled his horse and loped back to Fort Elliott.

Arrington's one-man welcoming committee had barely ridden out of sight when Lieutenant Colonel John W. Davidson himself rolled up to the Ranger camp in his wagon. The blue-coated 10th Cavalry officer seemed to be in "a terrible passion."

Seated after curt formalities, the colonel asked about Arrington's orders "in regard to Indians."

"I told him that my orders were always to give protection to life and property and preserve the peace whether from Indians or white men," Arrington later reported to headquarters in Austin.

The colonel's next question was whether Arrington intended to kill any Indians he might find.

"I replied that I most assuredly would if they were armed," Arrington wrote.

The two men, one speaking for the federal government, the other representing the state of Texas, then engaged in "a good deal of random talk" before the colonel took leave. The Ranger captain made no mention in his June 18, 1879 report of the incident or any invitation to join the colonel and his staff officers for dinner at the post.

Six days later Arrington was told by the Irishman—a clerk at the post sutler's store named Donnelly—that the garrison commander had said he would order his soldiers to fire on the Rangers or arrest them if they engaged any Indians in the Panhandle.

Hearing that, Arrington was mad enough to draw his Colt revolver. Instead, he whipped out a pen and wrote a note to the Fort Elliott commander:

Sir,

One John Donnelly...has said...that you would fire upon me and my men or put us in irons if we should kill or molest any Indians in the Panhandle. This man Donnelly is the one whom you honored as a messenger to me on the day of my arrival here—and for that reason I think his talk should be noticed.

I therefore desire to know whether or not Donnelly expressed your intentions in policy, not that I have any fears of you in the execution of the enterprise, but for the purpose of laying the matter before the Governor and the Legislature of Texas, which is now in session.

Ignoring Arrington, the colonel dashed off a copy of the Ranger's note to Governor Oran Roberts along with an affidavit from Donnelly witnessed by a first lieutenant.

The within statement as made by Capt. Arrington is not true. I said that if they did fire or kill an Indian that the Commanding Officer at Fort Elliott *should* [italics added] fire on them and put them in irons. I further said that the only object in getting these Rangers here was to provoke an Indian war.

The colonel's decision to call Arrington a liar—via mail to a third party—was a better idea than another face-to-face discussion of the matter. With two scars on his body left by Yankee bullets, Arrington was a little touchy when it came to dealing with military officers in blue uniforms.

Thirteen years had passed since the end of the Civil War, but being around Federal troops brought back memories the Ranger captain still fought hard to suppress. His men knew he had fought for the South during the Civil War, but there was more to Arrington's past than most people knew about. For one thing, he had not been born George Washington Arrington. The captain's real name was John C. Orrick Jr. The reason he changed his name had nothing to do with not liking how it sounded. The change was a matter of expediency.

Born in Greensboro, Alabama, on December 23, 1844, Orrick was not yet seventeen when he joined the 5th Regiment, Alabama Infantry on April 13, 1861. Wounded in the Battle of Sharpsburg on September 17, 1862, he recovered and rose from foot soldier to cavalryman. As a private in Company E, Jeff Davis Legion, Houston's Brigade of Cavalry, he survived the bloody fighting at Gettysburg but was taken prisoner at Funkstown, Maryland, a week after the battle.

As the trainload of captured Confederates approached Baltimore, where he and his fellow soldiers were to be imprisoned at Fort McHenry, Orrick and several other men jumped from the train. A rifle ball cut down one of the fleeing prisoners next to him, but Orrick escaped. He made his way to his grandparents' home in Maryland, but, sympathetic to the Union cause, they turned him away.

Still recovering from his wound, which had reopened during his escape, Orrick managed to reach Virginia. There he joined Company C, Mosby's Rangers, 43rd Virginia Battalion.

John Singleton Mosby, an expert practitioner of guerrilla warfare, became known as the "Gray Ghost" during the war. He and his men, including Orrick, wrecked Union supply trains, cut Federal troops off behind their lines, disrupted communication, and in general played havoc with the U.S. Army. Under Mosby, Orrick learned tactics that would serve him well as a Texas Ranger.

When the war ended in April 1865, Orrick, now a hardened young veteran of twenty-one, was paroled in Virginia to return to civilian life. Back in Greensboro, he worked for a time in a store, but fighting was a hard habit to break. When Orrick heard of the French imperialist adventure in Mexico, he and seven others headed south to join Emperor Maximilian's mercenary forces. The movement was popular in the South, where some saw it as another hope for the Confederacy, even though the fighting ended at Appomattox. But before Orrick got to Mexico, Maximilian was executed.

Back in Greensboro, Orrick soon became involved in what nineteenth-century journalists liked to refer to as a "difficulty." On June 13, 1867, he shot and killed a black businessman. "We infer from the few facts we have been able to gather," a newspaper reported two days after the shooting, "that something had previously passed between them through a third party, which was particularly offensive to Orrick."

Whatever the circumstances of the case, local authorities considered it more than a mere "affair of honor." Orrick was charged with murder. But the ex-Rebel did not stay in Alabama and try to clear his name. He fled to Honduras, where he hid out for about a year. Back in the United States in July 1868, he traveled around some before coming to Texas in 1870. By that time he was George Washington Arrington. How he came by his new first and middle name was obvious enough. He took his mother's maiden name for his new last name.

Landing in Galveston, Arrington walked to Houston where he got a job in a sawmill. In the span of four years he hired on for a time with a railroad, worked in a commission house in Galveston, farmed, and then took up cowboying. That occupation took him to Brown County on the edge of settlement.

There, in April 1875, he tried to enlist in the Rangers, but he was denied a commission because of the Alabama murder indictment, which he owned up to. After hearing Arrington's side of the story, Frontier Battalion commander John B. Jones urged him to go home and stand trial to clear his name. But Arrington, clearly fearing conviction, decided to stay in Texas. Recognizing talent when he saw it, Jones hired him as a civilian scout.

Somehow—the details are not known—Jones changed his mind about accepting Arrington into the Rangers. On September 1, 1875, Arrington was able to enlist in Company E under Captain Neal Coldwell. Later, when Coldwell took over command of Company A, Arrington went with him. By 1876 Arrington had been promoted to sergeant. On Christmas Day 1877 he was named lieutenant in command of Company C.

Arrington was notified of his promotion to captain in a letter written by Adjutant General Jones on May 7, 1879. "I trust," Jones wrote, "that your conduct and services and management in the future will be such that I will never have cause to regret having made the recommendation."

So far as is known, Jones never did. Nothing of consequence came of the friction between the U.S. Army officer and the Ranger captain, but among certain parties at Fort Elliott, Texas Rangers were not welcome. They, and the government they represented, were seen by some as an impediment to good business.

"Lee and Reynolds, who were post traders and who handled all the mail that came here, were in opposition to the movement for [county] organization and were doing everything in their power to prevent [it], even to holding up letters which they thought might be instrumental in bringing new conditions about," Arrington wrote years later.

To get his letters back to Ranger headquarters in Austin, a trusted ally carried Arrington's correspondence westward across the Panhandle to New Mexico Territory. From there, the letters went to Austin by U.S. mail. "I knew it [his mail] would not reach its destination if it had to go through the trading post at Mobeetie," Arrington recalled.

In addition to his problems with the post traders at Fort Elliott, someone writing the *Ford County (Kansas) Globe*, one of two newspapers covering the thinly populated Panhandle, denounced Arrington and his men.

A correspondent for the other newspaper, the *Dodge City Times*, replied on August 25:

> Capt. Arrington certainly never injured any one in this section of the world but Indians found depredating on Texas soil, and had it not been for the timely arrival of this company, the horrible scenes and deeds of bloodshed perpetrated in your country by the barbarous Cheyennes last fall, would have surely been reenacted in the Pan Handle.
>
> Arrington has not only thanks of people but their everlasting gratitude in not only doing his duty but doing it so nobly. Within 30 days after his broad brimmed sombreros entered the Pan Handle country not an Indian remained alive on Texas soil; and they have stayed put.

Not that Arrington and his men actually killed any Indians. The captain stayed in camp near the fort for ten days, then scouted farther west.

Shortly after the Rangers broke camp, a group of Pueblo Indians from New Mexico rode into Fort Elliott. They had been on a trading expedition to meet up with the Cheyennes in Indian Territory, but Arrington and his Rangers found them before they got all the way through Texas.

The Pueblos, according to the *Dodge City Times*, "sought protection under the Stars and Stripes at Elliott. The commanding officer gave them protection for a day or two, then gave them an escort to take them beyond the scope of the Rangers. These Indians were heavily loaded with various commerce to trade, but had to return to from whence they came."

Arrington may or may not have known the Indians had gone to the fort for protection, but the fact they arrived at all must have meant he did not consider them hostile, merely unwelcome.

Soon, the captain was pleased to hear that Colonel Davidson had received orders to rejoin his old regiment, the

2nd Cavalry, in Montana Territory. If Arrington had any trouble with Davidson's successor at Fort Elliott, he did not report it.

From Fort Elliott, Arrington moved his company diagonally across the Panhandle to scout for Indians and cattle thieves. The captain liked to ride ahead of his men and let them trail him. It was prudent and good practice for the younger Rangers.

Arrington's men knew he was headed toward Blanco Canyon, but they lost his trail.

While waiting for the rest of his men at Charles Goodnight's JA Ranch in Palo Duro Canyon, Arrington did not immediately identify himself as a Ranger. But Goodnight, who had once ridden as a Ranger himself, suspected Arrington was not just another cowboy. After a few days in respectful observance of that part of the unwritten Western code that held against asking too many questions of strangers, the old cattleman finally asked Arrington who he was.

When Arrington told him he was a Ranger captain, Goodnight's next question was whether he held warrants for any of his employees.

"I said that I did want a man who was working in a blacksmith shop...but that I didn't believe I would risk taking him, since he had done such a good job a short time before of hanging a horse thief...I didn't think he ought to be bothered," Arrington wrote years later. That sentiment was a clear reflection that Arrington, like other Rangers, believed that there were degrees of justice.

Leaving the JA with a promise from Goodnight that he could raise seventy-five armed men "any time" to lend the Rangers a hand if he ever needed the help, Arrington and his company rode beneath the Caprock through Briscoe, Motley, and Floyd Counties. The Rangers found that the country was settling up rapidly.

Arrington wrote Austin on July 12, 1879, to suggest that he be authorized to establish a semipermanent camp on the High Plains. He received the necessary approval, and on September 9 he set up Camp Roberts—named in honor of the governor—on Catfish Creek about eight miles from the mouth of Blanco Canyon in Crosby County. Using the camp as a base, Arrington and his Rangers scouted as far as 300 miles to the west, well into New Mexico Territory, along the Canadian River to the north and to the Devil's River 500 miles to the south.

Leading twelve men, Arrington rode from the camp in January 1880 on a forty-day scout of unexplored territory in search of the so-called Lost Lake in eastern New Mexico. The Rangers endured a hard march of more than 500 miles in the dead of winter but succeeded in identifying previously unknown Indian water holes and rendezvous points. Strategically, the completion of the scout made any successful Indian raid into Texas virtually impossible.

For a man who had engaged in guerrilla warfare during the Civil War, Arrington was a strict disciplinarian. The surviving written special orders he issued reflect that he did not tolerate excessive drinking or other behavior unbecoming a Ranger, including the way they talked to superior officers. "Members of this company in addressing the non-commissioned officers will address them by the rank to which they are entitled," Arrington ordered. In the spring of 1879, when his company was stationed in Throckmorton County, Arrington discharged a Ranger private for "disobedience of orders," specifically "by having women from Fort Griffin Driving around the herd [presumably a cattle outfit the Rangers were escorting] to meet him, and for trying to pursuade [sic] other members of the company to go with him to meet them."

When one of his men took up with a good woman, however, the captain was happy to issue the Ranger an honorable discharge. On July 15, 1879, Arrington approved one private's request for an honorable discharge "for the purpose of 'trying the sweets of a married life'" while another Ranger was honorably discharged "from the Service of the State" so that he could enter "the bonds of matrimony."

In the summer of 1882 the captain sought his own discharge from the service. His reason for leaving the Rangers was not impending matrimony—though he married Sarah C. Burnette a year later—but to take up ranching. Arrington ended more than seven years of Ranger service when his resignation became effective on August 31. As a Ranger, Arrington had trailed both hostile Indians and outlaws, serving during the time the Rangers were making the transition from a paramilitary body to an organization more concerned with enforcing criminal laws.

Arrington soon hired on as a deputy for Wheeler County sheriff Henry Fleming. He probably had in mind running for the office himself at the next election. Fleming resigned in November 1882, and Arrington was appointed to fill his unexpired term. He stood for the office at the next election and began a two-year term on January 1, 1883.

As sheriff, he did not have the statewide jurisdiction he held as a Ranger, but Arrington's effective territory included more than Wheeler County. For judicial purposes, the county also included all the land covered by ten surrounding unorganized counties: Collingsworth, Gray, Greer, Hansford, Hemphill, Hutchinson, Lipscomb, Ochiltree, and Roberts.

When campaign time rolled around every two years, Arrington set out in his buggy to stump for votes, though in the nearly treeless Panhandle the expression was strictly figurative. In the back of his wagon he carried a gallon of whisky in a wicker demijohn. What earned him more votes than his oratory was his reputation—and free whiskey.

During his last race for sheriff in 1888, Arrington spent his first night on the campaign trail in Ochiltree. "Next morning," he later wrote, "when I took a friend out to my buggy to do some 'electioneering,' we found that when I started to pour the whisky out into a tin cup that someone had stolen all the whisky and put water in its place."

Even though he was happy to offer a drink to prospective voters and never minded a nip or two himself in the name of Democracy, the ex-Ranger would not tolerate the illegal sale of alcohol. When he found the town doctor selling whiskey at ten cents a shot without a license, he ordered the physician to get out of town.

"As I passed down the street in my buggy leaving for Hansford," Arrington recalled, the doctor "came out and stopped me and put a package in the back of the buggy. Two or three miles out of town I found it was a quart of whisky."

But the doctor did as he was told and left Ochiltree, presumably with the rest of his whiskey supply. Twenty-two ballots were cast in Ochiltree County. When the election results came in, all but two votes were for Arrington's opponent. The rest of his counties carried him back into office.

In 1886, while the sheriff attempted to arrest George and John Leverton for cattle theft, John shot twice at Arrington. The sheriff shot at Leverton with a shotgun, but the wanted rustler ran from the cabin, firing at Arrington again as he attempted to flee. Arrington also fired again, dropping John Leverton. Four hours later, he died.

A grand jury found sufficient cause to indict Arrington for murder in the death, but in a short jury trial in July 1887 he won acquittal.

After serving four terms as sheriff, Arrington decided to leave law enforcement in 1890, fifteen years after he first joined the Rangers. His chief deputy was elected Wheeler County sheriff and Arrington concentrated full time on his ranching interests. By then he owned 37,000 acres along the Washita River in Hemphill County and a smaller spread in Gray County. In addition to overseeing his own ranching operations, in 1893 he was hired to manage the 250,000-acre British-owned Rocking Chair Ranch.

At the age of fifty in 1894, Arrington was appointed sheriff of Hemphill County after the incumbent was mortally wounded in an unsuccessful railway express robbery. Arrington tracked down the killer, who got a life prison sentence.

When the Rocking Chair Ranch was sold, Arrington returned to the management of his own holdings. He was active in Masonic affairs and became one of the Panhandle's civic leaders.

In 1922 Arrington's longtime friend Charles Goodnight put together a reunion at the old JA Ranch. Goodnight, well aware that he and his friends were the last of a breed, arranged for a photographer to take pictures of the old-timers. The *Dallas Morning News* published one of the images on June 18, noting they were men "who helped to make history in West Texas."

Arthritis plagued Arrington in his final years. He believed the hot, mineral-laden waters available at various health resorts in Mineral Wells eased his discomfort, and he usually spent his winters there. Heading back to the Panhandle on a train from Mineral Wells in March 1923, the old Ranger had a heart attack. He died on March 31 at his home in Canadian. He was seventy-eight.

In 1930 cowboy historian J. Evetts Haley, then field secretary for the Panhandle-Plains Historical Society at Canyon, tried to pin down the date Arrington legally changed his name. He believed it had been

This historical marker commemorating Captain Arrington stands outside the old Wheeler County Jail in Mobeetie. (Photo by author)

accomplished by legislative act but could find no record of it in H. P. N. Gammel's *Laws of Texas*. Haley wrote Arrington's widow seeking information on the matter.

"I appreciate the interest you take in the life of my late husband," Mrs. Arrington replied on July 13, 1930, "but I feel that what you want is too personal, and I am sure were he living he would refuse, as I am doing. I know that his friends who are now living would understand, but the coming generation might not. I feel that I owe it to his memory to refuse."

One of the captain's old friends was W. S. Mabry of Selma, Alabama. Mabry collected information on Arrington's Alabama roots and furnished it to Haley.

"For many years I knew Captain Arrington well," Mabry wrote. "There is much to his career worth preserving, without dwelling on the tragedy he enacted in Greensboro, causing him to leave there. He was one of the best peace officers in Texas and deserved great credit."

107

The old Ranger had lived two lives—one as John C. Orrick Jr. and one as George Washington Arrington. He packed a lot in both.

Shortly after Arrington's death in 1923 he was featured on the cover of J. Marvin Hunter's *Frontier Times*. (Author's collection)

Sources

Arrington, George Washington. "Organization of Panhandle Counties." Unpublished manuscript, n.d., George Washington Arrington Papers, Panhandle-Plains Historical Museum, Canyon, Texas.

_____. Papers. Panhandle-Plains Historical Museum, Canyon, Texas.

Haley, J. Evetts. "Arrington's Life-Sketch." Unpublished interview of Mrs. G. W. Arrington, n.d., George Washington Arrington Papers, Panhandle-Plains Historical Museum, Canyon, Texas.

Hunter, J. Marvin. "Captain Arrington's Expedition." *Frontier Times*, Vol. 6, No. 3, December 1928, pp. 97-102.

Mabry, W. S. Papers. Panhandle-Plains Historical Museum, Canyon, Texas.

Sheffy, L. F. "The Arrington Papers." *Panhandle-Plains Historical Review*, Vol. 1, No. 1, 1928, pp. 30-66.

Sinise, Jerry. *George Washington Arrington: Civil War Spy, Texas Ranger, Sheriff and Rancher*. Burnet: Eakin Press, 1977.

White, Lonnie J., ed. *Old Mobeetie 1877-1885: Texas Panhandle News Items From The Dodge City Times*. Canyon: Panhandle-Plains Historical Society, 1967.

Being Robbed: A Vested Right

By most measures West Texas was downright civilized in 1884. The vast herds of shaggy buffalo were gone. The Rangers had not fought any Indians in three years. The Legislature convened in special session and made it a felony to cut any of the barbed-wire fences that were rapidly partitioning the once open range. And two years had passed since workers drove the last spike on the tracks of the Texas and Pacific Railroad, connecting the region with the rest of the nation.

The closest the T&P came to San Angelo, however, was Abilene, eighty-nine miles to the northeast. In the mid-1880s, to get to the seat of sprawling Tom Green County, which at that time stretched all the way to New Mexico, a person had only three practical choices of transportation: horse, wagon, or stagecoach.

This is how San Angleo looked when stage robbing was common.
(Author's collection)

110

A daily stagecoach connected San Angelo with Abilene. Business was good for the stagecoach company—and for stagecoach robbers. In the winter of 1884, holdups seemed almost as regular as the stages. Seven robberies occurred in one three-month period. San Angelo residents appreciated having dependable transportation to and from the railhead, but they were getting a little skittish about using it. Even the ranking military officer in West Texas, Colonel Benjamin Grierson, a man who had survived the Civil War and fights with Apaches, would not ride the stagecoach out of San Angelo.

Looking down the barrel a six-shooter in the hands of a masked bandit was unsettling but not usually life threatening. Assuming the victims were cooperative and did not pay too much attention to what the holdup men looked like, most robbers were content to collect money and valuables from stagecoach travelers without harming them in a physical way. Some robbers were even relatively polite.

The two robbers picked a bad night to hit the Abilene-San Angelo stage. Here, latter-day re-enactors ford a stream. (Photo courtesy Austin History Center, Austin Public

Stage robbery was so common in West Texas in the early 1880s that journalist Alexander Sweet joked about it in his humor sheet, *The Texas Siftings*:

> There are only nine stage robbers in jail in San Antonio now, and the Lord knows how many on the outside. Why, at one time, the traveling public became so accustomed to going through the usual ceremonies that they complained to the stage company if they came through unmolested. Being robbed came to be regarded as a vested right.

What happened in the early morning hours of February 4, 1884, however, was not funny.

The two men waiting patiently for the westbound stage expected to complete their work quickly and efficiently and then double back to King's Saloon in San Angelo for another round or two. They had already robbed the eastbound stage and sent it on its way. That half of their night's work netted them $25 in cash from a passenger plus some money collected from the registered mail the stage had been carrying.

But while it was reasonable to assume that the driver and passengers of the stage heading toward San Angelo would be carrying varying amounts of money, the robbers had no way of knowing who the passengers were. Neither, apparently, did the robbers anticipate the possibility that the stage they had just detained would soon meet up with the stage they intended to rob next.

When the eastbound driver hailed the westbound stage to report the holdup, two passengers on the stage from Abilene listened with particular interest: Texas Ranger Sergeant J. S. Turnbo of El Paso-based Company A and Deputy Sheriff W. L. Jerrell of Las Cruces, New Mexico. Jerrell's brother-in-law was El Paso County sheriff James White.

The two lawmen were on their way to San Angelo with a warrant for a man wanted in New Mexico for armed robbery. Four other passengers, including a soldier with orders to report to Fort Concho, shared the coach with the officers.

After hearing of the robbery, the driver of the westbound stage thought it best to turn around and spend the night at the nearest stage stop. The Ranger saw it differently and told him to keep going. Before proceeding, however, the passengers did change their seating arrangements. Ranger Turnbo moved to the window on the left side of the coach with the New Mexico deputy taking the opposite window. The two officers put their pistols in their laps. Reluctantly, the driver jiggled his reins and the horses started moving.

A mile down the road—still about five miles from San Angelo—two masked men brandishing pistols emerged from the mesquite thicket on Jerrell's side of the stage and yelled for the driver to stop. As the driver reined the team and pulled the brake lever, Jerrell raised his six-shooter and fired at one of the robbers. He missed.

Though they had not expected resistance, the outlaws reacted quickly. Jerrell saw two flashes of orange as a pair of bullets slammed him back against the leather seat. As the other passengers ducked, Turnbo sprang to the right side of the stage and aimed at one of the gunmen. When the Ranger fired, he saw the man's pistol fly from his hand. The robber grabbed his stomach and went down but quickly got back to his feet.

Lead tore through the wooden sides of the coach as Turnbo and the robbers continued to shoot at each other. The soldier, traveling unarmed, picked up Jerrell's pistol and joined the gunfight.

From above came shots fired by a passenger in the shotgun seat next to the driver. His .32 revolver did not have the knockdown power of the officers' .45s, but at close range the difference was negligible.

All the shooting spooked the horses. As the driver struggled to control the team, the stage jerked into motion. Still the robbers kept up their fire. With the horses running in fright, Turnbo opened the door of the coach and leaned out to shoot back at the robbers. A newspaper later called the Ranger a man of "dauntless courage and untiring energy." Considering the amount of lead that flew in Turnbo's direction during the attempted robbery, in describing the Company A sergeant the correspondent could as easily have added the word "lucky."

The outlaws decided to leave well enough alone and not give chase, but they kept shooting at the stage until it rolled out of sight in the darkness. "Firing from and into the stage continued with great rapidity," the *Galveston News* later reported.

When the stagecoach reached San Angelo, Turnbo and others helped carry the wounded Jerrell to the San Angelo Hotel and placed him on one of the beds. Someone ran to awaken Dr. S. L. S. Smith, who quickly dressed, grabbed his bag, and rushed to the hotel to examine the officer. The doctor determined that Jerrell had a wound in his lower abdomen and one in his shoulder blade. He had bled considerably, and one of the rounds had pierced his bowels. The doctor realized the only thing he could do for the moaning deputy was give him morphine and try to stop the bleeding.

Next to be treated was passenger Sam P. Cochran of Dallas, who had a minor flesh wound on his back from an inert round. The doctor bandaged the wound and assured Cochran he would be fine.

"Brave and fearless," as the *Police News* later reported, "he [Cochran] was compelled to sit idly by and be shot at without being able to reply as he was entirely unarmed."

Onlookers counted six bullet holes in the stage and three in Cochran's overcoat.

Tom Green County sheriff James D. Spears and his deputies, along with Turnbo and armed volunteers, soon rode out in search of the two gunmen. When they reached the scene of the attempted robbery, they found a small amount of blood on the side of the road but no other sign of the outlaws. Clearly Turnbo had hit one of them, but the robber and his colleague had managed to get away. The Ranger figured his round must have struck the robber's pistol or deflected off his belt buckle, causing only a minor wound.

Deputy Jerrell died about 2 A.M. on Wednesday, February 6. He was buried at 4 P.M. the same day, "it being impossible to convey his body to the railroad," the *San Angelo Times-Enterprise* reported. "His remains, in time, will be removed to his home in New Mexico," the newspaper continued. "His sad death has thrown a gloom over our town that can only be removed by bringing his murderers to justice."

The residents of San Angelo had had enough of stage robbers. The holdup that claimed the lawman's life was the fourth since the first of the year. Within thirty minutes after learning of the robbery, citizens subscribed $700 in reward money.

"The dastardly outrage has at last fully aroused our people and induced them to realize the situation," the *Times-Enterprise* declared. "The blood of a brave officer and valuable citizen," the newspaper continued, "called for vengeance. The cowardly conduct of the murderers in getting behind the stage and emptying their pistols into it, regardless of the fact that it might have contained innocent women and children adds, if anything could add, to their crime. There is no excuse for this affair to go unpunished."

Unknown to the good people of San Angelo, the robbers lived in a tent only about fifty yards from the Tom Green County jail. After the shooting, the two men had circled around the stage and galloped back to town. They changed clothes, patched the minor wound one of them had suffered, and joined the crowd that met the bullet-riddled stage when it arrived. They acted as indignant as the other townspeople.

How long Turnbo stayed in San Angelo after the shooting is not known, but it probably was not long. With responsibility for the entire Trans-Pecos, the nineteen men of Company A had no shortage of work. The prevented holdup was just another incident in a busy year during which Rangers killed seven outlaws in various incidents and two of their own were wounded. When the adjutant general compiled his report for 1884, the abortive stage robbery was mentioned briefly, but Turnbo was misidentified as another Ranger, F. W. DeJarnette. Company records show DeJarnette had been discharged from the service nearly a year before the attempted robbery.

Meanwhile, despite the tough talk in the San Angelo newspaper, the two robbers kept up their work. But they did change scenery for a while. Three weeks after killing the New

Mexico deputy, the outlaws robbed the post office at Pipe's Creek in Bandera County, west of San Antonio. Their take was only 75 cents in silver. Back in Tom Green County that spring, on May 3 they hit another stage.

That robbery finally led to their downfall. When the men stopped the stage, they found it crowded with eleven members of a variety troupe. None of the performers had much money, but the five women in the traveling show wore expensive-looking jewelry. It was only the cheap costume variety, but the robbers were not particularly sophisticated in their judgment of finery.

One of the robbers gave the jewelry to his girlfriend, who also happened to be his partner's sister. The young woman did not realize the jewelry was as phony as her lover's story of how he acquired it. Quite naturally, she showed off the glittering evidence of her sweetheart's affection. Eventually, someone who viewed the jewelry as evidence of another sort informed the authorities.

The woman's brother, Lewis Potter, and James McDaniel were arrested in Mitchell County by Sheriff Dick Ware for murder and robbing the U.S. mail. Ware sent a telegram bearing the happy news to Sheriff Spears in San Angelo.

"Officers leave here next week and will bring the criminals to San Angelo for a preliminary examination," the *San Angelo Standard* reported on June 21, 1884. The next week's issue of the *Standard* noted that Potter and McDaniel had been returned from Colorado City to Tom Green County by Sheriff Spears and a deputy and were in jail "awaiting further developments."

On July 5, 1884, the suspected stage robbers were taken to San Antonio—by stagecoach—to face the federal mail robbery charges. The *San Antonio Express* reported during their examining trial that the two accused robbers were "a pair of as bad-looking men as one would wish to see."

Both men received life sentences on May 14, 1885, and were remanded to the Bexar County jail to await transfer to the prison at Chester, Illinois. The prison was a state facility but accepted federal prisoners on a contract basis.

In June, McDaniel escaped from jail and made it to the Boerne area. Kendall County deputy sheriffs James Van Ripper and Ed Stevens Jr. found him at a goat camp about eight miles from Boerne on July 1. The escaped stage robber violently resisted arrest and was shot and killed by the two officers.

Six days after McDaniel's demise, Potter left San Antonio in the company of deputy U.S. marshals to begin his prison sentence in the land of Lincoln.

The removal of Potter and McDaniel from society significantly reduced the number of stage robberies along the Abilene-San Angelo road, but in their absence others were willing to give it a try. Fort Concho began providing soldiers for escort duty, but only for coaches carrying U.S. mail.

"Army starts escort of 2 men with driver in a buck board to attend the stage from San Angelo to Abilene and return," noted diarist George W. Wedemeyer, an officer stationed at Fort Concho. The purpose of the escort, he continued in his January 7, 1886 entry, was "to prevent frequent stage robberies on that route."

Six months later, Wedemeyer observed that the situation had improved: "The tough element is pretty well cleaned out. The citizens have done much to encourage the officers of the law and by that means discouraged the rowdy elements."

The smell of money, however, attracted "rowdy elements" like flies to fresh cow patties. When economic activity in and around San Angelo picked up with the approach of the Santa Fe Railroad in late 1887 and early 1888, robbers started hitting the stages again.

One of those holdup men was a criminal with particular verve. On April 20, 1888, he detained the westbound San Angelo stage—at gunpoint—near what is now the town of Miles in Runnels County. Ordering the passengers to alight, he courteously handed them sacks to place over their heads. That done, he collected their cash and other valuables.

Somewhat apologetically, he explained he would have to hold them until the eastbound stage passed so he could rob it, too. For the next four hours, he regaled his captive audience

117

with tales of his exploits in outlawry. He falsely claimed he was Rube Burrows, a celebrated train robber from Alabama.

When the stage did not show as scheduled, the robber released his captives. Conscious of the importance of good public relations in all business operations, "Burrows" wrote out a certificate duly attesting that the passengers had bravely held up during a stagecoach robbery and would have tried to prevent it if they had been armed. One of the victims even offered the robber a drink of whiskey for the road, but the holdup man politely declined. Though relieved of their valuables, the robbery victims at least completed their journey richer in experience.

The Rangers had some success in thwarting stagecoach robberies, but there was too much Texas and too few Rangers to eliminate the problem altogether. In the end, the expansion of the railroads is what put stagecoach robbers—and stagecoach companies—out of business.

With the Santa Fe tracks nearing San Angelo, the last stage robbery on the Abilene-San Angelo road occurred on June 23, 1888, three miles east of Willow Water Hole. The spot was not far from the place "Rube Burrows" liked to stop stages, though it was a different robber this time. Someone recognized the gunman, and by July 15 he was in jail. "Rube Burrows," a robber with a sense of humor if not honor, was never caught.

The *Mason News* summed it up pretty well on September 18, 1888:

"San Angelo is now a railroad point, and the lone highwayman has gone to California, seeking better fields."

Notes

Lycurgus S. Turnbo first joined the Rangers on October 1, 1876. He enlisted in Clay County as a private in Company C, Frontier Battalion, under Captain J. C. Sparks. After seventeen months of service, he was discharged on February 28, 1878.

The Ranger's name was frequently misspelled as "Turnbow" and "Trumbo." Records in the adjutant general's papers at the Texas

State Archives show two other men named Turnbow, A. E. and N. Turnbow, served under Captain Baylor about the same time as Turnbo. Possibly they were brothers.

In 1882 Turnbo was hired as a deputy city marshal in El Paso under former Ranger J. B. Gillett.

Enlisting in Captain G. W. Baylor's Company A, Frontier Battalion, on December 1, 1882, at Pecos, Turnbo stayed in the Rangers until the company was disbanded for lack of funds on April 15, 1885. By that time he had risen in rank to lieutenant. His last mission as a Ranger was leading seven men to Fort Davis in March 1885 after a group of soldiers about to be transferred from the cavalry post threatened to burn the town down when they left. The Rangers' show of force must have caused the soldiers to change their minds, because there was no trouble.

On August 20, 1885, Turnbo was appointed as the second sheriff of newly created Reeves County. The office had been vacated when Sheriff J. T. Morris was shot to death by a Texas Ranger after the sheriff, during a drinking spree, shot and killed another Ranger. Turnbo was elected to a full term on November 2, 1886, and served until November 6, 1888.

What become of Turnbo after he left office in Pecos has not been determined.

Sources

"1884: The Year In Review." *Fort Concho Report*, Vol. 16, No. 4, Winter 1984-85, p. 42.

Austin Statesman, February 6, 1884.

Cude, Elton R. *The Wild and Free Dukedom of Bexar*. San Antonio: Munguia Printers, 1978, p. 110.

"Daring Hold-up Between Fort Concho and Abilene." *Frontier Times*, March 1924, p. 11.

"A Dead Desperado." *San Antonio Express*, July 2, 1885.

Holden, W. C. "Law and Lawlessness on the Texas Frontier, 1875-1890." *The Southwestern Historical Quarterly*, October 1940, pp. 188-203.

L'Aloge, Bob. *Riders Along the Rio Grande: A Collection of Outlaws, Prostitutes and Vigilantes*. Las Cruces, N.M.: RCS Press, 1992, pp. 144-154.

The Lone Star, El Paso, Texas, February 9, 1884.

"Masked Men. More Doings of the Stage Robbers." *Galveston News*, February 5, 1884.

San Angelo Standard, June 21 and 28, 1884.

San Angelo Times-Enterprise, February 9, 1884 as reprinted in the *Rio Grande Republican*, February 16, 1884.

San Antonio Express, July 5, 7, 8 and 15, 1885.

Sweet, Alexander Edwin. Virginia Eisenhour, ed. *Alex Sweet's Texas: The Lighter Side of Lone Star History*. Austin: The University of Texas Press, 1986, p. 85.

"Tells of Depredations of Early Day Robber." *Frontier Times*, July 1929, pp. 423-424.

Thalis Cook and the "Steer" Branded M U R D E R

On his way to the chuck wagon after a hard day in the saddle, a cowboy spotted a solitary brindle yearling standing broadside about a hundred yards away. Thinking to round up one more maverick, he rode close enough to check for a brand. What he saw made his eyes widen in disbelief. From neck to flank, someone had burned the brute's hide with six letters: M U R D E R.

At the sound of iron horseshoes striking rock, the animal spooked and suddenly cut away, disappearing down a draw. By the time he rode into camp, the cowboy wondered if he'd seen anything at all.

The story of the steer branded M U R D E R has been told around many a campfire. With the help of a string of romanticizing wordsmiths, beginning in 1896 with a newspaper story by Alpine judge Wigfall Van Sickle and continuing with work by the venerable J. Frank Dobie in 1940 and other writers since, it has joined the herd as one of the West's more enduring tales. Whether a steer with such a chilling brand ever actually roamed ghost-like in the high country of Brewster County in far West Texas is open to debate. Nevertheless, the tale took root like Johnson grass.

But what happened to longtime Ranger Thalis T. Cook was no romantic fantasy. A participant in the climax of the bloody event that triggered the M U R D E R brand legend, Cook would suffer for the rest of his life from an outlaw's bullet.

Like many good stories, the case of the M U R D E R steer is a rickety windmill of legend built with only a few solid facts. For one thing, the bovine in question was a bull, not a steer. But the story did start with a murder.

During a roundup at Leoncita in Brewster County on January 28, 1891, Finus "Fine" Gilliland gunned down a one-armed Confederate veteran, Henry Harrison Powe, in front of Powe's son and other witnesses. The shooting erupted in the midst of a heated argument over the ownership of an unbranded brindle bull. After the shooting Gilliland fled the roundup, riding off into the Glass Mountains.

As Gilliland left at a run, Powe's son mounted his horse and rode hard for Alpine to notify the sheriff, former Ranger James B. Gillett. Gillett hurried to the scene with former sheriff John M. Rooney, who knew the area well. They covered many miles searching for Gilliland but finally concluded, as Gillett later wrote, that the cowboy had "left the country."

When he returned to Alpine, Gillett sent a description of Gilliland to every sheriff in West Texas. At the time, Thalis Cook was living in Marathon and working as an inspector for the Texas and Southwestern Cattle Raisers Association. He had not taken part in the initial search for Gilliland, but he had an intense interest in the case: Powe had been a friend.

An unrelated investigation connected Cook to the case. Someone in the Fort Stockton area was long-roping cattle and using a running iron to alter the legal owner's brand. Cook asked Ranger J. M. (Jim) Putman, stationed at Marfa, to join him on a scout to Pecos County to look into the matter. With a good dog and a pack mule loaded with supplies, on January 30 the two officers rode out of Marathon in a snowstorm.

At thirty-three, Cook had been a lawman half his life. Born in Uvalde County on March 10, 1858, he joined the Frontier Battalion on June 4, 1874. He was only sixteen—likely the youngest Ranger ever on the state's payroll. Cook served under Captain Neal Coldwell in Company F for two months, then left to work as a cowboy. But two years later, on September 16, 1876, he re-enlisted in Company F. By this time the unit was under the command of Lieutenant Pat Dolan, Cook's brother-in-law.

Although his brother-in-law enjoyed a distinguished career as a Ranger, another of Cook's many relatives—his cousin, Tom O'Folliard—planted his boots firmly on the wrong side of the law. After leaving the Uvalde country for the New Mexico Territory in 1878, O'Folliard became friends with a young cattle rustler and hired gun named Henry McCarty, alias

William Bonney. The two stole cattle in New Mexico and the Texas Panhandle and participated, beginning on July 15, 1878, in the protracted four-day gun battle in Lincoln, New Mexico, that marked the violent climax of the Lincoln County War.

Cook, a deeply religious man, stood solid as a mesquite stump in his determination to live the right kind of life. Having a relative riding with Billy the Kid—as McCarty became known—was a matter of considerable concern and embarrassment to the young Ranger. Cook wrote a letter to his cousin urging him to surrender, but it did no good.

Mustering out of the Rangers again on March 30, 1879, Cook took up ranching in Uvalde County. In December 1880 he got word that his outlaw cousin had been killed at Fort Sumner, New Mexico, by Sheriff Pat Garrett and several posse members. The Kid's sidekick, O'Folliard, mortally wounded from a shot in the chest, begged Garrett to put him out of his misery. Garrett of course refused, and O'Folliard died in less than an hour. He was buried at Fort Sumner.

Four years later, still trying to make a living as a rancher, Cook married Ella West on Christmas Eve in 1884. But married life did not dull Cook's interest in the Rangers. On April 25, 1889, he enlisted again, this time in Company D under Captain Frank Jones. He stayed on through the end of November that year. Following his discharge, Cook moved to Marathon and began working as a cattle inspector.

Now, on a cold winter day, he was about to run into a killer. Riding northeast from Marathon in the snow, Cook and Putman worked their way up into the Glass Mountains. Putman was in the lead, followed by the state-owned pack mule. Cook brought up the rear.

The two men knew the terrain, but they were operating with one major disadvantage: Neither had any idea what Fine Gilliland looked like. All they knew was that he was a young cowboy, a description that fit just about every male in the Trans-Pecos.

When they met up the next day with a lone rider on the trail through the mountains, they had no immediate reason to be suspicious. Still, it was not weather to be riding without a pressing reason.

When Ranger Putman offered the man a polite "Good evening," Cook pulled his horse off the trail. The former Ranger saw that the man was carrying a gunnysack of corn for his horse. Obviously he planned on doing some traveling.

"Are you Fine Gilliland?" Cook asked, his breath steaming in the cold mountain air.

Indeed he was. But in lieu of a verbal reply, Gilliland pulled a .45 from behind his back and snapped off a shot.

The bullet shattered Cook's left knee, leaving him with a bullet wound only slightly less painful than a gut shot. Before Cook could clear his pistol from his holster, a second bullet tore into Cook's horse. As the kicking, screaming animal went down with Cook still in the saddle, Cook's revolver fell out of his hand.

Gilliland quickly fired off another shot, hitting Putman's horse in its thigh. Then the cowboy kicked his horse's flanks and tried to run.

"Shoot his horse!" Cook yelled to Putman as he struggled to get out from under his dead pony and retrieve his gun.

The Ranger, a good shot, probably could have hit Gilliland. At that point, he certainly had every legal right to shoot to kill. But Cook's advice was sound, based on twenty years' experience dating back to the frontier Indian wars. A savvy fighter always directed his first shot not at the man but at the fleeing man's horse. Without a horse, an opponent could not go far.

At the crack of Putman's rifle, Gilliland's horse tumbled down on the rocky trail, a bullet hole in its neck. Uninjured, Gilliland rolled with the fall and took cover behind his dead horse.

"State Ranger!" Putman shouted. "Surrender!"

Again, Gilliland replied with his six-gun, firing two more shots at the officers. Cook, meanwhile, recovered his pistol. Though in terrible pain, he managed to shoot at Gilliland while Putman sought cover. Soon the Ranger had his rifle leveled at the shooter's fallen horse. When Gilliland raised up to fire another round, the Ranger blew the top of his head off.

Putman stood, his rifle still trained on Gilliland, and walked slowly toward the dead horse and the still form behind it. Satisfied that he had no need to shoot again, the Ranger turned his attention to his wounded partner.

After stanching the flow of blood from Cook's leg with a makeshift tourniquet, Putman removed the pack from the mule, threw Cook's saddle across the animal's back, tightened the cinch, and helped the cattle inspector to mount. Moaning in agony, Cook kept his good leg in the stirrup as Putman led them out of the canyon, leaving Gilliland and two dead horses lying on blood-covered snow. Putman soon realized his horse was too badly wounded to carry him. Dismounting, he walked the rest of the way, leading the mule.

The Ranger left Cook at the Iron Mountain Ranch and saddled a fresh horse for his ride to Marathon. He wired Sheriff Gillett that Gilliland was dead and Cook was badly wounded. Putman returned to the ranch with a hack to carry Cook back to town.

In Marathon, the officers boarded the westbound Texas and Pacific for the short ride to Alpine. At the train station a large crowd met the officers. A hack took Cook to the home of Mrs. Powe, recently made a widow by Fine Gilliland. Mrs. Powe's brother, a doctor, was in town to attend Henry Harrison Powe's funeral.

The brother had served as a surgeon for the Confederate army during the Civil War, but he had no medical instruments. County Judge Van Sickle hurried to a blacksmith's shop and returned with a brace and bit, a poor substitute for a probe and scalpel. The veteran sawbones tried to work the slug out of Cook's knee but succeeded only in further mangling it.

"Cook was finally sent to Santa Rosa Hospital in San Antonio," Van Sickle later wrote. "He recovered partially but refused to have his limb amputated and was ever afterwards a cripple."

Not only did Cook reject a doctor's advice that his leg be removed above the knee, he later made another doctor break the bones and reset them at an angle. When the break healed, Cook was better able to sit a horse.

With the Powe murder case closed by gunpowder adjudication, only a coroner's inquest for Gilliland and a couple of funerals were needed to wrap things up.

When Sheriff Gillett heard of the shooting, he caught a freight train and reached Marathon about 1 A.M. on February 1. He hired a wagon and driver and left to retrieve Gilliland's body.

"We reached the battleground at sunup and what a sight it was!" Gillett later wrote. "We came to Cook's black W-Bar pony first, then about thirty or forty feet away was Fine's pony with his neck broken from Putman's shot, and crumpled behind the pony was the dead body of Fine Gilliland, his pistol at his side. The pack outfit was scattered around over the ground where Putman had hurriedly unpacked the [mule]."

Putman's boss, Captain Jones, did not find out until the following day that Cook had been shot. The day the two officers ran into the fleeing killer, January 31, Jones had been working on his monthly report to Adjutant General W. S. Mabry in Austin. He apologized to Mabry for having cut short his previous communication to headquarters. "I was just starting out after Gilliland, who murdered an old one-armed ex-confederate soldier, and perhaps did not particularize sufficiently in my report on State property," the captain explained.

Jones' next report to Mabry, sent from Alpine, had an account of the final disposition of Gilliland:

> Sir: The man Gilliland, referred to in my report
> and letter of yesterday, was killed about 20 miles
> from here yesterday by Private Putman of my Co;
> and a Deputy Sheriff. Gilliland made a desperate
> fight, wounding the Deputy, killing his horse and
> wounding Putman's horse. He was a very desperate
> man.

Jones ordered Putman to shoot his wounded horse to end the animal's suffering. On February 9 the captain sent an appraisal of the horse's value to Austin, the first step in the state's reimbursement for the loss of his mount.

From the state's standpoint, the case was closed. But the legend began to grow. Powe's son later maintained that some of his father's friends roped the young bull that had been the object of the argument and branded the word M U R D E R on its side. On the animal's other flank, so the story goes, the cowboys burned the date "Jan. 28, 1891."

The bull branded M U R D E R supposedly roamed between Fort Davis and Alpine, reminding anyone who saw him of murder most foul. In the telling and retelling of the story, somewhere along the way the bull became a steer, though the survivors of the incident all agreed that the branded bull had not been castrated. Some headline writer, unschooled in animal husbandry, probably thought bull and steer were synonymous.

Some said this bull prowled West Texas ghost-like for years after the cowman's murder. (Drawing by Roger Moore)

Five years after Powe's murder, as the legend grew, the bull was rounded up and put into a herd shipped from West Texas to Montana. One old-timer, however, later said the bull never made it beyond Odessa. Eventually, the bull that folklore turned into a steer morphed again: It became a ghost steer. In truth, beyond the uncontroverted facts of the murder and the subsequent killing of Gilliland and wounding of Cook, the whole story of the branded brute was mostly just bull.

Walking with a limp the rest of his life, Cook lived the reality of the story. Despite his stiff leg, Cook returned to the Rangers again. On May 24, 1894, he enlisted in Company D under Captain John R. Hughes, who had been promoted following the slaying of Captain Jones in El Paso County the year before. Cook stayed on the state payroll for six months.

He worked for a while as an El Paso County sheriff's deputy but carried a Special Ranger commission as well. On March 10, 1896, he returned to the Rangers once more, serving as Hughes' first sergeant until November 30, 1898.

Cook's decision to leave the Ranger service for good may have had something to do with his final gunfight, a shootout that filled two graves in Fort Davis' cemetery.

In September 1896 two brothers, Jude and Arthur Frier, along with a third person, stole a dozen horses in Reagan County near Big Lake. They also stole guns and supplies from a farmhouse. Such a crime in later years would be called an armed robbery and would take precedence over the theft of animals, but back then stealing horses was a capital offense often involving little formal litigation.

The young men headed west, pushing their stolen stock past Fort Stockton and Alpine, adding more horses to their remuda as they passed through. Horses were beginning to be missed by their owners, but no one had realized yet that the two boys from Reagan County were the culprits.

Sheriff Gillett did get wind that a couple of questionable characters were seen camped in the Glass Mountains. None of the ranchers in that part of the county knew who they were. Thinking they might be planning a train robbery, Gillett notified the railroad. The railroad, in turn, contacted Captain Hughes at Ysleta and asked if the Rangers would look into it.

Hughes, with Cook and Ranger R. E. Bryant, came to Alpine by train, their horses and pack mule in a baggage car. By the time the Rangers arrived, arrest warrants for horse theft had been issued. From Alpine, the three Rangers along with Brewster County deputy sheriff Jim Pool and two concerned citizens (one of them recently having lost a valuable horse, stolen by parties unknown) rode toward the Glass Mountains.

Soon they picked up a trail and began following it toward the distant Davis Mountains. When the Rangers reached the McCutcheon ranch on September 28, Hughes split the group into three parties, each with one Ranger.

Heading up a canyon about twenty miles northeast of Fort Davis, Cook and Beau McCutcheon soon encountered two young men, both armed. From behind a boulder, they shouted to Cook and ordered him to turn around and head back the way he had come or be killed. The Ranger did two smart things: He did not identify himself as a Texas Ranger, and he pretended that he thought the two men were joking. With that, the men cursed him soundly and said seven rifles were pointing in his direction. Cook, making a big show of being frightened, wheeled his horse and rode for cover.

Safely out of range, Cook told McCutcheon he intended to go back and call their bluff. McCutcheon graciously offered to go notify the captain. After McCutcheon left, the Ranger waited for a while but grew impatient. Finally, he back-trailed the rancher, thinking maybe he was having trouble locating the captain and the other men.

Cook had not covered much ground before he saw Hughes and several others riding hard in his direction. The men let their horses blow for a moment while Cook parlayed with the captain. Judging from the tracks they had followed, the Rangers did not believe they were up against seven men. Cook had seen only two. But the strangers had the advantage of high ground and plenty of big rocks for cover.

Cautiously, with their Winchesters out, the two Rangers and several of the volunteers rode back up the canyon. As soon as they passed the point where Cook had waited after first being confronted, rifle fire echoed off the rugged walls of the canyon. Cook, Hughes, and the others fired back and kept coming.

Cook called for the shooters to surrender, but the horse thieves opted to shoot it out.

Van Sickle, the judge who issued the warrants for the boys, later described what happened:

One of the outlaws was directing all of his fire at Cook. When he exposed himself to get a more direct aim, Cook fired a second sooner.

A younger brother of the outlaw, seeing his brother was killed, called out a desire to surrender and threw up his hands. Cook started to him, but when he thought Cook was off his guard, he opened fire, but again Cook was too quick and his bullet reached its mark.

There had not been seven gunmen, only three. The third member of the group wisely chose to take a fast horseback ride in the opposite direction.

Jeff Davis County justice of the peace Nick Mersfelder summed up the matter in his inquest docket:

The above named deceased persons came to their death by gun shot wounds inflicted at the hands of the afore mentioned persons, Capt. John R. Hughes, T. T. Cook, state Ranger, and a posse of citizens in self defense, the aforesaid officers having warrants of arrest for the deceased persons issued by proper authority from Brewster County, State of Texas, for the theft of horses, and upon attempt to execute same the within described deceased persons resisted arrest by firing upon the officers and posse with the above result. Therefore the coroner and justice of the peace finds no blame attached to the foregoing homicide and finds so according to this inquest.

The bodies of the two brothers were carried back to Fort Davis where the county expended $13 in public funds for two pine coffins and an additional dollar to have two graves dug. The Frier brothers were buried as they died, with their boots on. The killing of the boys clearly had been justified, but Cook felt badly about the one he had shot. As Judge Van Sickle later wrote, Cook "grieved over having to kill this lad [the one who had raised his hands]—said it was one of the saddest memories in his life—but it was kill or be killed."

Even though the shooting of the two young men bothered Cook, it added to his reputation as a tough Ranger. "When

Thalis Cook comes to the east side of the Pecos," so a saying in West Texas went, "the outlaws go to the west side."

Cook stayed in the Big Bend Country for only a few years afer leaving the Rangers. His name occasionally appeared in the *Alpine Avalanche,* which referred to him as a cattle inspector. After December 7, 1900, the Brewster County newspaper made no further mention of Cook. He may have gone back to his home range in Uvalde County for a time, but eventually he moved to the piney woods of Arkansas. There, close to relatives, he spent the last third of his life.

His only son, Johnny, lived near Marshall in East Texas. There, in the summer of 1918, Cook finally consented to have his bad leg amputated. As it turned out, it was not a good decision. He died during the procedure on July 21 at the age of sixty. Other complications contributed to the death, but he would not have needed the operation if he had not been shot by Gilliland twenty-seven years before.

A few years later, after reading an account in the *El Paso Herald* of Cook's shootout with Fine Gilliland, one of the old Ranger's childhood friends was moved to write a letter to J. Marvin Hunter, editor of the Western history magazine *Frontier Times.*

"He served all the useful years of his life as a Ranger on the frontier of Texas," Joe T. McKinney wrote. "There never lived on earth a braver bunch of men than the Texas Rangers, and there was never a braver one than he or one who did more valuable service for his native state."

McKinney viewed Cook as "a manly man, absolutely fearless, strictly honorable, generous, witty, a good story-teller, a fine entertainer, and a man who could be relied on at all times."

Cook's life story, McKinney went on, "would be a great book....I am ready to contribute liberally to one who will look up his record and write it." Unfortunately, no one ever took McKinney up on his offer.

What has endured is not the memory of Thalis Cook, but the story of a brindle bull branded M U R D E R.

Notes

For someone who was so well known as a Ranger, Cook left frustratingly few footprints in his later years. Though the *Alpine Avalanche* and his friend Captain J. B. Gillett referred to Cook as a cattle inspector around the turn of the twentieth century, the Texas and Southwestern Cattle Raisers Association in Fort Worth has no record that he ever worked for their organization. Association historian Cheri Wolfe said Cook's name is not on the list of some six hundred known cattle inspectors, many of whom were former Rangers. The association did lose some records in a 1949 flood of the Trinity River, so, as Wolfe put it, "All we can say is that according to the records we have, he was not an inspector."

Cook may have worked for some local stockman's organization or ranch, performing the generic duties of a cattle inspector. Another account of his role in the M U R D E R bull story identified him as a Brewster County sheriff's deputy.

Cook's son died less than three months after his father. Since he was a young man, a logical suspect in his death is the influenza pandemic of 1918, which killed hundreds of thousands of people in the United States alone. Father and son are buried in the Nesbitt Cemetery in Harrison County.

Sources

Alpine Avalanche. Index. Center for American History, The University of Texas at Austin.

Casey, Clifford B. *Mirages, Mysteries and Reality: Brewster County, Texas*. Hereford: Pioneer Book Publishers, 1972, pp. 220, 326-327.

Dearen, Patrick. "Horsehead Crossing." *Persimmon Hill*, Summer 1991, p. 42.

"Fort Davis Not a Badman's Town." *Fort Davis Exchange*, Vol. 1, No. 1, Spring-Summer 1966, p. 8.

Gillett, J. B. "The Law Rides." *The Cattleman*, June 1936, pp. 31-32.

Jacobson, Lucy Miller and Mildred Bloys Nored. *Jeff Davis County, Texas*. Fort Davis: Fort Davis Historical Society, 1993, pp. 131-132, 163-165.

Martin, Jack. *Border Boss: Captain John R. Hughes—Texas Ranger.* San Antonio: The Naylor Co., 1940, pp. 131-142.

Miles, Elton. *Tales of the Big Bend.* College Station: Texas A&M University Press, 1976, pp. 90-99.

Scobee, Barry. *The Steer Branded Murder.* Houston: Frontier Press, 1952, pp. 43-44.

Shipman, Mrs. O. L. "The Red Murder Yearling of West Texas." *El Paso Herald*, December 17, 1922.

Stephens, Robert W. *Texas Ranger Sketches.* Dallas: n.p., 1972, pp. 43-47.

"Thalis T. Cook, Texas Ranger." *Frontier Times*, December 1927, p. 107.

Wolfe, Cheri, historian, Texas and Southwestern Cattle Raisers Association, Fort Worth, Texas. Interview with the author, February 10, 1999.

The Other Half of the "Four Great Captains"

The muzzle of the double-barrel shotgun the drunk saloon-keeper held to his shoulder looked as big as two railroad tunnels to Ranger Captain John Rogers.

Standing in the door of the saloon, Rogers faced the man who had the scattergun pointed straight at him. The bar was one of several such establishments in Cotulla, a rough and tumble South Texas town between San Antonio and Laredo. A company of Rangers commanded by Rogers had recently set up camp nearby.

Plainly, the proprietor had sampled too much of his inventory. A well-known mean drunk, he'd already let fly with a load of buckshot at someone whose only offense was riding by the saloon on his horse. Before Rogers got there, the bartender had emptied a few other shells. The bar smelled of stale beer, tobacco, and cordite.

Noting that the saloon man had both barrels cocked, Rogers realized that walking in the front door had not been a particularly wise move. But then the Ranger thought of something else. Going around to the back would show weakness, "and that might cause more trouble."

"There was but one thing to do," Rogers later recalled, "and that was go in and get him right then and there."

Rogers offered a silent prayer and slowly walked toward the man with the shotgun.

"You have been getting by with this stuff too long," the Ranger said. "You'll have to cut it out."

The drunk looked on in disbelief as the Ranger drew closer and closer. Rogers grabbed the end of the shotgun and pushed it away. With his other hand, the Ranger caught the bartender by the collar.

"Come with me," he said.

As Rogers later said, "My time just had not come."

Another Ranger who knew something of close calls was W. W. "Bill" Sterling. He survived the turbulent days of the border bandit wars and then managed to cheat death one more time in another way—by finishing his memoir only a year before he died.

His *Trails and Trials of a Texas Ranger* remains one of the better Ranger narratives. In the book, Sterling beatifies four Rangers as the "Four Great Captains." He picked the men, he wrote, "by virtue of their long, outstanding, and unhampered service." These men—listed alphabetically—were John A. Brooks, John R. Hughes, William "Bill" McDonald, and John Harris Rogers, the Ranger who backed down the shotgun-wielding bartender.

Hughes and McDonald have been the subject of books and numerous articles. But no books and few articles have been written about Brooks and Rogers, the other half of Sterling's quartet of great captains. This lack of attention on the part of historians and writers has not been because Brooks and Rogers were not deserving. Indeed, the record well supports Sterling's estimation of the two Rangers. But Brooks and Rogers were not talkers. They were low-key lawmen who did not seem to crave public attention and tended to downplay their accomplishments.

Hughes and McDonald, on the other hand, were not embarrassed to see their names in print. McDonald, particularly, was a man who shot from the lip as well as the hip; and Hughes, while professing modesty, never appears to have turned down an interview request, photo opportunity, or the offer of a parade marshal job.

Walter Prescott Webb, in his classic but now dated history of the Rangers, was the first writer to bestow the adjective of greatness on selected Ranger leaders and to outline qualities that in his opinion led to that greatness.

A Ranger captain, Webb believed, had to emerge as a leader. "All that the state could do was to confirm and legalize a fact," he wrote. "It is not too much to say that a Ranger captain had to prove his leadership every day, in every battle, and in every campaign." That was accomplished, Webb continued, not only by courage, but by having "a complete absence of fear." Finally, a Ranger captain needed intelligence, good judgment, and something that would seem at odds with that good judgment—youth.

Both Brooks and Rogers measured up to Webb's benchmark.

Rogers and Brooks (seated, second and third from left) joined the Rangers about the same time. (Author's collection)

Brooks was the older of the two men, born November 20, 1855, in Bourbon County, Kentucky. Rogers was born nearly eight years later on October 19, 1863, in Guadalupe County, Texas.

Aside from the difference in their ages and place of birth, the two Rangers had several things in common:

★ Both became Rangers about the same time. Brooks joined Company F, Frontier Battalion, on January 15, 1883, at age twenty-seven; Rogers signed up as a private in Company B on September 5, 1882, a little more than a month shy of his nineteenth birthday.

★ Both survived desperate gun battles in which they were wounded, each overcoming physical disabilities associated with their wounds.

★ Both rose in rank quickly. Brooks became a captain in May 1889 at age thirty-three, only six years after joining the Rangers. Rogers was appointed captain on October 19, 1892, the day he turned twenty-nine.

★ Both had lengthy careers in the Rangers. Brooks served twenty-three years, Rogers almost three decades.

★ Both continued in public service after leaving the Rangers, Brooks as a politician, Rogers as a U.S. marshal and police chief. Rogers, in fact, went back into the Rangers at an age most men would be content to retire.

★ Both survived dangerous careers to die naturally. Brooks lived the longest, dying at the age of eighty-eight. Rogers died when he was sixty-seven.

Brooks came to Texas in 1876, settling in Collin County. He did some cowboying, then drifted to Laredo where he worked at a coal mine for a time. He signed up with the Rangers at Cotulla in La Salle County, then "the toughest town in Texas or in the West" in the opinion of Sterling.

Rogers, who had blue eyes, dark hair, and a fair complexion, joined the Rangers at another tough cowtown, Colorado City. When he signed up, he listed his occupation as farmer.

As young Rangers, Brooks, Rogers, and their captain all were seriously wounded in a wild gun battle in East Texas. Ranger James H. Moore died in the same fight.

Adjutant General W. H. King got first word of the shooting in a telegram from Nacogdoches "via Houston" at 9:11 A.M. April 2, 1887:

> Am just in receipt of following Capt Scott Co F state Rangers & two of his men Brooks & Rogers severely wounded & one man Moore killed dead in a fight with the outlaws Conners[1] in Sabine County yesterday morning A Winchester ball entered apex of Capts left lung & come out at lower border scapular hope to save his life (signed) Frank H. Tucker MD.

Tucker must have been a very good doctor and Scott, Brooks, and Rogers three very tough Rangers. Barely a week after the gun battle, in a clear and steady hand, Captain Scott wrote General King from Hemphill with an account of the incident. He and his Rangers reached Sabine County on March 29, the captain reported. A day later, the Rangers set out into the timber "scouting for the Conners."

About 2 o'clock on the morning of March 31, the Rangers reached the general area of the Conners' camp. Scott divided his men, sending part of them to the houses of Conner and some of his associates "to guard and prevent them from rendering aid to the Conners during the raid."

Three hours later the captain and the rest of his Rangers approached within three hundred yards of the outlaw camp, deep in the pine trees. At daybreak, Scott divided his men again, detailing two Rangers and four private citizens to move to the left of the camp while Scott and five other Rangers —including Brooks and Rogers—took the right flank. The two groups were about eighty yards apart.

But the vegetation was thick, and the Conners knew the woods better than the Rangers. The officers walked right into an ambush. Hiding behind trees less than thirty feet away, the gang opened up on the Rangers. As Scott told the story:

> Private Moore fell dead from the first volley fired
> by the Connors. Myself, Sergt. Brooks & Private
> Rogers, each fired two or three shots before being
> disabled, each of us having received serious wounds.
> The fight continued some seconds longer; Private
> [Frank] Carmichael shooting whenever he could see
> one of the Connors.

Private William Treadwell's gun jammed, the captain continued in his report, and he "rendered but little assistance during the fight, the citizen squad none. They [the citizens] being more accustomed to hunting deer than desperadoes held their stand [kept behind cover], not being more than 80 yards distant from the fight and not even coming to our assistance for minutes after the fight was over, having then to fire signal guns and call them."

When the two Rangers with the citizens tried to come to the aid of their fellow officers, the man in charge of the civilians told them to stay put, saying, "Stop, stop. We are now in the right place." The Rangers apparently trusted the man's judgment and stayed on the left side of the camp.

"Had the squad come to our assistance," the captain went on, "we would have captured the entire Connor gang."

But the Rangers did drop Bill Conner with four bullets. The other three Conners escaped, though one was wounded. The outlaws' packhorse also went down in the return fire of the Rangers.

"After the fight we killed their four dogs, which were so well trained that they did not give us any signal whatever. I then had their camp equipage & effects destroyed," the captain wrote at the conclusion of his three-page letter to King.

Brooks lost the two middle fingers of his left hand in the fight. An account book Rogers had in a pocket probably saved his life. The bullet, which struck him on his left side, penetrated the book, deflected, and went out through his hip.

The gunfight with the Conners had not been Rogers' first. Years later, required by the adjutant general to fill out a three-page printed biographical form, including a blank for "details of your actual service in riots, skirmishes or battles" Rogers responded:

Had skirmish with fence cutters in Brown Co. Two of them killed. Rangers not hurt. Caught them in act. [Rogers then summarized the Conner fight in two sentences.] A Horse Thief resisting arrest near San Angelo was shot by me, wounded and captured [in 1887].

In filling out the same form, Brooks noted that his "service in riots, skirmishes or battles" included a railroad strike in Fort Worth in 1886, a shootout a year later along the Red River in which he was "compelled to kill a man in self-defense," the Conner fight in East Texas, "the fence cutting trouble in Brown County," a railroad strike in Temple, "the Garza trouble on the Rio Grande," and the capture of a band of horse thieves in Kinney County.

"The Garza trouble" occurred in 1891-92 when the Rangers and U.S. Army tried to prevent Mexican journalist Catarino E. Garza from continuing his Texas-based revolution against Mexico. During the trouble, flamboyant newspaper correspondent Richard Harding Davis came to Texas to ride the border with elements of the Third Cavalry. While on the border, Davis met Adjutant General W. H. Mabry and Captain Brooks, visiting their camp as the Rangers breakfasted on bacon and coffee. Davis later described his encounter in his book *The West from a Car Window*:

> General Mabry told me some very thrilling tales
> of their deeds and personal meetings with despera-
> does and "bad" men of the border; but when he
> tried to lead Captain Brooks into relating a few of
> his own adventures, the result was a significant and
> complete failure.

Indeed, neither Brooks nor Rogers was overly wordy in describing their shooting scrapes. Of the two, Brooks may have been a bit more inclined to talk, but only to close acquaintances—certainly not some Yankee outsider like the writer Davis.

One person who heard at least a couple of stories from Brooks was C. V. Terrell, who served in the Texas Legislature, as state treasurer, and later on the Railroad Commission. Terrell's 1948 memoir included two anecdotes relating to Captain Brooks.

Brooks, Terrell said, had known Sam Bass before Bass took up train robbing. West of the Collin County community of Bolivar, Brooks once ran a horse race with Bass. Terrell did not report who won, but it was probably Bass and his legendary Denton mare.

Terrell said that as a young cowboy on a drive headed up the Chisholm Trail, Brooks almost was arrested by the Decatur city marshal when he "got a little too much 'Tangle foot' liquor under his belt" after coming to town to replenish his outfit's grocery supply. The kindly grocer interceded in

Brooks' behalf, and the marshal agreed to let him go. On the way to the herd, however, Brooks fell asleep on his horse.

He woke up when his horse started drinking out of a water barrel some Wise County settler was hauling on a sled. The man took Brooks to his house, put him to bed for the night, and took care of his horse while the young cowboy slept it off. In the morning, the settler's wife cooked Brooks "a fine breakfast, hot biscuits, butter, coffee, and country-fried ham with red gravy." When Brooks stood to leave, he asked what he owed for the lodging and meal. "Not one cent," was the reply. "Just don't drink anymore."

Though there is nothing to suggest that Brooks was anything but a gentleman, despite his story to Judge Terrell about being overserved as a young cowboy, Rogers was a teetotaler and deeply religious. The Presbyterian Ranger carried two "bibles" on his scouts through the brush country: the King James version and the so-called Book of Knaves, an annual listing by the Adjutant General's Department of wanted felons. As one old Ranger said, "if Rogers couldn't preach the fear of the Lord into 'em, he was prepared to shoot the Hell out of them."

"He never opened fire unless he had to, and when opportunity arose he used both gun and Bible on his prisoners with telling effect," one writer said of Rogers. "More than once he has brought wayward youths to Christianity while they were his prisoners by reading them passages of Scripture."

The straitlaced Rogers—his only vice was a liking for cigars —must have taken particular pleasure when he, Brooks, and McDonald were dispatched to El Paso in early 1896 to back up Captain Hughes and his men in the state's effort to prevent a prize fight between Peter Maher and Robert Fitzsimmons. This may have been the first time—and it has only happened a couple of times since—that virtually the entire Texas Ranger force was concentrated on one specific trouble spot.

Fourteen "stalwart, bronzed, and determined-looking men"—including Brooks and Rogers—alighted from the train and strolled over to the nearby Pierson Hotel for breakfast on the morning of February 9, the *El Paso Herald* reported. Those

Rogers was one of numerous Rangers sent to El Paso in 1896 to prevent a prize fight. (Author's collection)

"resolute-looking strangers," the newspaper continued, were soon determined to be Texas Rangers. And other Rangers were on their way to town.

Despite the show of force on the part of the state, the much-ballyhooed "fistic carnival" was staged on an island in the Rio Grande near Langtry. The Rangers were helpless to stop the match. The promoters had picked a perfect location, a spot as close as West Texas could come to being on the high seas. History, at least, benefited from the beefed-up Ranger presence in El Paso, even though the fight went on. Someone took a photograph of thirty-one Rangers standing in front of the El Paso County Courthouse, an image that has become a classic.

Three years later, with far fewer Rangers to back him up, Captain Rogers got into the second serious shooting scrape of his career. In the spring of 1899 his shoulder was shattered in a melee that broke out as the captain and other officers worked to enforce a smallpox quarantine in Laredo. The captain wrote: "On 21st day of March 1899 while assisting State Health officer...to enforce quarantine regulations at Laredo, we met with opposition and had a brush with Mexicans resulting in the death of one Mexican in this engagement. I received two wounds. One serious and one slight wound."

Rogers was taken by train to San Antonio, where at Santa Rosa Hospital a doctor told him that while he could save the captain's arm, he would have to remove some bone. The operation was successful, but the Ranger was left with a shorter arm. After a nine-week convalescence, Rogers rejoined his company at Cotulla.

The captain was given a custom-made rifle with a curved stock, a weapon specially designed to fit his bad shoulder. Thus armed, as one writer said a short time later, Rogers returned to "business at the same old stand."

In a case that became part of South Texas folklore, Captain Rogers led the posse that tracked down Gregorio Lira Cortez. The chase began June 12, 1901, after Cortez shot and killed Karnes County sheriff W. T. "Brack" Morris, a former Texas Ranger who had served as a sergeant under Rogers. Morris and two deputies had gone to Cortez' residence to question him in connection with a horse theft. The situation got out of hand partially because of misunderstandings born of poor English-Spanish translation. Cortez fled toward Mexico after the shooting. Three days later, as the posse closed in on him near the Gonzales County community of Belmont, Cortez killed Gonzales County sheriff Robert M. Glover. A county constable died in the gunfight that followed, possibly from friendly fire. The pursuit of Cortez, who was finally captured in Webb County on June 22, was widely covered in the press and eventually became the basis for a nonfiction book and a somewhat fictionalized movie. Captain Rogers downplayed his role in Cortez' capture and refused to take any share of the reward money. "No especial credit is due to me for the capture," the captain told the *San Antonio Express*. "Somebody else would have got him if I hadn't."

Though Rogers was far from loquacious, he could talk when it counted. Trailing a hard case outlaw near the New Mexico line in June 1904, the Ranger almost caught up with the man, but as Rogers later reported, "he ran out of shooting distance from me, thereby avoiding arrest." The outlaw, Hill Loftis, knew the lawman would stay on his trail and laid an ambush for the Ranger. He shot Rogers' horse in the jaw, then leveled his Winchester at the captain, relieving him of the only weapon he had, a pistol. "I was completely in his power," Rogers reported, "and it looked as if he would kill me in spite of all I could do or say."

But Rogers managed to say just the right thing, warning the outlaw that if he killed him, other Rangers would never stop tracking him to avenge his death. Rogers even talked Loftis into giving him his pistol back. The outlaw emptied the weapon, tossed it into a sand dune, and rode off into New Mexico. Several killings and nearly two decades later in Montana, Loftis committed suicide.

The incident with Loftis occurred when Rogers was in command of a Ranger company stationed at Fort Hancock in Hudspeth County. While in far West Texas, he invested in lands in the El Paso valley, a move which provided financial security for his family.

At some point in his mid to late forties, Brooks, like most middle-aged men, must have begun thinking about how he was going to spend the rest of his life. While he was a widely respected Ranger captain, he nevertheless had to accept the reality that he was a low-paid state employee with no retirement benefits in place. In 1904, with the arrival of a new railroad into what was then northern Starr County, Ed C. Lasater subdivided some of his immense pastureland and called it "The Falfurrias Farm and Garden Tracts." Brooks was one of the first persons to buy acreage. In June 1904 he purchased eighty acres for $1,200, putting down $240 in cash and agreeing to pay the balance in four years at 7 percent interest. A little more than two years later, on November 15, 1906, the fifty-one-year-old Brooks resigned his Ranger commission.

Rogers remained with the service another four years, resigning effective January 31, 1911. The reason was Texas' newly elected governor, Oscar B. Colquitt. He campaigned on an anti-prohibition platform, leading some to say the governor's middle initial stood for "Budweiser." The nondrinking Rogers wanted no part of an administration not opposed to booze, believing, as his children later told Sterling, that "whiskey was to blame for the majority of all crimes."

When President Woodrow Wilson appointed Rogers U.S. Marshal for the Western District of Texas in 1913, the *State Topics* applauded the move. Rogers and his Ranger colleague McDonald, appointed at the same time as U.S. Marshal for

144

the Northern District of Texas, "are known throughout the breadth and length of Texas as fearless Ranger captains… and it goes without saying that they will make good U.S. marshals."

While Rogers' appointment certainly had political overtones, Brooks sought and achieved a more active role in the democratic process. He served two terms in the Legislature as a member of the House. When the northern end of Starr County was organized into a new county—an effort that had been led by Brooks and Lasater—the new county was named in the retired Ranger captain's honor. Brooks became its first county judge in 1911 and continued in that capacity until 1939. He died on January 15, 1944.

This painting of Brooks hangs in museum in Falfurrias, seat of the county named in his honor. (Photo by author)

Long after Brooks hung up his six-shooter to be an elected official, Rogers continued in law enforcement or in private sector work where his experience as a peace officer was important. He served as a U.S. Marshal in El Paso until 1921. From 1921 to 1923 he worked for the Railway Express Agency as an investigator and guard. On April 1, 1924, he was appointed chief of the Austin Police Department. He got crosswise with the city council, however, apparently pushing too hard for a city ordinance making possession of "hop" (marijuana) illegal and for an ordinance giving city police more control over gambling in domino and bingo halls. His career in municipal law enforcement lasted only one month before he was fired.

The no-nonsense Rogers might not have been the man those who ran Austin wanted for their police chief, but when former Williamson County district attorney Dan Moody was elected as governor in 1927, he soon hired Rogers once again as a Ranger. At the age of sixty-four, Rogers took over command of Company C in South Texas.

Three years later, when a doctor diagnosed Rogers' chronic indigestion and chest pains as nothing more serious than a bad gallbladder, the old Ranger traveled to Scott and White Hospital in Temple for surgery. The operation to remove the diseased organ was successful, but as Rogers dressed to leave the hospital on November 11, 1930, he suffered a fatal aneurysm.

The men of Rogers' company served as his pallbearers and insisted on handling the closing of his grave themselves.[2]

As his grandson later recalled, John Rogers was "A man totally without fear. . . . He was shot four or five times, but he died of a tiny blood clot."

Notes

[1] The Conner gang is referred to here by what seems to have been the more common spelling. Ranger reports of the incident, however, spelled the name Connor.

[2] Funeral services for Rogers were held at Austin's First Presbyterian Church, followed by burial in Oakwood Cemetery.

Sources

Lasater, Dale. *Falfurrias: Ed C. Lasater and the Development of South Texas*. College Station: Texas A&M University Press, 1985, p. 76.

Miletich, Leo N. *Dan Stuart's Fistic Carnival*. College Station: Texas A&M University Press, 1994, pp. 148-149.

Paredes, Americo. *"With His Pistol in His Hand," A Border Ballad and Its Hero*. Austin: University of Texas Press, 1958, pp. 67-72, 81.

Peyton, Green. *For God and Texas: The Life of P. B. Hill*. New York: McGraw-Hill Book Co., 1947, pp. 126-128.

"Police Chief Wants Ordinance to Prohibit Hop Weed." *Austin American*, April 1, 1924.

Reeves, John. Interview with the author, March 1, 1999.

Sowell, A. J. *Early Settlers and Indian Fighters of Southwest Texas*. Austin: State House Press, 1986, facsimile reproduction of 1900 edition, pp. 624-633.

Sterling, William Warren. *Trails and Trials of a Texas Ranger*. Norman: University of Oklahoma Press, 1968.

Terrell, C. V. *The Terrells: 85 Years - Texas From Indians to Atomic Bombs*. Austin: 1948, pp. 34-35.

"Two New U.S. Marshals." *State Topics*, Houston, April 12, 1913.

Van Demark, Harry. "Religion and Bullets: Two Factors Which Have Figured Prominently in the Making of a Famous Texas Ranger." *The Texas Monthly*, Vol. III, No. 2, March 1929, pp. 349-351.

Webb, Walter Prescott. *The Texas Rangers: A Century of Frontier Defense*. Boston: Houghton-Mifflin, 1935, pp. 79-80.

"When Rogers Courted Death." *Frontier Times*, Vol. 4, No. 3, December 1926, p. 8.

Whispering Tom and the Plan of San Diego

From atop the white stucco headquarters of the Santa Gertrudis unit of the King Ranch, the long beam of a searchlight powerful enough for an oceangoing vessel played across the flat landscape, illuminating mesquite and scrub oak and shining off the eyes of startled livestock and deer.

Men with rifles at their sides held field glasses to their eyes, searching the brush to the south for riders as a nearly full moon rose over South Texas. Their grandfathers, fathers, and even some of them had known a time when Texans dreaded what they called a "light moon" because it drew hostile Indians to the settlements as surely as moths to a kerosene lantern. Now, more than three decades after the last fight with Indians and fifteen years into the twentieth century, men and women who lived within a few hours' horseback ride of the Rio Grande feared a new threat: Mexican raiders.

Bandit raids turned the Rio Grande Valley into an armed camp. Here, a plucky U.S. soldier poses with armed revolutionaries. (Author's collection)

A terrible war raged in Europe. Closer to home, Mexico was in the fifth bloody year of revolution. The consequences of both events led to a virtual state of war along the Texas side of the border, particularly in the sparsely populated Rio Grande Valley and to the west in the rugged mountains of the Big Bend. By the fall of 1915 many men had already died violently along the big river and many more would.

Armed conflict often is undeclared, as in the Indian wars of the nineteenth century. But this little war—it never had a name other than "the bandit troubles"—actually began with the execution of a formal document, though few had taken it seriously at the time. The instrument was signed in secret behind prison bars in Mexico, but some of its points may have been worked out earlier over bottles of beer in a bar in Duval County, Texas. It was a statement of intentions as chilling as the Declaration of Independence had been ennobling—a plan urging race war, genocide, and the ripping apart of sovereign territory. Its authors called it the Plan de San Diego.

A tall lawman most folks knew as Whispering Tom, a man who eventually would be sworn in as a Texas Ranger, was the one who discovered it.

Thomas Shannon Mayfield was born in the small community of Leesville in Gonzales County on June 16, 1880. He grew up on a dry land farm, but he figured out pretty early in life that he did not much care for that lifestyle. Those were the days, he liked to say in his later years, before the government told a farmer how much cotton he could plant. Back then only the boll weevil had the final say-so when it came to the cotton harvest.

Mayfield soon learned that roping a horse was easier than picking cotton. When Teddy Roosevelt came to San Antonio in 1898 to recruit and train men for duty in the war with Spain, Mayfield saddled up and rode to the Alamo City.

"I heard he wanted to buy horses for the United States Volunteer Cavalry, and I took two horses up and met him," Mayfield later recalled. "He saw that I could tell how old a horse was by looking in its mouth and could judge its weight."

Though Mayfield was old enough—and at six feet two inches tall certainly big enough—he settled for horse trading with Roosevelt rather than serving under his command and going to Cuba.

A railroad grade-leveling project at the town of Alice in Jim Wells County lured Mayfield to South Texas around the turn of the century. When that work played out, he hired on with a stagecoach line that operated between Brownsville and Alice, a 138-mile, day-and-a-half-long trip through arid brush country.

By 1901 Mayfield—newly married to a schoolteacher—was working for Valley pioneer John Closner as assistant manager of his San Juan Plantation, a section of irrigated land in Hidalgo County that produced bountiful sugarcane crops. The job was perilously close to farming, an avocation Mayfield had foresworn. But Closner also was sheriff of Hidalgo County. Mayfield handled some security work for his boss and eventually got a commission as a deputy. In the fall of 1908, county records were hauled in mule-drawn wagons from the old county seat of Hidalgo to the new town of Chapin. Some men in the county opposed the change. As one of the armed guards, Mayfield went along to make sure the transfer was accomplished without incident. It was. The town later was renamed Edinburg.

When the elections of 1914 approached, Closner opted to run for county treasurer instead of sheriff. He was succeeded in office by former Ranger A. Y. Baker. After Baker took office, Mayfield stayed on as one of his deputies. Early in 1915, in his capacity as a Hidalgo County lawman, Mayfield made the most important arrest of his career.

Occasionally a peace officer arrests a suspect for a relatively minor offense, only to discover that the person has been up to more than it appeared. That was not the case with Basillio Ramos Jr. The twenty-four-year-old Ramos, a native of Nuevo Laredo, Mexico, had worked as a secretary at the customs house there. When the Mexican revolution broke out in 1910, national leadership changed so quickly—three times in four years—that it was easy for someone to be a loyalist one day and an enemy of the state the next. Ramos had supported

150

General Victoriano Huerta. When Huerta resigned in 1914, creating a power vacuum that General Venustiano Carranza hastened to fill, Ramos found it expedient to come to Texas. Along with three other newly displaced colleagues, Ramos opened a wholesale-retail distributorship for the Royal Brewing Company of Kansas City in the Texas town of San Diego.

A longtime stopping point on the road from Corpus Christi to Laredo, San Diego was the seat of Duval County. The population of 2,500 was about 75 percent Hispanic. Among many of those, anti-American sentiment ran strong.

Though Ramos and his associates operated a saloon, their preoccupation with certain radical political concepts far exceeded their interest in capitalism. While they supported the need for new government in Mexico, they also envisioned a brand new republic on the continent—one reclaimed from the United States. For like-minded men interested in the concept and expressing their disdain for Anglos, Texas, and the United States, Ramos offered beer on the house or priced below market cost. By December a bold plan was afoot. But Ramos' generosity did not leave enough money in the saloon's till to meet business expenses, much less to cover the cost of their ambitious plot. Ramos and his colleagues left the local Masonic Society holding the bag for their surety bond and slipped out of town, leaving rent and other bills unpaid.

Ramos returned to Mexico, where he soon was arrested by the Carranzistas. Jailed for five days in Monterrey, he was released near the end of the first week of January 1915. From there he went to Matamoros and then across the river into Brownsville. After spending one night in a boardinghouse run by a movement sympathizer, he traveled west to the four-year-old town of McAllen, a community that developed when the railroad moved west from Brownsville.

At McAllen, the young Huertista approached Dr. Andres Villarreal, hoping to enlist his support in the execution of the revolutionary plan. The doctor was not interested. When the physician told McAllen merchant Deodoro Guerra, former sheriff of neighboring Starr County, about Ramos' scheme, the ex-lawman passed the information on to Hidalgo County sheriff Baker.

Over the years, two widely disparate motivations for the tip-off have been ascribed to Guerra. An old friend, former Ranger and state Adjutant General W. W. "Bill" Sterling, later wrote that Guerra was "one of the Valley's best citizens." Unstated by Sterling but inferred was that Guerra provided the information to Sheriff Baker simply because it was the right thing to do.

Affidavits filed in connection with the case told a different story. Though Guerra had indeed worn a sheriff's badge in Starr County from 1906 to 1910, he happened to be the target of a smuggling investigation at the time of Ramos' appearance in McAllen. Guerra eventually was named in a criminal complaint charging him with smuggling and receiving stolen goods, but about a year after Ramos' arrest the case was dropped for lack of witnesses. Perhaps Guerra believed it to be his civic duty to report the conspiratorial conversation to Sheriff Baker. Perhaps a more personal consideration was involved.

Whatever the motivation for Guerra's cooperation, Baker asked the merchant to schedule a meeting with Ramos. When the Mexican came to Guerra's grocery store, Baker intended to step in and arrest him. But Ramos did not show up at the appointed time, and the sheriff departed. However, Mayfield stayed on the case. When Ramos finally appeared, the deputy arrested him, possibly with the assistance of former sheriff Guerra and his son. The date was Sunday, January 24, 1915.

Found in Ramos' possession was an assortment of papers, including a thousand-word document in Spanish bearing eight signatures. Mayfield, who was bilingual, read enough of it to realize its content was inflammatory.

The document contained fifteen points, the first of which stated, "On the 20th day of February, 1915, at two o'clock in the morning, we will arise in arms against the Government and Country of the United States of North America, ONE IS ALL AND ALL AS ONE, proclaiming the liberty of the individuals of the black race... and at the same time and in the same manner we will proclaim the independence and segregation of the States bordering upon the Mexican Nations."

Those states, the document continued, were Texas, New Mexico, Arizona, Colorado, and "Upper California." In reclaiming this territory, the "Liberating Army for Races and People" would execute all captured opponents, every "stranger who shall be found armed and who cannot prove his right to carry arms" and "every North American over sixteen years of age."

Land taken from the Apache and other Indians would be returned to them in exchange for their participation in the campaign, the plan went on. Once the Liberating Army had control of former Mexican territory, it would assist blacks in "obtaining six states of the American Union, which States border upon those already mentioned," so they could form their own republic.

The Hidalgo County Sheriff's Office had no jurisdiction in a matter involving a planned attack on the United States. Ramos soon was turned over to Deputy U.S. Marshal T. P. Bishop and Immigration Service agent Frank J. McDevitt. The two federal officers took the prisoner and the seized documents to Brownsville where an agent stayed up all night translating the papers into English. The matter was handed over to Immigration Service Inspector E. P. Reynolds, who took a sworn statement from Ramos on January 28. Ramos freely admitted signing the document and acknowledged that he had the authority to organize revolutionary *juntas*.

A day after Ramos signed his statement, an agent with the U.S. Department of Justice filed a complaint charging Ramos and the other seven signatories to the document with conspiracy to levy war against the United States. Bond was set at $5,000.

Grave as the Plan of San Diego read and even though federal charges had been filed against its signers, no one seems to have taken it very seriously at first. Since the beginning of the Mexican revolution in 1910, inflammatory rhetoric had been as common as prickly pear along the border. At Ramos' arraignment, the federal magistrate said Ramos was more in need of a psychiatrist than a defense attorney.

The man arrested with the revolutionary plan was taken to the federal court-house in Brownsville. (Author's collection)

Less than a week before Ramos' arrest, James Ferguson was inaugurated as governor of Texas, replacing Oscar B. Colquitt. Ferguson soon learned that among the many responsibilities of office, he had inherited a particularly worrisome situation along Texas' long border with Mexico. The Adjutant General's Department already had most of its sixteen-man Ranger force in South Texas. Before the end of the year, Ferguson would have sixty Rangers patrolling the Valley.

Despite the fact that no one put much stock in the revolutionary manifesto seized by Mayfield, an effort was made to keep it quiet. The motive was not to avoid public panic, but to give federal agents a better chance of arresting the other men who had signed the plan. But on February 2 the Associated Press got wind of it, and newspapers across the state published the story.

U.S. troops along the border went on alert, and the Rangers kept their eyes out for trouble. However, the day the revolution was scheduled to start passed without incident.

The news that nothing of consequence happened on February 20 was not as good as it seemed. The plan had been amended by others involved in the movement, which investigators eventually found had connections to a left-leaning Mexican newspaper editor in Los Angeles, California. The new plan was more socialist in nature but still called for the violent separation of Texas and other Southwestern states.

While all this was going on, Ramos languished in the Brownsville jail. A federal grand jury indicted him in May, but his bond was reduced to an easily raised one hundred dollars. He soon was in Mexico and, so far as is known, was never heard from again.

When the war did begin on July 4—the 139th anniversary of a more distant North American rebellion—the people of South Texas still did not realize the significance. They thought the Mexican raiders stealing horses and supplies were connected to the revolution under way across the river, not the vanguard of a separatist effort on the American side of the river.

"The raid by this band is the first instance of the kind in this section since the early seventies, when the notorious bandit Cortina terrorized the lower coast," the *Houston Post* noted in a dispatch from Brownsville.

The perception clearly held that the incursion into Texas was an act of outlawry. In truth, the foray was a guerrilla operation, as were other raids in South Texas that followed throughout the summer. On August 8, fifty or more Mexicans attacked the Norias division headquarters of the King Ranch, seventy miles north of Brownsville. Three ranch employees were killed and two U.S. soldiers were wounded in the attack. At least five of the bandits were killed. More than a dozen Rangers had been at the Norias headquarters a short time before the raid, but they had ridden off to check a report of suspicious Mexican horsemen on another division of the ranch.

As a Hidalgo County sheriff's deputy, Mayfield rode with the Rangers as they sought out and skirmished with the raiders believed to be responsible for the Norias raid and other incidents.

In their efforts to cope with the situation in the Valley, the Rangers had their critics and their supporters. In early

November, when twelve of Captain J. J. Sanders' Rangers stopped in Kingsville for supplies, the *Kingsville Record* summed up the opinion of many Valley residents:

> What a sight for sore eyes they were! It's no won-
> der Mexican bandits tremble in terror at the word.
> Strong, determined men they are, with courage and
> daring written on their faces, dead shots, tireless on
> the trail, cunning as cunning is judge on the border
> paths, true Texas Rangers of the old school... a
> mighty army within themselves, the State's best gift
> to her people.

The *Alice News,* reprinting the Kingsville article, added that "Captain Sanders and his force of rangers... are a fine lot of gentlemen and Alice is proud to have them as citizens."

Sanders may have been a gentleman in his dealings with Anglos in the Valley, but he and the other Rangers approached the bandit situation with an attitude similar to their predecessors of the old Frontier Battalion: Bullets solved problems quickly and permanently.

The bandit trouble born of the Plan of San Diego lasted about a year. Roughly thirty raids had claimed twenty-one American lives, but the envisioned redrawing of the North American map never happened.

Several factors went into the eventual pacification of the Valley. Under pressure from U.S. president Woodrow Wilson, Mexican president Carranza helped suppress anti-American activities on his side of the river. The activities of the Rangers and other law enforcement officers, though at times contrary to the Constitution they were trying to protect, clearly had a chilling effect on the adherents of the Plan of San Diego.

"They were good riders, trailers, and excellent rifle and pistol shots," former Cameron County deputy sheriff John Peavey said years later of the Rangers. "Whenever they made contact with a bandit gang, they wiped it out.... They did much and talked little."

Whispering Tom was one of those who "talked little."

In 1915 the Hidalgo County deputy sheriff found the dead bodies of fourteen Mexican men in the city park in the small town of Alamo. The Rangers got the blame or credit, depending on who was talking, for the mass killings.

"Tom states that neither he nor any of the Rangers in the Valley had anything to do with it," an Edinburg High School student who interviewed Mayfield a few years before his death wrote for the Texas State Historical Association's *Junior Historian* magazine. "He gave his version of the story, which was accepted by law enforcement agencies at the time as the truth, but it was never published for many reasons. Mayfield has requested that it not be put into print."

Mayfield did tell the young writer that he and several Rangers were the ones who buried the bodies.

"As far as he [Mayfield] knows," the student wrote, "they are still buried in the same spot near [the town of] Alamo."

Tom Mayfield found fourteen dead bandits in the city park at Alamo, Texas. (Author's collection)

As a sheriff's deputy, Mayfield worked with the Rangers for years, but he had never held a Ranger commission. On June 6, 1918, the thirty-seven-year-old lawman was sworn in as a

Ranger. His enlistment, which was without pay because of the war emergency, could have run for two years. Records in the state archives do not reflect when his service ended, but he probably gave up the commission after the armistice in November 1918.

By 1921 the Rio Grande Valley had become a relatively peaceful place, at least in comparison to the previous ten years. Mexico, which still had not recovered from the chaos of its decade-long revolution, was not a peaceful place. Mayfield took a job as a guard with the American Oil Company in Mexico.

Later that year the forty-one-year-old former Ranger found himself facing a five-soldier firing squad. Just as the presiding officer was about to give the order to fire, Mayfield ran for it. He managed to reach a nearby *cantina* despite a horizontal hailstorm of lead aimed in his direction that killed three innocent bystanders. None of the slugs hit Mayfield, who was escorted to Tampico by several more amicable citizens.

His employers, however, already had released details of his "execution" to the press. Safely back in Texas, Mayfield had the pleasure of reading his own highly laudatory obituary. He kept a framed copy of the newspaper account of his violent demise hanging on his office wall for the rest of his life.

Mayfield never went into great detail discussing his close call south of the border, other than to say the matter stemmed from a disagreement over a horse. Others said his interrupted execution had to do with ill feelings on the part of certain parties due to his previous law enforcement work in Texas, particularly his role in exposing the Plan of San Diego. The Mexican official who ordered Mayfield's execution later was found shot to death.

Some said that Whispering Tom Mayfield's voice had been hoarse ever since his Mexican captors tortured him by pouring hot grease down his throat. He did talk in a whisper in his later years, but it was the result of a laryngectomy, not torture. While Mayfield was well known for his voice, the arrest he made on a January night in 1915 is what made him famous in the Valley.

The historical significance of Basillio Ramos' arrest probably explains why it has been attributed to others over the years. Some accounts incorrectly have Deodoro Guerra taking Ramos into custody. The date is sometimes wrongly given as February 1915, and Guerra is described as still being a sheriff. Federal authorities also have been credited with Ramos' arrest. While they were soon involved in the matter, Mayfield put the handcuffs on Ramos. As Walter Prescott Webb said in *The Texas Rangers: A Century of Frontier Defense*, "It is important to give Tom Mayfield credit for this arrest because the agents of the federal government assume all credit for the act and do not mention Tom Mayfield's name."

Sterling called Mayfield "one of the greatest officers who ever served on the Rio Grande." The former adjutant general, who seldom lacked an opinion, said Whispering Tom "did more than any living man to suppress the Bandit War."

Mayfield, Sterling wrote, was *puro hombre*. A border officer, Sterling continued, gained such a reputation by surviving gunfights. "If one or two of the attackers are killed…his reputation is established and he usually has no further trouble. The former enemies often become good friends. Tom Mayfield did so well along this line that many of the natives named their fighting bulldogs and game roosters" in his honor, Sterling wrote.

Long after Mayfield's Ranger service ended, he still was enforcing the law in South Texas and living up to his reputation. In 1938 he was hired as a deputy by Precinct 8 constable Grover Brady. Two years later he ran against his boss and was elected.

One night in the 1940s, George J. Brown and several teenaged friends were playing "ditch 'em," chasing around Pharr in their cars and trying to lose the person in the car behind them.

Fairly soon the person behind Brown was Constable Mayfield.

"He stopped me and told me to go home and tell my dad what I'd done," Brown recalled. "He said he was going to check with him the next day to make sure I'd told him. Well, I went right home and told him. But if Mayfield ever checked with my dad, I never heard about it."

Mayfield retired in 1963, nearly half a century after he first started legally toting a gun. A widower, he spent all but two of the last years of his life at the San Juan Hotel in Pharr. The management, happy to have a man of Mayfield's reputation as a permanent guest, charged him only one dollar a day in rent. His meals usually were on the house anywhere in town. When he got too feeble to live alone, he was moved to the nearby San Juan Hospital. He liked to sit in his room and look down on the town's busy main thoroughfare, still keeping an eye on things.

When Mayfield turned eighty-five in 1965, Governor John Connally honored him with a proclamation presented by Senator Jim Bates of Edinburg. The old lawman died on November 26, 1966.

In 1993 the Texas Historical Commission approved a historical marker about Mayfield for placement at the old hotel where he had spent so many years.

Notes

Finding dead Mexicans on the Texas side of the river during the bandit troubles became so commonplace, the *San Antonio Express* reported, that it "created little or no interest." U.S. Army general Frederick Funston estimated at least three hundred Mexicans were summarily executed in the Valley by Rangers, posse members, and vigilante groups during the unrest that followed the inception of the Plan of San Diego. As the incident involving Mayfield reflects, an exact accounting will never be known.

Sources

Alice News. November 14, 1915.

Anders, Evan. *Boss Rule in South Texas: The Progressive Era*. Austin: University of Texas Press, 1982, pp. 221-230.

Brown, George J. Interview with the author, May 31, 1998.

Coerver, Don M. and Linda B. Hall. *Texas and the Mexican Revolution: A Study in State and National Border Policy 1910-1920*. San Antonio: Trinity University Press, 1984, pp. 85-108.

Curl, Tom. "Whispering Tom." *Southern Living*, July 1985, p. 142.

Hoover, Larry. "Tom Mayfield, Dean of Law Enforcement." *The Junior Historian*, Vol. XXII, No. 5, March 1962, pp. 13-16.

"Mexican Raiders Eluded Posse in Cameron County." *Houston Post*, July 7, 1915.

Peavey, John R. *Echoes From the Rio Grande*. Brownsville: Springman-King Co., 1963.

Robertson, Brian. *Wild Horse Desert: The Heritage of South Texas*. Edinburg: New Santander Press, 1985.

Sandos, James A. *Rebellion in the Borderlands: Anarchism and the Plan of San Diego, 1904-1923*. Norman: University of Oklahoma Press, 1992.

Sterling, William Warren. *Trails and Trials of a Texas Ranger*. Norman: University of Oklahoma Press, 1968.

Webb, Tom and Robert Norton. "Tom Mayfield." Report prepared for the Hidalgo County Historical Commission, August 10, 1992.

Webb, Walter Prescott. *The Texas Rangers: A Century of Frontier Defense*. Boston: Houghton-Mifflin, 1935, p. 484.

A Killer Bullets
Couldn't Stop

Fannie Pennington was a charter member of the Women's Study Club in Holland, a small town in Central Texas. Since 1914 Fannie and the other ladies had been meeting once a month to discuss good books and significant issues of the day. Fannie knew that the behavior of the characters in the novels she and her women friends read and talked about was based on motivation. Surely she knew as well what now can only be speculated on: what motivated her fifty-six-year-old husband Ben, at an age when most men start thinking about slowing down the pace of their lives, to become a Texas Ranger.

Maybe in the patriotic fervor that followed America's April 2, 1917 entry in the Great War (not for more than two decades would it be known as World War I), Pennington believed it was the least he could do for his country. After all, his father had died in the service of the South in 1863. Too old to enlist in the army or navy, Ben Pennington may have thought that as a Ranger he could protect the border from Mexican bandits or German spies and saboteurs. If he could not take on the Huns himself, at least he could help round up slackers (those young enough to fight but unwilling to do so) or jail anyone who spoke disloyally of America.

Beyond the notion of duty to state and country, the rugged, mountainous landscape of West Texas could have a powerful pull on a man, especially one born in the gently rolling farmland of Central Texas. To a man well past middle age, any of those considerations must have seemed more interesting than being a constable in Bell County.

For whatever reason, on October 4, 1917, Pennington was sworn in as a Texas Ranger under Captain J. M. Fox in Brewster County. Though new to the Rangers, Pennington had toted a pistol for twenty years, twelve years as marshal of

Holland and eight years after that as a Bell County constable. Heavyset, he stood five feet ten inches tall. He had light hair, a fair complexion, and brown eyes.

Bob Hunt was a younger man, only thirty-four, but he had seniority on Pennington in terms of Ranger service. An easy-going cowboy from San Angelo with light brown hair and blue eyes, Hunt stood as tall as Pennington if shorter in over-all experience as a lawman. He had first signed on with the Rangers in El Paso on June 8, 1915, as a private in Company B. The following spring, on April 11, 1916, he resigned for reasons not noted on his records. But on August 20, 1918, the affable bachelor rejoined the Rangers. This time he was a private in Company L under Captain W. W. Davis.

Even before they met, the two Rangers shared common ser-vice under Captain Fox, who had joined the Rangers as a private on October 5, 1911. That same day, Governor Oscar B. Colquitt appointed him captain. It was the beginning of a controversial career that would end in Fox's resignation nearly seven years later over an event in which Pennington may have been a participant. No one will ever know for sure. Fox refused to identify the Rangers involved.

What little is known is that on Christmas Day of 1917, Mexican bandits raided the L. C. Brite Ranch in Presidio County near present-day Valentine—twenty-five miles above the Rio Grande into Texas. Early that morning Sam Neil, an old Texas Ranger, had just poured himself a cup of coffee and walked out to the woodpile to watch the sunrise over the mountains when he spotted at least two dozen armed horse-men approaching. Neil ran back to the ranch house, shouted a warning to his son Van, the ranch foreman, and grabbed a Winchester. When the riders opened fire on the ranch house, the elder Neil leveled his .30-30 and dropped one of the ban-dit leaders with his first shot. Father and son, protected by thick adobe and good marksmanship, held off the bandits for several hours. With them were their wives, two of Sam Neil's nieces, and two women who worked at the ranch. The attack-ers sent one of two captured ranch hands to tell the Neils that the other man would be killed if they did not surrender. The former Ranger and his son were inclined to keep fighting. But the foreman's wife suggested a life-saving compromise: Give the attackers the key to the ranch store. Her idea worked. The raiders turned their attention to the store and began looting. About that time, the mail wagon from Candelaria arrived. The bandits robbed and shot the two passengers and then took driver Mickey Welch inside the store, hung him upside down, and slashed his throat.

While this was going on, the Reverend H. M. Bandy and his family arrived at the ranch for Christmas dinner. The bandits, not wanting to kill a *padre* and still preoccupied with their sacking of the store, let the Bandys join the Neil family inside the ranch house. The preacher fell to his knees and led everyone in prayer. In the firm conviction that the Good Lord helped those who helped themselves, he stood up and asked for a rifle. Sam Neil—who already had a rifle—asked for a drink of whiskey. Horrified that her husband mentioned drinking in the presence of a preacher, Mrs. Neil reproached the old-timer. "Let him have his whiskey," Bandy said. "If there ever was a time a man needed a drink, this is it."

In the end, twentieth-century technology may have played as big a role as anything in saving the Neil and the Bandy families. The sound of prolonged gunfire that morning brought a concerned neighbor to see what the trouble was. Riding close enough to see that the ranch was under attack, James L. Cobb rushed back to his farm, gathered his family, and went to the Gourley Ranch where he knew there was a telephone. Cobb reported the raid to Sheriff M. B. Chastain, who in turn contacted Captain Fox. Soon, sheriff's deputies, Rangers, soldiers, and armed volunteers raced to the Brite Ranch in a thirty-car caravan. Ben Pennington, then stationed at Marfa, probably was one of those riding to the rescue.

The posse reached the ranch almost in time to catch the raiders, but the advantage returned to those availing themselves of a more traditional mode of transportation. Men on horseback could move down trails that men in Model Ts could not. Unable to continue the pursuit, the posse watched as the bandits escaped in a shower of long-range rifle shots.

Texans were outraged by the Christmas Day attack and the murder of three people. Fox's Rangers mounted up to search for the bandits, who had escaped with goods from the Brite store along with cattle and horses. In the days following the raid, the Rangers of Company B scouted the well-worn trails leading to the Rio Grande, looking for any sign of the raiders and interrogating Mexican-American residents along the river.

Suspicion centered on the outlaw Chico Cano, who a couple of years earlier had ambushed and killed Texas Ranger Eugene Hulen and former Ranger Joe Sitters. Though he lived in Mexico, Cano and his bandits spent a lot of time in and around the small village of El Pourvenir on the Texas side of the river. When Fox learned that many of the children in the village seemed to be wearing new clothes and that some of the local men had been seen in Hamilton Brown shoes—the same brand of shoes that had been among the goods taken from the Brite store—the captain sent Sergeant Bud Weaver and seven Rangers to investigate.

On January 29, 1918, the Rangers conducted a house-to-house search of Pourvenir. They found new shoes, Crystal White soap, and Barlow pocket knifes—all items listed as having been taken from the Brite Ranch—and rounded up fifteen men they suspected of participating in the raid. The only uncontroverted fact concerning what happened next is that by the following morning, all fifteen men were dead.

Captain Fox reported that the Mexicans had been "carried out on the edge of town" so the Rangers could determine their identity. While that process was under way, Fox continued, "some of their comrades…fired into the Rangers, the Rangers [sic] horses breaking loose and leaving them all on foot. They immediately lay down returning fire on all moving objects in front." The fifteen men the Rangers had been questioning apparently were among those "moving objects."

A Presidio County grand jury found no cause to indict any of the Rangers over the matter.

Though the extent of Pennington's participation in the Pourvenir affair may never be known, he saw more action in less than a year than in his previous two decades as a lawman

165

in Central Texas. He had jailed his share of fighting drunks back in Holland, but keeping the peace in Bell County was easy compared to Ranger duty in the Rio Grande country. Like most Rangers, Pennington did not talk much about his business, but since first stepping off the train in far West Texas in the fall of 1917, he had heard the whine of bullets more than once. And more than once a bullet sent in his direction came close to ending his career. One of those bullets, though sparing his life, cost him an eye. Still, he rode the river for Texas, keeping his one good eye out for trouble. He deserved his reputation for fearlessness.

Another source of trouble along the border—though far from the worst—was El Paso's Fort Bliss, a seventy-year-old cavalry post. On payday, when the soldiers hit the city's 250 bars and numerous houses of prostitution, El Paso police often called on the Rangers to help keep the rowdy soldiers in line. The sentiment in El Paso was to let the boys have a good time, but not too good. The U.S. War Department, however, wanted El Paso and other Texas cities with large military posts to clean up their act. So did Congress, which passed wartime legislation prohibiting the sale of alcohol as a food conservation measure. (The 18th Amendment to the Constitution, the beginning of more than a decade of violence associated with national prohibition, would come later.)

While America dried up in the social sense, in the desert around El Paso spring was quickly turning into summer. As nature began one of its quarterly transitions, another form of change—but one that was quite random—occurred. Seven hundred miles northeast of El Paso, in a biological process that would not begin to be even partially understood for decades, a normally stable avian virus somehow was transmitted from a bird to a pig. When the pig's immune system attacked the invader, the virus mutated to survive. The resultant new strain proved particularly deadly for its next host: human beings.

On March 11, company cook Albert Mitchell reported to the infirmary at Camp Funston, Kansas, a subpost of Fort Riley. He had a slight headache, a mild sore throat, and a low-grade fever. His appetite was off, and his muscles ached. A post doctor put the cook on sick leave and ordered him to spend the day in his bunk. By mid-day 107 Camp Funston soldiers were ailing. Two days later the number of sick soldiers at the Kansas camp had increased to 522.

The disease quickly stretched across the United States —from the isolated prison on Alcatraz Island in San Francisco Bay to sailors aboard ships in ports along the East Coast. Despite the rapid spread of the disease, the medical community and the general public did not take it too seriously at first. Recovery seemed as rapid as its onset. At first doctors referred to it as "three-day fever," but they finally came to realize it was a new strain of influenza. Soldiers in the trenches "over there" in Europe began calling it the Spanish Flu, believing it had originated in Spain. But in Spain, people referred to it as the French Flu.

Newspapers published in the spring of 1918 were crowded with war news—President Woodrow Wilson had just given his famous 14 Points speech—but little if any attention was paid to the flu epidemic. The flu spread from post to post in the military. Soon the virus was well embedded into the general population.

In West Texas, ranchers also were getting sick of incursions by Mexican bandits. The Neville Ranch was raided on March 25, and two people were killed. The next day, U.S. troops —accompanied by some of Captain Fox's Rangers—crossed the river and struck the suspected bandit stronghold in Pilares, Mexico. As many as thirty bandits and some innocent bystanders were killed in the attack.

In the wake of the Pilares raid, Governor William P. Hobby ordered Adjutant General Jason Harley to discharge five of Fox's men. The other seven Rangers were transferred to other companies. Pennington was assigned to Company L, joining Ranger Hunt. Captain Fox, citing politics as the only reason for the firing of nearly half of his company, resigned from the Rangers.

A little more than a month after his resignation Fox sent the governor a letter that would have cost him his job if he had not already quit:

This company was formed to replace Captain Fox's disbanded company.
(Author's collection)

Do you not think I would be an ingrate to send
my men out on a duty and because they unfortunately had to kill any number of Mexican bandits
to let them be discharged for carrying out my orders? You may be built in that way but I am not. I
think more of my men and friends than any job I
ever heard of. Why do you not come clean and say
that this is purely politics just to gain some Mexican votes?

That letter brought a reply to Fox from Adjutant General
Harley, which the *Marfa New Era* soon published:

The evidence disclosed, after a thorough
investigation...that fifteen Mexicans were killed
while in the custody of your men after they had
been arrested and disarmed....The right of trial by

> jury cannot be denied by any organization.... You
> were not forced to resign by the Governor for politi-
> cal reasons, but your forced resignation came in the
> interest of humanity, decency, law and order, and I
> submit that now and hereafter the laws of the con-
> stitution of this state must be superior to the
> autocratic will of any peace officer.

Whatever role Pennington had in all this, he at least kept his job.

The flap eventually died down, overshadowed by other events. As the great armies of Europe and America battled that summer in the deadliest war the world had ever known, each side gained another vicious enemy. Symptoms of the flu became more severe. A fifth of all sufferers developed life-threatening secondary infections: bronchial pneumonia or septicemic blood poisoning. With antibiotics yet to be invented, a large percentage died. Those who developed heliotrope cyanosis turned blue from lack of oxygen and within a day or two, 95 percent of them were dead. In America, many blamed the sickness on a secret biological weapon developed by the Germans. But the disease knew no flag or boundary. It decimated an already war-weary German army as well as that nation's civilian population. From the Western front to the home front, thousands of people died. The disease proved deadlier than bullets, shrapnel, or mustard gas.

In El Paso, east-west railroad traffic and the routine rotation of troops at Fort Bliss carried the disease to the southwestern desert, an area generally noted for its healthfulness because of its high, dry climate. On September 30, 1918, El Paso papers casually noted that some people in the city had the flu. A week later, nearly a thousand people were sick. Flu sufferers began dying.

The situation worsened daily in early October. The city's board of health ordered the closing of all schools, churches, theaters, lodges, pool halls, and other public places. All public meetings were canceled by edict of the board. In addition, soldiers at Fort Bliss were essentially confined to the post, forbidden to pass beyond the intersection of Overland and

El Paso Streets. Some other cities imposed even more severe restrictions, requiring passes for entry and limiting funerals to only fifteen minutes.

To help enforce their quarantine, El Paso officials called on the Rangers for help. Rangers Pennington and Hunt, along with others, were pulled in from border duty to see to it that the soldiers of Fort Bliss, normally an economic asset, stayed on the military reservation. Armed with six-shooters that could do no harm to the real enemy they faced, Pennington and Hunt followed orders and tried to keep people put for their own good.

Soon, both men began feeling ill. In following their orders, the two Rangers had contracted the flu. The disease progressed rapidly in both officers. Pennington went first, dying on October 12, only four days after his flu symptoms first appeared. "Famous Fighter of Border Guard Finally Downed," the *El Paso Times* reported the next morning.

> Pennington was one of the oldest and best known men of the border guards. The story is told of one fight in which he and another Ranger entrenched themselves in the sand near the river and stood off alone a body of raiders, doing such deadly work with their rifles that the attacking bandits finally beat a retreat across the line. He carried 16 wounds in his body, the marks of various frays. . . . Among his associates he was known as one absolutely fearless and one who could be depended upon to stick out any fight in which they were engaged.

The lawman's body was shipped by one of El Paso's busy funeral homes back to Central Texas for burial.

Ranger Hunt lived only four days longer than his older colleague, dying in an El Paso hospital on October 16. In five days his disease had progressed to pneumonia. With many of its reporters, editors, and printers also sick, the *Times* barely noted Hunt's passing. A one-paragraph article reported only that "Robert Hunt, state ranger, from Fabens, Tex., died in a local hospital Wednesday morning."

The Rangers and others afflicted with the Spanish flu died hard. One doctor wrote that the pneumonia associated with the flu was "the most vicious type...that has ever been seen." Once cyanosis appeared in a patient, the physician continued, "it is simply a struggle for air until they suffocate."

The second week of October 1918 saw the worst one-week death toll in the city's history. In the seven-day period from October 9 to October 16, El Paso mayor Charles Davis announced that 131 people, including the two Rangers, had died, most from the flu. Thirty-one people died in one day, October 12. Davis said the one-week count amounted to nearly as many deaths as had been reported for the entire month of October in 1917.

Nationwide, 6,122 civilians died of the flu during the week ending October 12, with another 4,439 claimed by flu-induced pneumonia. Those figures did not include military personnel. Hospitals across the country were full but short-staffed, since many doctors and nurses were sick or dying. El Paso and other cities were short of funeral directors, grave-diggers, and coffins. The American Red Cross mobilized to meet a domestic crisis as severe as the one abroad.

Children, struggling to understand what was happening, reduced the epidemic to a rhyme chanted while skipping rope:

> I had a little bird,
> Its name was Enza.
> I opened the window,
> And in-flu-enza.

The quarantine the Rangers helped enforce probably saved lives. In El Paso, death was more common along the river where most of the Hispanic population lived and at Fort Bliss. "Army and civilian doctors continue confident that they have the situation under control," The *El Paso Times* reported on October 14. "That the Spanish Influenza epidemic among the civilians has not been as serious as it might have been is indicated by the fact that only one death has occurred among the 1,500 members on the roll at St. Patrick's Cathedral."

In addition to the quarantine, good hygiene and wearing gauze facemasks also may have helped some. Other methods, however, were ineffective. In Britain, streets were sprayed with chemicals dangerous in their own right. Some thought tobacco smoke would kill the virus, or brisk walks, or eating plenty of porridge, or forcing yourself to sneeze once each morning and night after thoroughly washing the inside of your nose with soap and water.

In El Paso, the epidemic finally began to abate in November. On November 9, though only seventeen new cases had been reported, three people a day were still dying. But that was a significant improvement from October. The viral siege was declared at an end, and public places were allowed to reopen. But Fort Bliss, with 2,000 cases, remained under quarantine.

Three days later, at one o'clock in the morning on November 11, El Pasoans were awakened by pistol shots and whistles. Soon the city's two newspapers had extras on the street declaring in huge type that an armistice had been signed. The war was over. A wild, spontaneous celebration swept the city, continuing through daybreak. Though the onset of prohibition was only months away, local saloons did a flourishing business. Those not inclined to offer a toast to liberty headed for church, where special services were offered. Honking cars jammed the streets. At 9 A.M. the commander of Fort Bliss sent his soldiers—mounted, in vehicles, and on foot—into town. Townspeople fell behind the troops as a victory parade worked its way through downtown.

People in El Paso and all across Texas and the rest of the nation may not have realized it, but they were in truth celebrating two victories—a military triumph over Germany and, for the time being, a defeat of death. America had won a war, and its people had endured a terrible epidemic that had been even worse than they fully realized. Spanish flu infected 28 percent of all Americans, killing somewhere between 675,000 and 850,000 people. The virus had claimed the lives of more American military men and women than German warfare had killed. Worldwide, one-fifth of the planet's population had been infected. An estimated 20 to 40 million people died in the worst pandemic the world had known.

Though the epidemic peaked in Texas during the fall of 1918, it continued elsewhere through the first few months of 1919. Suddenly, eighteen months after it appeared, the virus vanished. Except for their families and friends, few remembered Pennington and Hunt—two horseback-era Rangers who died in the line of duty trying to protect the people of Texas from a killer bullets couldn't stop.

Notes

Pennington married Miss F. E. Blair on September 6, 1882, in Bell County. Records in the Bell County Courthouse show he was sued twice for debts during the near-national depression in 1892-93; both cases ended in judgments against him. On November 3, 1898, while he served as marshal of Holland, a six-man county court jury found him not guilty of an unknown misdemeanor offense. Precinct 3 voters in Bell County elected him to a two-year term as constable in November 1908, and he was returned to office three times, serving until November 1916. There is no probate record for Pennington.

Sources

Adjutant General's Records. Enlistment records of Ben L. Pennington and R. E. Hunt. Texas State Library, Archives Division, Austin, Texas.

Bell County Historical Commission. *Story of Bell County, Texas* (2 vols.). Austin: Eakin Press, 1988, pp. 134, 138, 820-821.

Billings, Molly. "The Influenza Pandemic of 1918." Stanford University Web site, 1997.

El Paso Herald, various issues.

El Paso Times, various issues.

Lockwood, Tomasin. "Influenza Pandemic." www.spartacus.school.net.co.uk, 1998.

Metz, Leon. *El Paso Chronicles: A Record of Historic Events in El Paso, Texas.* El Paso: Mangan Books, 1993, 1994, pp. 193-194.

Miller, Rick. Interview with the author, January 28, 1999.

Ritter, Al and Chick Davis. "Captain Monroe Fox and the Incident at Pourvenir." *Oklahoma State Trooper*, Winter 1996, pp. 35-41.

Thompson, Cecilia. *History of Marfa and Presidio County, Texas 1535-1946* (2 vols.). Austin: Nortex Press, 1985, pp. 144-148, 154-155.

Cowboy Tom Hickman

The ladies loved Captain Tom Hickman. And so did the press.

Hickman, a tall, lanky former cowboy with a smile that seemed almost as wide as his Stetson, received the undivided attention of most women when he walked into a room. He was married, but as one female reporter wrote: "His presence causes a vague discontent in women and frank admiration in men."

Newspaper reporters liked Hickman because, as they put it, he was "good copy." Unlike his boss, Senior Ranger Captain Frank Hamer, Hickman did not mind talking to journalists. Most of the time, anything he said was on the record. He had a sense of humor and liked practical jokes.

Ladies and the press liked Captain Tom Hickman. (Author's collection)

When the Democratic Party chose Houston for its 1928 national convention, Texas governor Dan Moody dispatched Hickman and fifteen other Rangers to serve as assistant sergeants at arms. Of course, the lawmen were in Houston to do what they always did, which was to prevent trouble.

The gathering in Houston was the first national political convention held below the Mason-Dixon Line since the Civil War. The historic decision to have the convention in the South was helped along by a $200,000 cash offering from Houstonian Jesse Jones, who owned the *Houston Chronicle* and numerous other Bayou City businesses.

With scores of reporters from around the nation in Houston to cover the proceedings, Hickman was in his element. In addition to keeping the peace, Hickman decided to have a little fun with an old friend in the convention press corps, nationally known humorist Will Rogers.

"I'm going to see that his name is placed before the convention for the vice presidential nomination," Hickman confided to "some of his newspaper friends," as the *Chronicle* soon reported.

But Rogers was wise to the scheme. The cowboy columnist, the newspaper related, "sent word out all over the country that he didn't care anything about being nominated for the vice presidency."

Once he discovered that he had lost the element of surprise, Hickman went public with his sentiments on the matter.

"You can just tell Will Rogers that us Texas Rangers have done made up our minds," Hickman said. "He might as well quit his beefing now and get in line. We've done held our caucus and decided he'll make a good running mate for Al [Smith]. He might as well prepare to serve. We ain't going to stand any foolishness from that fellow."

Or anyone else in Houston, for that matter. One-Eyed Conley, a nationally known gate crasher, was tossed out of Sam Houston Hall. The six-acre convention facility, built of Texas pine in only sixty-four days, could seat 16,000. Tobacco smoke and thousands of sweaty people packed into an un-air-conditioned structure in the middle of Texas summer quickly overpowered the piney smell of freshly cut lumber. As tempers rose along with the heat and humidity, the Rangers and Houston police broke up numerous fistfights on the convention floor.

Fort Worth newspaper publisher Amon Carter had to be settled down by the Rangers after demonstrating his annoyance at a slow elevator by firing a six-shooter in the lobby of the Rice Hotel, Houston's largest and best known hostelry. The flamboyant Carter popped off another three rounds through the window of Baltimore journalist H. L. Mencken's room. The bullets struck a hotel across the street, near enough to a room full of caucusing Ku Klux Klan members to cause something of a commotion. Again, some of Hickman's Rangers had to referee the matter. In the same hotel two days before the convention, the Rangers broke up a crap game and arrested fourteen men. The next morning the shooters paid $185.50 in fines.

Meanwhile, Hickman saw the dice rolling up sevens for Will Rogers.

"The job's as good as his whether he wants it or not," Hickman continued in his interview in the *Chronicle*. "I have fifteen Rangers here and they're all with me backing him for the vice presidency.... No joking. I look on Will Rogers as the man best qualified for the job.... He'd pile up a powerful vote."

In retrospect, the Ranger captain's joking suggestion that the convention delegates lasso Rogers as a dark horse vice presidential candidate does not seem all that unreasonable. After nominating New York governor Alfred E. Smith for president, the delegates in Houston picked Senator Joseph T. Robinson of Arkansas to join Smith on the ticket. In November, Republican Herbert Hoover won the presidency.

The Ranger with the cheek to "nominate" Will Rogers for the vice presidency—even if it was largely a tongue-in-cheek proposition—enjoyed a long law enforcement career that proved far more successful than his brief entry into the field of political strategy.

Born on his family's 2,300-acre ranch about twenty miles northwest of Gainesville in Cooke County on February 21,

1886, Thomas Rufus Hickman was sitting a saddle at an age when most city boys were learning how to stay upright on their bicycles. He soon made his father a good hand as a cowboy. He was not bad at sports, either. In 1905 and again the following year, the six foot one inch Hickman played on the Gainesville Athletic Club's football team. Both years the team went undefeated.

Graduating from Gainesville Business College in 1907 with a diploma saying he was "an intelligent and competent accountant," Hickman could have pursued a career in business. But the country still was recovering from the financial panic of 1906, and besides, getting paid to ride a horse was much more fun. When Zack Miller's 101 Ranch Wild West Show came to Gainesville, Hickman hired on. Traveling with the show for a year, he met and became friends with Tom Mix and an Oklahoma cowboy and trick roper named Will Rogers. Hickman never lost his love of rodeo or his flair for showmanship.

Hickman's law enforcement career began in 1908 when he returned to Gainesville from the performance circuit and went to work as a deputy constable. In 1911 Sheriff Louis Bringham hired him as a deputy. Five years later, when Bringham did not seek another term, Hickman made a run for the office. In a close election, he lost to Tom M. Ford. He did not have any better luck when he first sought a commission as a Texas Ranger.

"I tried for two or three years to get in," he later recalled. "Then they changed the Ranger force...raised the pay to sixty dollars a month and tried to get a better bunch of men. And I got in on that better bunch."

Hickman entered the Ranger service on June 16, 1919, as a private in Company A. At the time the state had six Ranger companies, and Governor William P. Hobby ordered every one of them stationed along the Rio Grande. Company A, commanded by Captain Jerry Gray, was based at Marfa in Presidio County. Should trouble arise, only seven Rangers working out of the headquarters in Austin were available for duty anywhere else in the state.

This is how a newspaper writer described the Rangers of 1919:

> These ranger men are all good shots; they have to be because the rules require it. They are allowed only 30 cartridges a month for target practice with revolver; but it is mighty seldom that a ranger confines himself to that number despite the fact that the cost must come from his pay check. They understand practice makes perfect.... They are not killers in the sense of the word that they are bloodthirsty or that they seek causes for slaying their fellow man. But they realize that their calling brings with it dangers—and they are ready.

Hickman and a partner patrolled the Rio Grande for bootleggers and bandits for a time, but Hickman soon was transferred to headquarters in Austin and placed in charge of rifle practice at the Camp Mabry range. The plan called for him to organize a Texas Ranger shooting team to compete in national matches, but the team never materialized. There was too much work to do. In short order, Hickman saw service in Galveston during labor difficulties in 1920, in Denison during a railroad strike in 1922 as the newly appointed captain of Company B, and in Mexia during a period of lawlessness at the height of its oil boom.

Hickman also did town-taming duty in Breckenridge, Burkburnett, Borger, and Kilgore during their respective oil binges.

At Burkburnett, in addition to coping with the typical problems of an unruly oilfield town, in 1920 Hickman found himself injected into a dispute between Texas and Oklahoma over which state owned the wildly prolific oil wells along the broad bed of the Red River. In support of Texas' claim to the wells, Hickman led his horse through shallow water to a small sandbar. Unloading his camping gear, the Ranger put up a tent and made himself at home on territory claimed by Oklahoma while officials hundreds of miles away argued the finer legal points of just exactly where the boundary lay between the two states.

The U.S. Supreme Court finally settled the controversy in 1923. Texas won claim to the one hundred fifty or so oil wells in question.

In the summer of 1924, following the tragic death of his first wife in an accidental shooting, Hickman went overseas to be a judge in the first American rodeo ever held in England. An estimated one and a half million people took in one of the show's thirty-three performances. While there he presented a pony named "Tejana" to the Prince of Wales as a gift from the Texas Rangers. The prince, delighted with the horse, said British law prohibited a member of the royal family from accepting expensive gifts and paid Hickman thirty pounds for the animal.

When promoter Tex Richard put on the first rodeo in Madison Square Garden in New York two years later, Hickman was there as a judge.

Despite his ready smile and a propensity for showmanship, Hickman could be as serious as a train wreck when necessary. His growing reputation as a tough Texas Ranger was solidified in early September 1926.

Robbers knocked over the Irving State Bank on August 25, 1926, and Hickman assisted Dallas County sheriff Schuyler Marshall and his deputies in the investigation. While not learning anything that pointed directly to the identity of the robbers, Hickman got word that the Red River National Bank in Clarksville might be the next financial institution on the robbers' "to-do" list.

Acting on that tip, on September 9 Hickman was in Clarksville. He contacted Stewart Stanley, a former Ranger sergeant, and told him of his belief that the bank was about to be robbed. Shortly before noon that day, the two men sat in Hickman's parked car, watching the bank on the northwest corner of the courthouse square.

The Ranger saw a car with two men in it pull up to the curb facing west on Broadway. Leaving the motor running, they got out of the vehicle and casually walked into the bank. Nothing about that aroused any suspicion on the part of the Ranger captain. Next two little girls walked up to the front of the bank. Suddenly, a man with a mask over his face emerged from the bank, grabbed the children, and pulled them inside.

"We immediately got busy," Hickman later told a reporter. "We turned my car around so that it faced north and prepared to meet the men as they came out."

When Hickman saw two men wearing masks coming out of the bank a few moments later, he was relieved to see they did not have the young girls with them as hostages. One of the men strained to carry a suitcase in both arms. Looking up and down the street, the second man walked slightly behind the first.

Hickman waited until the pair moved off the sidewalk and turned toward their vehicle before he and the former Ranger at his side jumped out of the car with their rifles leveled.

"We commanded them to halt, drop the suitcase, and hold up their hands," Hickman said.

The Ranger must have seen a flash of metal but would not remember hearing the crack of a pistol shot or the tinkle of falling glass behind him. Time froze and his field of vision constricted on the men, excluding anything around them. Hickman at first had not noticed the approach of town constable B. Q. Ivy and Sam Stanley, father of the former Ranger who had staked out the bank with him. Hickman gave the elder Stanley his pistol, and all four men fired on the robbers.

The man with the suitcase dropped in his steps in a fusillade of rifle fire. His companion went down less than four feet away.

"When we were satisfied they were dead we ran over to them and then rushed into the bank to see what conditions there might be," Hickman said.

At first Hickman did not see anyone. Then he noticed the bank employees, several customers, and the two young girls all lying on the floor in front of the vault.

After making sure that everyone inside the bank was safe, Hickman went back out to try to identify the two dead men. One of the men had a poll tax receipt in his pocket bearing the name of A. M. Slaton, forty-five, from Fort Worth. The other dead man had no identification on his body, but he was soon determined to be T. L. Smallwood, also forty-five and also of Fort Worth.

Inside the suitcase one of the robbers dropped when he was hit, Hickman found a mixture of silver coins and cash. Many of the bills were perforated by a neat round hole. One of the officers' bullets had traveled through the makeshift money-bag before hitting the robber.

The bag contained $33,125—including $3,000 in silver —taken from the bank, plus $3.65 that evidently had been in the bag at the time of the robbery.

Hickman noticed a crowd of people looking at two cars parked behind where he and the other officers had stood while firing at the robbers. The back windows of both vehicles were shattered.

"For the life of me I can't now tell whether either of them fired a shot," Hickman told the *Fort Worth Record-Telegram* that evening, "but they must have, for the glass in two autos to our back was shot out." To another reporter, Hickman added, "I was taking no chance."

Contemporary newspaper accounts of the robbery never described the weapons the robbers had on them when they were killed. Neither did the stories report whether one or both of the pistols contained empty shells or smelled of having been fired. One story did note that the officers found a double-barreled shotgun and a rifle—both loaded—in the car the men had left running outside the bank. Witnesses confirmed that the men pulled pistols when they entered the bank and demanded money. While one man collected money from the vault and tellers' cages, the other held a gun on five employees, two customers, and the two children inside the bank, assistant cashier T. E. Williams told the officers. The robbery had taken about five minutes, its bloody ending only a few seconds.

No one in Clarksville was particularly interested in the finer legal points of the case. Texas law at the time made it clear that deadly force could be used to protect property as well as life. What counted to the people of Red River County was that a Texas Ranger had prevented the area's largest bank from losing a small fortune in uninsured deposits.

No one seems to have thought about it at the time, but the double killing in Clarksville underscored both the strength and weaknesses of the Rangers in the Roaring Twenties and into the mid-1930s. On the whole they were as fearless and quick on the trigger as ever, but with no technological support to back them up, Hickman and his colleagues continued to operate as nineteenth-century peace officers nearly three decades into the twentieth century. When the Rangers needed fingerprints collected or crime scene photographs taken, they had to rely on assistance from the few big city police departments with fingerprint bureaus and rudimentary crime laboratories. As Hickman sought to link the dead Clarksville robbers with other bank jobs, he had to request help from the Dallas and Fort Worth police departments.

But the people of Texas were clearly content with Hickman's old-fashioned crime fighting. In less than a week, the state senate unanimously adopted a resolution praising Hickman and noting that the frequency of bank robberies in Texas had been causing "considerable alarm among bankers and business interests in the state." Introduced by Senator Walter C. Woodward of Coleman, the resolution proclaimed that "the courageousness of his action, together with his fidelity to duty, warrants the public commendation by the senate of Texas, and we express to him our appreciation of his services."

The Texas Bankers Association expressed its appreciation as well. Hickman received a $500 reward for each of the dead robbers. Various banks in Red River County presented other rewards amounting to $1,300, bringing the Ranger's total compensation for killing the two robbers to $2,300. Newspaper reports did not reveal whether the Ranger shared any of the reward money with the other three men involved in the shooting.

"I commend and endorse the Hickman method of preventing bank robberies," Bexar County district attorney C. M. Chambers said in a telegram to the Red River County sheriff's office. The San Antonio DA also asked for mug shots of the dead robbers. "A few incidents like the one in Clarksville will do much to discourage this form of outlawry in Texas," the *Houston Post Dispatch* editorialized on September 13.

The Clarksville bank robbery was a minor incident compared to what happened in 1927 in the Eastland County town of Cisco three days before Christmas.

Hickman was in Austin at the Missouri, Kansas & Texas depot, waiting for the afternoon "Katy" to Fort Worth, when someone from the governor's office rushed up.

"Tom, the bank at Cisco has been robbed by a man dressed like Santa Claus," the messenger said. "He got away after a gunfight on the street. Get there as soon as you can."

Taking the "Katy" to Fort Worth was the fastest way to get to Cisco, an oilfield town about one hundred miles southwest of Tarrant County.

When he reached Fort Worth that night, Hickman learned that his old friend Cisco police chief G. E. "Bit" Bedford had died of wounds suffered in the gunfight with the robbers. Another Cisco police officer, George Carmichael, was shot in the head and not expected to live. One of the robbers, a man named Louis Davis, also was mortally wounded. The other three gunmen, including a not-so-jolly fellow in a Santa Claus outfit, had escaped.

Hickman learned that Davis had been driven to Fort Worth in a hearse, a funeral home vehicle also used as an ambulance in that day. A doctor had done all he could for Davis, which was little more than dressing his wounds and shooting him up with painkiller. The robber was going to die; it was only a question of how soon. His removal to Fort Worth was not to afford him better medical care—he was being kept in the infirmary at the Tarrant County jail—but to save him from an agitated citizenry not inclined to let nature take its course.

When the train pulled into Fort Worth that night, Hickman walked from the station down the street to the jail. Downtown was ablaze with Christmas lights and crowded with people caught up in the holiday cheer, but at the county jail Davis was not dying in a clean, well-lighted place. The cell used as an infirmary smelled of disinfectant, but whatever commercial preparation the county used did a poor job of masking a permanent odor built up over the years by drunks, vagrants, and law-breakers. A bare light bulb hung down on a long cord from the ceiling as Davis lay semiconscious on a bunk, covered with a thin blanket. He had lost a lot of blood.

The Ranger tried to get Davis to tell who his accomplices were and where they might be hiding. But Davis, a down-on-his-luck family man with no criminal history, was too far gone to talk.

Leaving the jail, Hickman saw the hearse from Cisco parked across the street. The driver, trying to keep warm, had the motor running. The Ranger flashed his smile and his badge and asked for a ride to Cisco. At barely twenty miles an hour on an unpaved road, the trip would take four to five hours. Hickman stretched out in the back to get some sleep.

Arriving in Cisco early in the morning the day after the robbery, Hickman took over the search for the suspects, directing one of the largest manhunts the state had ever seen. His sergeant, Manuel T. "Lone Wolf" Gonzaullas, went up in an airplane as an observer in what is believed to have been the first aerial search for criminals in Texas history.

When the three suspects were spotted near the Brazos River several days later, Ranger Cy Bradford wounded one, Marshall Ratliff, in a wild shootout. Two others—Robert Hill and Henry Helms—managed to escape but were taken into custody a few days later in Graham. In eight days the pair managed to make it only sixty-two miles from the bank they had robbed. Of the three, Hill got a ninety-nine-year sentence for armed robbery and Helms eventually died in the electric chair for the murder of the two officers. Ratliff, the man who had dressed as Santa Claus, also was sentenced to death for his role in the crime. He died, but not in the electric chair. On November 19, 1929, with his conviction under appeal, he was taken from the Eastland County jail by a mob and lynched from a utility pole.

The Santa Claus bank robbery went down as one of Texas' more spectacular criminal cases. Though Hickman led the search, it had been a joint effort. The Ranger may have harbored a belief that too many officers had been involved. He seemed to be hinting as much years later when he told a reporter: "There were officers in there from everywhere. Before it was over two of them had wounded themselves while unloading their guns."

When the Hardin-Simmons University Cowboy Band toured Europe in 1930, Hickman went along as the official State of Texas representative. The photogenic Ranger, wearing a big hat and with his pant legs stuffed into his boots, fulfilled European expectations of what the typical Texan looked like. He also helped build worldwide recognition for the Texas Rangers.

Hickman was on hand in 1931 for another incident that added to the international reputation of the Rangers—another war of words between Texas and Oklahoma. At issue this time was not oil wells but two bridges across the Red River, a toll bridge and a new free bridge.

The toll bridge crossed the river that forms the Texas-Oklahoma boundary north of Denison. With funding from both Oklahoma and Texas, a twenty-three-foot-wide free bridge was constructed parallel to the toll bridge. The new span was the first free crossing of the Red River.

While residents on both sides of the river welcomed this new governmental project, the owners of the toll bridge did not see the construction of the free bridge as a wise use of tax dollars. In an effort to resolve a dispute with the Texas Highway Commission involving the purchase of the toll bridge by the state, the Red River Bridge Company went to federal court in Houston and got an injunction barring the opening of the new bridge. Soon a barricade was set up across the south end of the new bridge.

Defying the federal order, Oklahoma governor William H. "Alfalfa Bill" Murray on July 16, 1931, instructed his state's highway department to remove the Texas barricade and open the new bridge to traffic. His argument was that the south bank of the river was the Oklahoma border, not the north bank. He also said Oklahoma's "half" of the bridge was linear.

The day before, Texas' Fifty-sixth Cavalry Brigade had begun its annual encampment at Camp Wolters, a National Guard facility outside Mineral Wells. Newly named Texas adjutant general W.W. "Bill" Sterling was there for the festivities. Hickman, down from Fort Worth, also was in town.

Near midnight on July 16, Sterling and his wife were guests at an officers dance on the roof garden of the Baker Hotel when a bell boy came up and said he had an urgent telephone call holding. The caller was Governor Ross Sterling (no relation to the adjutant general). The governor instructed Sterling to be at the Red River by daybreak to close the free bridge in compliance with the federal order.

Sterling summoned Hickman and briefed him. The two men left Mineral Wells immediately. They drove to Fort Worth, picked up two of Hickman's Company B Rangers, and headed for Denison.

The Rangers reached the Red River at daybreak on July 17. Soon the barrier that the Oklahoma highway workers had removed—a sign reading "Warning/This bridge closed by order of the United States District Court for the Eastern District of Texas"—was back in place.

"This time," Sterling later wrote, "the bridge stayed closed."

As word spread that Texas Rangers had closed the bridge, reporters rushed to cover the standoff, quickly transforming a legal dispute into an event placing Oklahoma and Texas on the brink of war.

The journalists got plenty of help from Oklahoma's governor Murray, who ordered his state's highway workers to bulldoze the asphalt roadway leading to the toll bridge. The governor also called out Oklahoma National Guard troops and sent them to the scene.

The adjutant general soon returned to Austin, leaving Hickman in charge. But before he left, Sterling obligingly invoked the moss-backed "one riot, one Ranger" line for the benefit of the press, observing that he would send a couple of his Rangers home if Governor Murray brought only one regiment to the scene. The tall former Ranger, ever mindful of the needs of the Fourth Estate, also graciously complied with a news photographer's request to stand defiantly in front of the "Warning" sign with a rifle in his hands. The photograph was published around the world. During World War II, it would be used as Nazi propaganda in an effort to show that the United States was not as united as the world believed.

With little else to do but pose for pictures and stand around in the summer heat swatting insects, Hickman and his Rangers honed their law enforcement skills with a little target practice on the riverbank below the bridge. Ranger Bob Goss amused journalists and bystanders by demonstrating his ability to cut playing cards in half with a .45 slug.

"Bob is just a new man we are breaking in as a Ranger," Hickman joked for the reporters.

The Texas Legislature passed a bill on July 23 allowing the toll bridge company to sue the state over the purchase controversy, and the company agreed to join the state in a motion asking that the federal injunction be lifted. Two days later Hickman and his men were allowed to go home. The rhetoric continued a bit longer, but on August 6 the injunction was permanently dissolved, and the Oklahoma troops guarding the bridge were dispatched elsewhere to quell a matter of oil-field lawlessness.

Sixteen months later Texas had a new governor, the wife of impeached former governor James Ferguson. After Miriam A. "Ma" Ferguson's election in 1932, many Rangers resigned in protest, but Hickman stayed on. Even so, after Ferguson took office in January 1933, she refused to reappoint any of the Texas Rangers still on the state payroll. Hickman and the remaining Rangers were discharged on January 18. Asked what he intended to do when he left the Rangers, Hickman told a reporter, "I'd downright enjoy doing a little mule-skinnin' again."

Hickman returned to Gainesville, running the family ranch and hiring out as a deputy for Sheriff B. B. Browning. As soon as Ferguson was out of office, replaced by Governor James V. Allred of Wichita Falls, Hickman rejoined the Rangers as captain in charge of his old company, listing his occupation as "peace officer Gainesville." His re-enlistment was effective January 23, 1935.

That spring, the Legislature passed a bill creating a new law enforcement agency for Texas to be called the Department of Public Safety. The Rangers moved from the Adjutant

General's Department to the new agency, which officially came into being on August 10. On September 1 Hickman was named Senior Ranger Captain at an annual salary of $1,854.

But soon Hickman found himself at odds with the Public Safety Commission, the three-member policy-making body of the new state agency. In October the commission turned down an invitation for Hickman to go to California to appear in a movie being made about the Rangers. The situation came to a head on November 7 when he was called to appear before the commission to explain an unsuccessful raid on a Fort Worth gambling joint, the Top of the Hill Terrace, five days earlier. The line of questioning in the hearing clearly showed that the commission believed the raid had been mishandled. And though the minutes contain no outright accusation of Hickman, the commissioners seemed to suspect that the operator of the club might have had forewarning of the raid. Testimony was clear that Hickman had said beforehand that he did not believe the raid would be successful and that he had previously been a guest at the club with his actor friend Tom Mix.

When questioned by the commission, Hickman pointed out that Fort Worth had always been lax in prosecuting gambling cases and that the only way to make an ironclad case against the club would entail an extensive undercover operation.

"After Captain Hickman left," according to the commission minutes, "the Commission and Director [R. G.] Phares discussed at some length Captain Hickman's past activities and the Top of the Hill Terrace raid. It was unanimously decided by the Commission that Captain Hickman was not suited for the place of Senior Captain of the Texas Rangers and that he be advised that the Commission would like to have his resignation by December 1st."

Hickman apparently refused to resign, because on November 12 the commission discharged the veteran Ranger. His replacement was Company C captain J. W. McCormick, a former police chief in Wichita Falls, Governor Allred's hometown. For the rest of his life Hickman believed Allred had been the driving force behind his difficulties with the Public

Safety Commission—not a botched gambling raid in a city where betting was more or less tolerated by local officials.

A legislative committee looked into the matter, but the newspaper coverage of the hearing did nothing but further tarnish the former Ranger's image.

"We fired Hickman in the interest of law enforcement and because he was inefficient and disloyal," Public Safety Commission Chairman Albert Sidney Johnson said. "He lost prestige with the peace officers."

Fired from the Rangers, Hickman remained in law enforcement. Soon he was back on the payroll of the Cooke County Sheriff's Office. He served for six years under two sheriffs, Luther F. McCollum and his successor, Carl Wilson.

Following the Japanese attack on the U.S. naval base at Pearl Harbor on December 7, 1941, Hickman went to work for Gulf Oil Company. His job was to protect Gulf pipelines from saboteurs. He recruited a force of former Rangers to help him cover a five-state area. Despite previous difficulties with the Public Safety Commission, the board—now made up of new members—tendered him a Special Texas Ranger commission.

After forty-eight years in law enforcement, Hickman retired from Gulf Oil in 1956. That January, Governor Allan Shivers appointed Hickman to the Public Safety Commission. For some reason, perhaps a lingering institutional fondness for the quotable old cowboy-Ranger by the capitol press corps, newspaper stories on his appointment did not indulge in the delicious irony of Hickman joining a policy-making board whose predecessors had fired him. Four years later, he was elected chairman of the commission.

"Captain Tom Hickman is a living symbol of law enforcement in Texas," Commissioner C. T. McLaughlin of Snyder said shortly after nominating Hickman to preside over the commission. "His colorful career as a peace officer covers a span of more than fifty years during which Texas has seen some of its most turbulent periods. We consider him one of the outstanding Texas Rangers of all time."

Hickman as a member of the Public Safety Commission, the same policy body which once fired him. (Photo courtesy of the Texas Department of Public Safety)

Not long after his election as commission chairman, friends from all across Texas descended on Hickman's Cooke County ranch for a barbecue in his honor on February 21, 1961, the occasion of his seventy-fifth birthday.

As usual, the old Ranger, still square-shouldered and tall but sporting a white goatee that made him look a little like Buffalo Bill, was happy to talk to reporters.

"The Rangers of today are better than those of my day," he told one journalist. "They are better trained and better equipped. We operated on a shoestring—the state didn't even furnish us a car—and at one time the force dwindled to twenty-six men."

Asked if he still felt there was a place for the Rangers "in the jet-powered, neon-lighted world of 1961," Hickman replied, "As long as there are men who break the law, there is a need for officers like the Texas Rangers to uphold it."

"Captain Tom," as his friends called him, died peacefully on January 28, 1962, at his home outside Gainesville.

Sources

Brewer, Anita. "The Day That 'Santa Claus' Knocked Off the Cisco Bank." *Austin American*, December 23, 1960.

"Captain Tom Hickman, 1886-1962." *The DPS Chaparral*, January-April 1962, pp. 7-13.

Flemmons, Jerry. *Amon: The Texan Who Played Cowboy for America*. Lubbock: Texas Tech University Press, 1998, pp. 127-131.

Gardner, William H. "At 75, Ranger Capt. Tom Hickman Still Stands Tall, Thinks Modern." *Houston Post*, February 26, 1961.

Hickman, Paul. "Life Story of Captain Tom R. Hickman." Unpublished manuscript, 1983.

"Mexican Buttons and Bandoliers: The Oral Memoirs of Captain Tom Hickman." *The Texas Ranger Annual* (Vol. II). Waco: The Friends of the Moody Texas Ranger Library, 1983, pp. 37-44.

Public Safety Commission Minutes, November 7, 1935.

"The Rangers and the Border." *Houston Post Magazine*, December 21, 1919, p. 10.

"Rangers Have Made Up Minds Will Is To Be Nominated, Captain Hickman Declares." *Houston Chronicle*, June 27, 1928.

Sterling, William Warren. *Trials and Trails of a Texas Ranger*. Norman: University of Oklahoma Press, 1968.

"Tall in the Saddle." *Houston Chronicle Rotogravure Magazine*, October 21, 1956, pp. 24-25.

Tise, Sammy. *Texas County Sheriffs*. Hallettsville: Tise Genealogical Research, 1989, p. 130.

The Sherman Riot

No citizen of this State shall be deprived of life, liberty, property, privileges or immunities, or in any manner disenfranchised, except by the due course of the law of the land.
— Article 1, Section 19,
Texas Constitution

The young newspaperman knew it would be a difficult shot. His flashgun could not put out enough light to illuminate the whole scene. His only hope of getting a picture was to use available light. To do that, he'd have to expose his film for a full ten to fifteen seconds. The camera would need to be motionless, but he had no tripod.

Looking around, he spotted a white picket fence. The corner post had a flat top. Pushing his way through the crowd, he placed his big Speed Graphic on that fence post, slid in a film holder, and pointed the camera toward the flames, checking his composition through the wire frame finder on top of the camera. Satisfied with the focus, he set the aperture on "T" for a time exposure, adjusted the diaphragm, raised the mirror, and gently pressed the curtain-release button. He repeated the process three times, bracketing his exposure to make sure he got the picture.

The upside-down image that came through the lens transferred itself to the four-by-five-inch film but burned even deeper in the journalist's memory. Hanging from a chain thrown over a tree limb was a charred human being, slowly twisting over a pyre built by a mob. Mercifully, the man had already been dead. His hanging was only symbolic.

In a later era, the photograph taken that night by thirty-two-year-old L. A. Wilke, the city editor of the *Fort Worth Press*, would have appeared on the front page of every newspaper in the world. But this was 1930. The dangling silhouette backlit by the fire that had transformed it from a person to a form only moderately reminiscent of a human was considered too stark for publication. Years later the photograph would seem practically tame: a black-and-white image reflective of a black-and-white time. As it was, a print of the image ended up in a box with other faded photographs, an artifact of an ugly period of history.

Wilke had rushed to Sherman that afternoon shortly after learning that Governor Dan Moody had ordered National Guard troops there to suppress a riot.

The trouble in Grayson County began almost as brutally as it would end. On Saturday May 3, a white farmer's wife was raped. Later that day a sheriff's deputy arrested forty-one-year-old George Hughes. In trying to flee, the black man fired two shots at the deputy. Despite being shot at, the officer was able to take Hughes into custody without having to use his gun.

The next morning the *Sherman Democrat* reported the crime under a banner headline: "Negro Held For Assault Near Luella, White Woman Victim Alone in Farm Home, Bart Shipp Fired on Twice in Taking Negro."

The arrest of a black man for the rape of a white woman usually had a familiar ending in the South, where men summarily adjudicated by "Judge Lynch" were referred to as "the fruit of the Dogwood tree." Tension built quickly in and around Sherman. Rumors—untrue—spread that the rape victim had been mutilated by her attacker.

Monday night, May 5, a few people gathered outside the jail on the courthouse square but took no action. Fearing trouble, District Judge R. M. Carter contacted Governor Moody the next morning and requested that two Rangers be on hand for Hughes' trial, which had been set for Friday May 9.

Tuesday night a bigger crowd built up, and its mood was ugly. Deputies fired several shots in the air to break it up.

Thursday, the day before the trial, Judge Carter telephoned Moody again and asked for two more Rangers. The governor told him that Rangers were en route.

Arriving in Sherman from Austin were Captain Frank Hamer, Sergeant J. B. Wheatley, and Privates R. W. Aldrich and Jim McCoy.

At 9 A.M. on Friday, Judge Carter called the case. The hall outside the courtroom was packed with county residents, but the judge decided to allow only those directly involved in the proceedings inside the courtroom. Meanwhile the crowd outside the courthouse was growing. Roads leading into Sherman were clogged with bumper-to-bumper traffic.

Jury selection took only two hours. When the panel was seated, the victim of the assault—who was still recuperating from surgery she had undergone prior to the attack—was carried into the courtroom on a stretcher. Seeing the prostrate woman further agitated the spectators, who believed she was on the stretcher because of injuries suffered in the attack.

The first witness was still on the stand when Hamer began to hear angry "murmurings" outside. Hamer motioned for one of his Rangers to go with him to one side of the double stairway leading to the second-floor courtroom. Hamer ordered the other two Rangers to take the other side of the landing.

"Then the leaders of the mob appeared in the central doorway," Hamer told a newspaper reporter later that day. "I was surprised and worried to see women in the first group. I could tell they were agitating the men, urging them to take [the defendant] from us."

Seeing that the Rangers had their pistols out, the mob quieted enough to listen as Hamer ordered their dispersal.

"The Negro is upstairs," Hamer said, "and there he stays. If you take him you'll have to come up these stairs. Don't try it."

"We're coming up to get him!" someone in the crowd shouted.

"Well, if you feel lucky, come on up," Hamer replied. "But if you start up the steps, there'll be a lot of funerals in Sherman tomorrow."

The young men in the front apparently believed they were lucky. When they moved forward, Hamer and the other Rangers started swinging the heavy barrels of their single-action .45s, "clubbing a man here and another there," as Hamer later described it.

The blows momentarily clarified the thinking of the mob leaders, and the crowd fell back. Pistols poised for more action, the Rangers pushed the mob outside the courthouse.

Back in the courtroom, Hamer found it now only contained the judge, Grayson County sheriff Arthur Vaughan, and Hughes. The judge, fearing the mob would try to get to the prisoner again, had ordered the courtroom cleared and the jury retired.

"Let's lock him in the big vault," the judge said.

Hughes may have had the same idea about the same time. "Lock me up in there," another account of the incident quoted Hughes as saying. "They can't get that open."

No matter who had the idea of locking Hughes in the vault, that's where he went. Hamer escorted the frightened defendant to the forty-square-foot walk-in vault in the county clerk's office and provided him with a large bucket of water on the assumption that he would be in there for a while. The heavy door swung shut, and the combination dial was given a twirl.

Thirty minutes later, one of the two Rangers still posted at the foot of the stairs yelled that the mob was reforming. Hamer and Sergeant Wheatley rushed down to join the men.

"Sure enough, the mob was coming again," Hamer said later that day. "This time I saw fifteen or twenty women scattered about in the crowd, half a dozen of them to the very front of the wedge that was preparing to enter the front door."

At the courthouse entrance the captain again warned the crowd against coming inside.

"The four of us prepared to withstand the assault, and as the leaders came within reach we raised our pistols and swung down, hard," Hamer continued. "I talked all the time I was swinging my pistol." So did the other Rangers.

For twenty minutes, the crowd would gain a few feet on the Rangers only to be pushed back. Finally, Hamer recalled, "The leaders lost courage, if mob leaders have courage." The Rangers succeeded in forcing the throng outside the door once again.

Leaving Wheatley, Aldrich, and McCoy at the door, Hamer went upstairs to check the situation there. He was worried that the mob might have thought of putting ladders on the back side of the building to come in through the second-floor windows.

By now it was noon, but the crowd was not stopping for lunch. The Rangers saw someone outside the courthouse parading an American flag around as if to suggest that a mob's intervention into the criminal justice system was some kind of patriotic act.

"We heard the rolling grumble again and knew that the third assault was to come," Hamer went on. "Meanwhile, someone had found some tear gas bombs. As the mob approached the entrance several of these bombs were thrown."

The irritating white fog delayed the crowd for a few minutes, but the gas had the same effect on the officers and courthouse employees. Many of those inside ran upstairs and climbed out on the window ledges for fresh air.

Realizing that the officers had used all the gas they had, the mob leaders pressed their attack. Hamer had ordered his men to continue using their pistols only as clubs. "I was sure we could handle the situation that way and did not want to shoot anyone," Hamer said.

Once again, the Rangers beat back the crowd with only minimal force.

The Ranger stand bought a couple of hours of quiet. But at 2:30 P.M. the mob made its fourth attempt to get to the prisoner locked on the second floor. This time Hamer had a shotgun in addition to the six-shooter on his hip.

When the mob began pushing through the door, Hamer leveled the shotgun at those in the lead, and that stopped them.

"I explained that this time if the charge were continued I would shoot," Hamer said.

Figuring that the Ranger was only bluffing, the crowd surged forward. When it did, a shotgun blast echoed through the courthouse, leaving ears ringing. Hamer deliberately shot low, sending a load of pellets into the legs of two of the instigators. The shot had its intended effect, and those who still could ran out of the building.

Realizing that Hamer would shoot if necessary to protect the prisoner, the mob decided on another tactic: setting the courthouse on fire.

A brick crashed through a downstairs window in the tax collector's office. Some later said a woman threw it. A couple of young men splashed gasoline into the courthouse through the broken window and then tossed in a torch.

Flames spread quickly through the seventy-one-year-old structure. By the time the fire department arrived, the fire raged.

Frank Hamer's threats, blows, and shotgun blasts only slowed the mob. (Author's collection)

As firefighters laid hose to battle the blaze, members of the mob grabbed axes from the fire trucks and began chopping the lines. The firemen did succeed in getting ladders up and rescuing the county judge and the county attorney, who had been trapped upstairs.

As the flames spread, Hamer frantically tried to find someone who knew the combination to the safe. No one seemed to know the numbers. Finally, realizing he and his men had to leave the building or burn to death, Hamer ordered the Rangers to head for the windows.

Soon the symbol of law and order for Grayson County lay in smoldering ruins. Stunned by the reality of what it had done, the mob became quiet for a time. When the first khaki-clad National Guardsmen arrived from nearby Denison, however, the passion of the mob rekindled. As word spread that Hughes had been locked in the vault, it occurred to some that he might still be alive, despite the fact that the courthouse had burned down around him.

Court House, Sherman, Texas.

A mob burned down this courthouse in its frenzy to lynch an accused rapist. (Author's collection)

Around dusk, when troops began marching toward the courthouse square, the mob attacked the soldiers. Several guardsmen and mob members were injured in the melee that followed. When the guardsmen retreated to the county jail, the rioters converged on the blackened shell of the courthouse. They still wanted Hughes.

The only way to get to the vault was to cut through the bars on a second-floor window. Using a blowtorch looted from a nearby garage, several men burned through the steel. Then they had to penetrate the steel and concrete vault. They cut the steel and drilled holes in the concrete large enough for several sticks of dynamite.

The first blast made a hole about a foot across, too small for a man to get through. A second detonation finally left a large enough opening. The crowd demanded the black man.

"Stand back, you people," yelled the young man who had emerged as the leader of the mob. "We can't get in the vault yet. It's full of gas and we've got to wait until the fumes drift away."

When the mob crowded closer, the man shouted: "Get back there, damn it, or I will not get him out."

After the smoke and dust cleared, the man scurried up the ladder and disappeared through the hole. When he did, the crowd grew silent.

"After an almost breathless silence from the mob," wrote a reporter who witnessed the scene, "he reappeared at the window. Without ceremony he pushed the Negro's body out through the hole, head first, and it catapulted to the ground, bumping along the rungs of the fireman's ladder with a sickening thud. The body alighted in a half-sitting, half-squatting position."

"Let's drag him through . . . town," one of the rioters yelled.

Someone appeared with a chain and lashed it around the dead man's upper torso, under his arms. The other end of the chain was attached to the bumper of a car. The corpse was then dragged to the black-owned Goodson Drug Store on East Mulberry Street across from the train station. From there, it was towed through the black neighborhoods of the city.

Soon the drugstore, which had a hotel on its top floor, was in flames. Taking burning wood from the fire, the mob built a bonfire and tossed Hughes into the flames.

The charred body was then removed from the fire and hoisted from a cottonwood limb while others in the crowd took burning lumber from the fire and began torching nearby houses.

More troops and three additional Rangers under Captain Tom Hickman arrived in Sherman early that morning. Finally, as a newspaper later reported, "comparative quiet was restored."

The riot and postmortem lynching of Hughes was not an isolated incident. No one kept records prior to 1885, but during the fifty-seven years between 1885 and 1942, a total of 468 persons were lynched in Texas. Of those, 72.4 percent (339) were black. That placed Texas as third among all the states, behind Mississippi and Georgia, in the number of unlawful killings at the hands of vigilantes or mobs.

The majority of Texans found such violence abhorrent. The most effective anti-lynching organization in the United States was the Georgetown, Texas-based Association of Southern Women for the Prevention of Lynching, founded by Jessie Daniel Ames. An anti-lynching law had been on the books in Texas since 1897, and Rangers were frequently called in to prevent trouble. More times than not, they succeeded.

"Sherman has been disgraced," the *Houston Press* editorialized the day after the incident. "All Texas hangs her head in shame.... The only encouraging thing in this terrible story, is the fact that Frank Hamer, brave Ranger captain, and his handful of men, repulsed the mob for hours and stood faithfully at their posts of duty until the courthouse was burning over their heads. All honor to them."

Though the Rangers had definitely delayed the mob, they had ultimately failed to protect Hughes. One researcher who delved into the incident years after the fact averred that the Rangers left Sherman as soon as they got out of the burning courthouse, implying that it was a less than noble act. They did leave town for a short time so Hamer could have a secure telephone connection to report to the governor. He believed that local telephone operators had listened to his earlier conversations.

But the Rangers returned that night. Years later, L. A. Wilke, one of the journalists who covered the riot and the one who took the photograph of Hughes' body, recalled how the Rangers had fortified themselves in the county jail along with the small contingent of guardsmen who had been attacked earlier in the evening. Wilke was with them inside the jail as .22 bullets fired from the mob ricocheted off the bars.

"Later that night Hamer and the others started getting hungry," Wilke remembered nearly a half-century later. "I volunteered to make my way through the crowd to a drugstore across the street to get something for us to eat. When I walked back toward the jail carrying a bucket of coffee and a big sack of sandwiches, somebody stepped in front of me and tried to stop me. I hit him on the side of the head with my flashlight, and he went down. No one else got in my way."

Given the size of the mob compared to the small number of soldiers and Rangers, about all the Rangers could do was hold the jail until more help arrived. That is what they did.

In *The Power Vested*, a well-researched study of instances of martial law in Texas, author Harry Krenek concluded: "Most accounts of the incident are not critical of the Rangers and express the view that there was little else the Rangers could do under the circumstances."

A rumor that Hamer had been ordered by Governor Moody not to shoot to kill in defending Hughes swept the city almost as rapidly as the flames that had destroyed the county's $60,000 courthouse. Hamer and the governor both denied it.

"At no time did he instruct me not to shoot," Hamer told a reporter for the Scripps Howard chain, which owned the *Fort Worth Press*, the *Houston Press*, and the *El Paso Herald Post*. "There were women in the crowd, and I naturally did not want to shoot until it was absolutely necessary."

Even if Hamer had started shooting to kill, he and his men did not have enough ammunition for everyone in the mob. Some estimated the crowd to be as large as five thousand.

The Sherman incident was an affront to anyone who respected the Constitution, particularly young Governor Moody, who had fought the Ku Klux Klan while serving as district attorney in Williamson County.

"The action of the Sherman mob in firing on the national guardsmen was treasonable in its nature," Moody said the morning after the riot. "The action of this mob in undertaking to set aside the laws of the country and making of itself a group of murderers by burning the courthouse in order to kill the Negro is a shame to Texas. It is an evil day when any group of persons combine to override the law."

In the aftermath of the incident sixty-five persons were arrested for riot, arson, or attempted murder, but only fourteen were indicted. Of those, only two were convicted of any crime. Each received a two-year prison sentence for arson and riot.

"Hamer's disgust at the cowardly actions of the townspeople of Sherman never abated as long as he lived," John

Jenkins and Gordon Frost wrote in their biography of the Ranger captain, *I'm Frank Hamer*.

The lawman at least lived long enough to see the end of an era. Two additional lynchings occurred in Texas in 1930, but it was happening less and less frequently. One lynching occurred in 1933, one in 1934, and two in 1935.

Though records were kept on lynchings, the occasions where mob violence was prevented by the presence of Rangers were not documented. However, one case in 1936 did make news. Rangers succeeded in saving five black men and four black women from a lynch mob of three hundred in El Campo in 1936. The last lynching in Texas was on July 13, 1942, in Texarkana when a black man accused of rape and murder was hanged by a mob.

In the years following desegregation in Texas, the lynching of blacks accused of crimes against whites was only an ugly chapter out of the past—fodder for novels and movies like *To Kill a Mockingbird*.

An 821-page history of Grayson County published in 1979 devoted only ninety words to the Sherman riot. "It wasn't the work of responsible citizens although the entire city will always bear the blame," one Sherman man who saw the courthouse burn that spring day was quoted in the book. Though the events leading to the riot and its results were not explained in the county history, the book did point to the only good that could possibly be said to have come out of it:

"While the tragedy is one that will never be removed from Sherman's history, it has been cited as a smoothing influence during integration of schools in the city in the 1960's."

On the sixtieth anniversary of the riot, the *Sherman Democrat* reported that by at least one measure—the number of black-owned businesses in town—the city had never recovered from the incident. In 1930, the newspaper found, Sherman had two black doctors, two dentists, a druggist, two lawyers, and two engineers. In addition, the city was home to a black-owned hotel, a theater, a restaurant, a grocery, a dance hall, two funeral homes, a transfer company, a dressmaker, and several tailors and shoemakers. Many of the businesses were located in the two-story brick Andrews Building, one of the structures destroyed in the fire. Six decades after the riot, the only black-owned businesses the newspaper could identify in Sherman were a few clubs, restaurants, janitorial services, and beauty shops. Only two black professionals—a doctor and a lawyer—were living in Sherman.

"I don't know why we never built it [black businesses] back up," the newspaper quoted one black Sherman resident who lived there at the time of the riot. "I kind of think some of the people never felt like putting their money back into it. I guess they were scared that the climate was bad and they could lose it all again."

Notes

L. A. Wilke, who covered the Sherman riot for the *Fort Worth Press*, was the author's grandfather. He was born in Travis County on June 16, 1897, and grew up in Austin and in the West Texas town of Ballinger, where his father served as a deputy sheriff and jailer. His first job in the communications field was as a printer's devil, melting lead type for reuse. Wilke was on the staff of newspapers in San Angelo, San Antonio, Corpus Christi, Fort Worth, Cleveland, Ohio, and El Paso before taking up Chamber of Commerce and association work in the late 1930s. He retired as editor of the Texas Game and Fish Commission's magazine in 1962. He died at the age of eighty-seven in Austin on December 11, 1984.

Sources

Grayson County Frontier Village. *The Story of Grayson County, Texas*. Grayson County Frontier Village, Inc. and the Hunter Publishing Company, 1979.

Horton, David M. and Ryan Kellus Turner. *Lone Star Justice*. Austin: Eakin Press, 1999, pp. 32-51.

Jenkins, John H. and Gordon Frost. *I'm Frank Hamer*. Austin: Jenkins Publishing Co., 1967, pp. 164-168.

Krenek, Harry. *The Power Vested: The Use of Martial Law and the National Guard in Texas Domestic Crisis, 1919-1932*. Austin: Presidial Press, 1980, pp. 113-137.

"Militia Rules Mob-Torn Sherman," the *Houston Press*, May 10, 1930.

"Moody Says Mob Action Was Treason," the *Houston Press*, May 10, 1930.

Wilke, L. A. Interview with the author, November 9, 1969.

Williams, Kathy. "Sherman left scarred by 1930 racial riot." Reprint from the *Sherman Democrat* in the *Dallas Morning News*, May 10, 1990.

The "Eyes of Texas" on the Balinese Room

One of the toughest jobs anywhere is being program chairman for a Rotary Club. All around the world Rotary Clubs meet once a week, and each week at each club, someone gives a speech. The pressure on a program chair is twofold: First, find someone willing to speak for a free rubber-chicken lunch, and second, find someone willing to make that trade who is actually a good speaker with an interesting topic.

But in the spring of 1957, when members of the Galveston Rotary Club read their club bulletin and saw that newly elected Texas attorney general Will Wilson was scheduled to be their luncheon speaker, they knew Wilson would have something to say. They also had a pretty good idea what it would be. Whether he would say it in an entertaining manner was not an issue.

During Wilson's campaign, a reporter in Houston asked the former district attorney for Dallas County and associate justice on the state supreme court what he intended to do about illegal gambling in Galveston if he were elected.

"I'm going to stop it," he said simply.

Shortly after taking office, Wilson arranged an invitation to speak to Galveston Rotarians. After lunch, prayer, and the pledge of allegiance, the program chair introduced the attorney general to a packed meeting.

"In my speech," Wilson later recalled, "I asked all the gambling establishments to close voluntarily and warned that if they did not, I intended to bring legal action against them. I suggested other tourist attractions, such as an old-time, three-masted sailing ship."

The Galveston businessmen had not realized that Wilson, in addition to being a lawyer, was a humorist.

His pitch to the community leaders of the island city, Wilson remembered, "went over with a thud."

No wonder. As one wag later put it, people on Galveston Island had been gambling since the first Karankawa Indian bet his fellow Native American that he could throw an oyster shell farther than the other. After people of European descent settled on the island, government officials paid lip service to the prohibition of gambling (during the days of the Republic of Texas games of chance were banned in 1838 by municipal ordinance and again in 1884 long after statehood), but over the years the local government's interest in enforcing gambling laws proved about as enduring as a sandcastle in an incoming tide. Galveston, a coastal city, offered visitors more than beaches, a balmy sea breeze, and good fishing. Galveston was a major international seaport with illegal drinking, gambling, and prostitution. Seasoned salts expected it, and many tourists enjoyed it.

In 1901, when a grand jury looked into illegal gambling on the island, it handed down a report urging only that children be barred from such establishments. The report mentioned nothing about shutting them down. Years later, when someone asked the county sheriff why he had not raided a well-known gambling operation at one of the numerous private clubs in his jurisdiction, he shrugged. "I wasn't a member," he said. The old line, blue-blooded families—all BOI (Born on the Island)—allowed gambling because it was good for business. On occasion, they even dropped by one of the nightspots themselves, though the bulk of the business always was from out-of-towners. City and county law enforcement saw no problem with the system as long as the operators and their employees did not break any laws the locals considered important. Occasionally, local law enforcement "discovered" gambling on the island and smashed a few slot machines for the benefit of newspaper photographers and selected local clergy. The joints soon reopened with no hard feelings. Business is business and politics is politics.

The island city was known as the Free State of Galveston, and it was not much of an exaggeration. Though even the state's interest in Galveston varied from governor to governor, the prevailing sentiment was that Galveston was still part of Texas. In 1920 Governor William P. Hobby flooded Galveston with Texas Rangers and National Guard troops, declaring a state of martial law. The basic issue was a violent longshoremen's strike, but while they were at it, the state endeavored to clean up the island. After all, Americans had ratified the 18th Amendment. Prohibition was the law. Twelve weeks after martial law had been declared, the soldiers left, but Texas Rangers managed the Galveston Police Department until January 19, 1921. After the Rangers pulled out, it soon returned to business as usual on the island.

Periodically in the 1920s, '30s, and '40s, Texas Rangers raided gambling operations in Galveston County, confiscating paraphernalia and arresting operators and patrons. The Rangers had statewide jurisdiction and thus were immune from local politics, but they were only one component of the judicial system. In the long run, no good came of making arrests and seizing evidence if local prosecutors did not do their part. Such raids amounted to little more than an annoyance to Galveston's gaming establishment.

During World War II, with the city packed with soldiers and sailors and with German U-boats prowling the Gulf of Mexico, Galveston may as well have been in Cuba. Scores of clubs did a flourishing business, but the flagship establishment on the isle was the Balinese Room, a former chop suey joint opened in 1942. Actually, the club was not even on the island. It extended from Seawall Boulevard at 21st Street on a pier some 400 feet out over the Gulf of Mexico.

The club, like most of the others, was owned by the Maceo brothers—Rosario (Rose) and Salvatore (Sam). The two Italians came to Galveston from Louisiana before World War I. Barbers by trade, with the advent of prohibition the Maceos saw another way to clip the customer. Galveston was a major port of call for rumrunners coming in from Cuba and Jamaica, and the Maceos soon gave up cutting hair.

By 1926 they had acquired enough capital to open one of the fanciest speakeasies in the South: The Hollywood Dinner Club. The club had a hardwood dance floor large enough to accommodate up to five hundred couples and a newfangled way to keep them cool: one of the first air conditioning systems in Texas. In addition to offering their customers ample beverage choices, the Maceos provided quality seafood and entertainment and gambling: slots and bingo for the shoe salesman crowd; roulette and sports books for the high rollers. The club attracted big name stars, including singer and bandleader Phil Harris. One of his band members, stimulated by the island scene, wrote a song called "My Galveston Gal" that became a national hit.

After the creation of the Department of Public Safety in 1935 during the administration of Governor James V. Allred, the Texas Rangers were ordered to rid Galveston of gambling. But it was the same old story: The Rangers kicked in doors and seized gambling paraphernalia and slot machines, but before long the casinos resumed business as before. Galveston had the most operations, but gambling also was a problem in Fort Worth, Houston, and San Antonio.

In 1947, a decade before Attorney General Wilson's appearance at the Galveston Rotary Club, DPS director Colonel Homer Garrison ordered the Rangers to turn their attention once again to gambling on the island.

Conventional wisdom holds that there is strength in numbers. But Garrison decided a lone Ranger—not one kicking in the gambling room door but one working undercover—could shut down the Balinese Room. Of the forty-five Rangers under his command, Garrison picked a rookie—albeit a rookie with charisma—for the job: Clint Peoples.

Like Garrison, Peoples began his law enforcement career as a sheriff's deputy in East Texas. Peoples joined the DPS in 1941, serving as a highway patrolman until December 1, 1946, when Garrison commissioned him as a Ranger private. The change in duty brought no change in pay. Both highway patrolmen and Rangers earned $175 a month, but Rangers received a clothing allowance and $4 a day for expenses.

Peoples' air of self-assurance went right to the edge of self-aggrandizement. That put people off, including some of his colleagues. Some thought he stretched the unwritten Ranger code thinner than a worn-out seersucker suit when it came to being available to the news media for statement-making and picture-taking. But being stationed in Austin as a highway patrolman, he had been expected to perform tasks a patrolman in Pampa or Pharr never had to worry about. He was a handy VIP escort, and Garrison periodically assigned him chores related to the legislature.

Garrison saw in Peoples a man who could do a little acting without much strain. But beneath the showmanship, Garrison knew, was a cold core of toughness and a willingness to work hard. He told Peoples to enter the Balinese posing as a gambler and build a case through his observations. When other Rangers came calling based on the probable cause he developed, Peoples would be on the inside.

"If anybody can get into the Balinese," the colonel told the young Ranger, "I believe you can. You work it any way you want to, but I think you will have to take a lady."

The woman who graciously agreed to fill that role was the Ranger's wife, Donna.

That settled, Peoples went about building a new identity. To do that, he called on a friend, Blanco County sheriff and tax assessor Frank Shelley. The sheriff knew a rancher, Robert Eberling, who was overseas and not due back anytime soon. Shelley dummied up a phony automobile registration for People's personal car and issued him a set of license plates. He also filled Peoples in on Eberling's personality. In Austin, the DPS issued the Ranger an undercover driver license bearing Eberling's name, with a physical description matching People's size and age.

With plenty of flash money to support his newly acquired lifestyle as a high-rolling Hill Country rancher, Peoples and his wife went shopping. He bought two tailored suits for himself and three fancy dresses for his wife. To complete the look, Mrs. Peoples borrowed some diamond jewelry from relatives while a friend loaned her husband a diamond ring and expensive cuff links.

In their new Chevrolet, "Mr. and Mrs. Robert Eberling" left Austin for Galveston. After crossing the causeway to the island, they drove down Broadway and then cut over to the Buccaneer Hotel, a high-rise overlooking the Gulf. The Maceo brothers had penthouses there.

Aerial view of Galveston Island, with the infamous Balinese Room flaring out into the Gulf of Mexico. (Author's collection)

Eberling asked for a good room with a view. The view he wanted was of the Maceos' balcony so he could begin to learn what their associates looked like. Once ensconced in the hotel, the couple tipped big, ate well, and spent the day as tourists. They played their parts even to the point of taking snapshots, though Mrs. Eberling did have a minor lapse when they took a roll of film to the Buccaneer's drugstore for processing. When the clerk asked their name, she answered "Clint Peoples." But her husband smiled big and loudly said "Robert Eberling." If the clerk noticed, he did not indicate it. It was not the first time in Galveston history that a couple staying in a hotel had a little trouble remembering the names they put on the registration card.

Two weeks into his undercover assignment, the Ranger approached hotel manager Jimmy Pilage about getting into the Balinese Room for a meal. He had heard, he said, that it had the best food in town. The manager politely said he would see what could be done.

The first thing the manager did, Peoples realized a short time later, was have someone discreetly check out the Eberlings' room while they were out taking in some of the salt air.

211

Anticipating that possibility, the Ranger carefully stored his badge and pistol in his car. He later found out that Pilage asked the local police to run his car tags to check the registration, but no one tampered with the vehicle.

Soon the manager contacted Eberling with good news. He had arranged a membership in the club for the Eberlings.

"I really want to go and eat some good food and shoot some dice," the Ranger told Pilage, "but my wife is not feeling well, and I don't know if we can make it tonight. You make the reservations, and if I see we can't go, I'll let you know."

Later that day, as he had intended all along, Peoples told the manager he would have to cancel. The next day Peoples called Pilage to report that his wife was much better. Pilage said he was glad to hear that and made reservations for them that night.

Around 9 P.M. the Eberlings left the hotel, crossed Seawall Boulevard, and walked up the steps to the entrance of the Balinese Room. The doormen graciously allowed the women to pass before flipping the switch on an electric eye that checked the gentlemen for any jewelry heavier than a diamond ring. Peoples noted the procedure for future reference.

Elegantly dressed men and women crowded the dining room. The excellent food was all the tastier on the state's nickel. After supper and some dancing, Eberling lit up a cigar and strolled with his wife to the smoky, noisy casino in the back. The Ranger immersed himself in a crap game while his wife started playing the slots. Soon she seemed as captivated by the one-armed bandits as any other robot-like player. Clink, pull, spin, clink, pull, spin. Occasionally, someone squealed in delight and surprise when the wheels tripled up and the machine paid off, but the slots, Peoples knew, were a sucker's game. With some concern, Peoples realized his wife wasn't acting. It showed the power of the lure of easy money, even if you were playing for law and order, not for profit.

While counting the dots on the ivory cubes, Peoples also took in everything else going on in the crowded room. The casino featured three crap tables, three blackjack tables, and two roulette wheels.

Ranger Peoples and his wife stayed at the Buccaneer Hotel while posing as high-rolling gamblers. (Photo courtesy Rosenberg Library, Galveston, Texas)

In a figurative sense, everything was coming up sevens for the Ranger until he spotted the son of the former sheriff of Montgomery County. The Ranger had been one of the sheriff's deputies and knew the young man. Fortunately, Peoples saw him first and was able to dodge him without blowing his cover in a place where Texas Rangers were not considered preferred customers.

The following morning, to play it safe, Peoples drove from Galveston to the DPS office in Houston to report by telephone to Garrison. The Ranger outlined what he had seen inside the Balinese Room—plenty enough to get a search warrant. They agreed that Rangers under Captain Hardy Purvis' Houston-based Company A would hit the club at 11 o'clock the next night, September 11.

"If anything goes wrong, I'll call by ten," Peoples told the colonel. "If you don't hear by ten, the raid is on."

On the night set for the raid, the Eberlings showed up for another evening at the Balinese. The Ranger had tipped well enough on the couple's first visit to be remembered by the staff, who treated them with particular courtesy as they made their entrance. Knowing his wife would not be checked,

Peoples had packed his .45 and his Ranger badge in the evening bag hanging from her shoulder. For dinner, they ate grilled steak presented on a flaming sword. After the delicious meal, the couple slid across the dance floor for a while, heartily enjoying the music and each other's company. In the casino behind them, the gambling continued in full swing.

With less than an hour before his colleagues would come crashing into the club, Peoples had one unresolved problem: His pistol and badge were of no use to him in his wife's purse.

The Ranger strolled casually up to his wife, who was busy on one of the slots. Quietly, he clued her in on his plan: They agreed to meet at the entrance to the restrooms. Donna would ask her husband to hold her purse while she went into the powder room. He, in turn, would take the purse with him into the men's room.

That part of the plan worked perfectly, but Peoples walked into the restroom and found two Maceo employees. They looked slightly askance at a big man carrying an alligator purse, but they must have figured his accessories were his business. Inside a stall, Peoples unzipped his wife's purse, covering the sound by flushing the commode. He flushed again as he zipped the purse after tucking his semiautomatic in his waistband under his coat and pocketing his badge. Back outside, he handed Donna her purse. She thanked him, making sure she was overheard. The two Maceo house men watched casually, any lingering suspicions allayed.

Donna Peoples went back to the row of slot machines while her husband returned to the crap tables.

Absorbed once again with the slot machines, Mrs. Peoples allowed time to slip by unnoticed. Suddenly bells rang. "Oh, my God," the woman next to her screamed. "This is a raid!" That brought the Ranger's wife back to reality. She scampered out of the casino just as the band struck up a rousing rendition of "The Eyes of Texas," the house's traditional greeting to raiding Rangers.

As Captain Purvis and his men hoofed it down the more-than-football-field length of the Balinese Club toward the casino on the Gulf side, Peoples displayed his badge and ordered everyone in the gambling room to freeze.

Unfortunately, not everyone obeyed the command. The dice table stickman, following standing orders, struck the Ranger across the arm. Peoples, as the story was related, "bounced the man across the table" and pulled his coat back to reveal his gun.

Though Peoples held the full attention of all those at his dice table, other Maceo employees followed standard raid procedure, a process they executed as smartly as Civil Defense volunteers in an air raid drill. The roulette wheels, the blackjack tables, and the other dice table were expertly stowed by employees, who then faded into the crowd and made for Seawall Boulevard. When Purvis entered the casino, Peoples had his crap table secured along with twelve house men and forty-eight gamblers.

It took the Rangers two hours to identify the people they held and catalog all the evidence: one roulette wheel, two dice tables, five electric slot machines, $1,700 in cash, and miscellaneous other gambling paraphernalia. When Peoples found his wife they checked out of the Buccaneer and drove to Houston. Dead tired, he got them a room downtown at the Rice Hotel. Their state-paid vacation was over.

Over breakfast in the Rice's coffee shop the next morning, Peoples read the front-page stories on the Balinese Club raid in Houston's three dailies, the *Chronicle*, the *Post*, and the *Press*. Captain Purvis, wisely choosing not to reveal that the Rangers had an undercover man inside when the raid was staged, said his men "just walked right into the place." To a newsman's query as to whether the band had been playing "The Eyes of Texas" when the Rangers rushed the place, Purvis replied: "To tell the truth, I didn't notice. We didn't go there to dance."

Despite the Rangers' penetration of the club's elaborate security setup, the raid was more symbolic than effective. Acting Galveston county attorney Sherwood Brown refused to accept felony charges against the club employees. The twelve Maceo men pleaded guilty to misdemeanor gaming charges and were assessed $109 in fines each. The gamblers pleaded out for lesser fines which club manager Victor Fertitta graciously paid.

Four years later, as the Kefauver Committee's hearings on organized crime hearings continued in Washington, the Texas Legislature began its own investigation of organized crime in the state. On June 25-26, 1951, the House's Crime Investigating Committee heard closed-door testimony about gambling in Galveston. Meanwhile, state auditor Charles H. Cavness began poring over a truckload of records subpoenaed from the Maceos. He found that in 1950 the Maceo brothers took in $830,586 from club rooms, $827,764 from coin-operated machines, $349,267 from bookmaking on horse races, $267,689 from the sale of drinks (at that time selling liquor by the drink was illegal), $122,817 from tip books, $91,055 from bingo, and $21,895 from baseball pools for a total of $2,511,073 in a single year of gambling operations.

Attorney General Price Daniel, armed with that information and testimony given before the House committee, went to court and obtained an injunction shutting down the Balinese and other Maceo operations in Galveston County. Gambling officially ceased in Galveston on June 15, and the Maceo family laid off 500 employees. By the end of the year, however, the club was back in business. So were the other gaming establishments in the county.

Garrison continued to send his Rangers on raids, but manpower was a problem. With only fifty Rangers to cover Texas' 254 counties, the DPS director could not justify committing a large force of men to only one county for the extended time necessary to achieve lasting results. Too, there was a communication problem. The DPS had the latest in two-way radios and a teletype system, but it was nothing compared to the gambling grapevine in Galveston.

"You've got an extraordinary communication system here," Garrison told a reporter for the *Galveston News*. "We can't raid one place and then go to another place down the street, because all evidence of violations disappears."

Beyond that, Garrison continued, there was yet another problem: "There is no use in raiding Galveston County as long as juries there won't convict on gambling charges." It was hard even to bring a case to a jury.

In gambling, the "house" sets the rules. In Austin, the House and the Senate changed the rules in a big way during the 1951 legislative session: Displaying, possessing, or even having the parts of a slot machine was considered prima facie evidence of felony gambling. While that new law made slot machines a more risky business enterprise, bookmaking on horse races was successfully attacked through an injunction sought by Attorney General Daniel to prohibit Southwestern Bell Telephone Company from using its lines to convey race-track results to Maceo family establishments.

Based on the new slot machine law, twenty-two felony indictments were returned against the Maceo interests late in 1951. But district judges continued the trial five times, and the county attorney moved for dismissal of the charges for lack of evidence. His motions were granted. Despite the new law, the injunction against the telephone company, periodic Ranger raids, and Internal Revenue Service action against the Maceo family, Galveston continued to operate as if the water around it constituted not a county line but an international boundary. In 1956 a grand jury lamented: "It is commonly known that open gambling, sale of intoxicants to minors, illegal sale of liquor, and prostitution exist in Galveston [County], but no charges were presented to the grand jury by law enforcement officers."

Not long after Wilson was sworn in as attorney general, he received a letter from Jim Simpson. Like Wilson, Simpson was a decorated World War II veteran. A former FBI agent with a law degree, he ran for county attorney in Galveston in 1954, losing the election by only eight votes. Though he opted not to run again in 1956, he still was interested in seeing Galveston rid of illegal gambling.

"I invited him to come to Austin to talk over the problem," Wilson later recalled. "We were in complete agreement: Wherever illegal gambling is allowed to flourish, honest government must suffer."

Since raids by Texas Rangers had never had lasting results, Wilson knew he had to come up with another strategy. The Rangers still could be used, but without strong local prosecution their traditional role was limited.

"I found a statute which stated that any establishment operating as a public nuisance could be padlocked until proper evidence was submitted to the court," Wilson wrote. "To substantiate a public nuisance and obtain a civil injunction, we needed to be able to prove a steady violation of the law involving the continued presence of illegal alcohol, gambling, and prostitution."

To get the evidence, Wilson recruited Simpson to coordinate an undercover sting operation. With $50,000 from "a generous private donation," operatives reporting to Simpson did as Ranger Peoples had done a decade before; they were able to gain access and gamble freely in the Maceo family joints. (Both Maceo brothers had died of old age by this time, but their businesses continued to flourish.)

By late spring in 1957, a two-couple undercover team had seen enough to swear and subscribe to a thick stack of affidavits describing all the illegal activity they had witnessed. An extensive series of raids including visits to the Balinese Room and the Turf Club—the Maceo flagship operations—was set for June 5. But on the night of the planned sweep, an operation involving dozens of Rangers and other DPS officers that Colonel Garrison intended to lead personally, someone made a telephone call. The raids were called off when Garrison got word that the gambling clubs had mysteriously shut down for the night.

Five days later Wilson and eleven assistant attorneys general showed up in Galveston seeking district court injunctions to shut down forty-seven gambling clubs or houses of prostitution. With Wilson came six Rangers. They seized nearly two thousand slot machines stored in the closed Hollywood Dinner Club on the west end of the city and discovered another 375 slots secreted away at Fort Travis, an abandoned Spanish-American War-era coastal artillery installation on nearby Bolivar Peninsula.

Soon the clubs in Galveston were padlocked, and all the slot machines were rusting in the bottom of Galveston Bay, having been tossed into the water by the Rangers. Many of those who had made their living from running the city's vice operations decided on a change of climate and moved from

Galveston to a new place where gambling was legal and there were no Texas Rangers—Las Vegas, Nevada.

Notes

By the time Galveston was finally tamed in 1957, Clint Peoples had become captain of Company F, headquartered in Waco. In 1969 he was transferred to Austin and promoted to Senior Ranger Captain. He held that position until his retirement from the DPS in 1974. As soon as he took off his silver star, he was sworn in as United States Marshal for the Northern District of Texas. Peoples retired again in 1987. On June 22, 1992, at the age of eighty-one, he died of injuries suffered in a traffic accident in Waco.

Peoples went on to become Senior Ranger Captain before retiring in 1974. (Photo by L. A. Wilke from author's collection)

Sources

Cartright, Gary. *Galveston: A History of the Island*. New York: Atheneum, 1991.

Chalfant, Frank E. *Galveston: Island of Chance*. Houston: Treasures of Nostalgia, 1997.

Day, James M. *Captain Clint Peoples, Texas Ranger: Fifty Years A Lawman*. Waco: Texian Press, 1980, pp. 83-90.

McComb, David G. *Galveston: A History*. Austin: University of Texas Press, 1986.

Wilson, Will R. Sr. "Gary Cartright's *Galveston: A History of the Island*." *Southwestern Historical Quarterly*, Vol. XCVI, No. 4, April 1993, pp. 543-546.

_____. Unpublished manuscript, 1998.

Ranger Grub

A frontier Ranger needed more than a fast gun and a good horse. He could not range far without food.

Rangers on scout in far West Texas ready to saddle up after their mid-day meal. (Author's collection)

In the fall of 1836, Rangers posted on the upper Brazos River lived on wild game, but corn was hard to come by.

Frightened settlers abandoned the year's spring corn crop during the "Runaway Scrape" and fled eastward to escape as Mexican general Antonio Lopez de Santa Anna and his army closed in on them. After the victory at San Jacinto and the revolution was won, settlers and Rangers returned to their scattered frontier communities to discover most of the cultivated fields trampled and eaten by buffalo and loose livestock.

"By going or sending out I could procure a few bags of nubbins," former Ranger George B. Erath recalled in his memoir, "and I issued my men an ear of corn apiece a day for bread, which they ground on a steel mill."

Corn bread tastes better with something on it. Early Texans were particularly fond of wild honey.

"Honey," Erath later wrote, "had to be kept in rawhide or deerskin sacks with the hair outside, and at Christmas we had several hundred pounds of it."

Rangers on a scout had a hard time passing up a bee tree. But shimmying up a tree to raid a beehive of its honey could be dangerous. A Ranger could get stung. Or worse.

When one of Captain John Hays' scouts discovered a bee tree on Sisters Creek, about fifty miles outside of San Antonio, Hays allowed Rangers Kit Acklin and John Coleman to climb the tree to rob honey from the hives for the company. The two Rangers were working away, thirty feet above ground, when Coleman chanced to glance around. Three hundred yards away, twenty-five Comanches sat silently on their horses, watching the sweet-toothed Texans up in the tree.

"Indians!" Coleman cried as he plummeted down the tree like a shot squirrel, Acklin following right behind.

Soon the Texans were engaged in one of the bloodiest fights Hays ever had with the Indians. When the shooting ended, the Rangers counted at least a half dozen dead Indians. Eight Rangers were seriously wounded, but Hays did not lose a single man. Although vastly outmanned, the Rangers were saved by new equipment they carried: Colt five-shot revolvers. Without the added firepower, the bee tree on Sisters Creek could have been their undoing.

A big appetite and a small knowledge of Spanish soon caused a problem for another of Hay's Rangers. While serving under Captain Hays in the early 1840s, "Bigfoot" Wallace walked into a Mexican eatery in San Antonio one morning and said he would like breakfast.

"*Quiere usted zorillo, senor?*" the proprietor asked as she emerged from the back of the place with a portion of broiled meat, some fresh-baked *pan* (Mexican bread), and coffee.

Wallace did not know what *zorillo* meant, but it looked good and tasted better to the hungry Ranger. He soon finished off everything but the head of the animal, washing the meat and *pan* down with strong, hot coffee.

Outside, after paying for the meal, Wallace ran into fellow Ranger Jim Dunn, who spoke Spanish, and asked him what kind of animal *zorillo* was.

"That means polecat," Dunn replied.

"What!" Wallace bellowed. "Did that damned woman give me a polecat to eat?"

Both Rangers went back inside as Dunn sought clarification from the woman who had served Wallace. Perhaps his Ranger colleague had misunderstood her.

"Oh, *si*," she said when Dunn asked her if she had fed Wallace a skunk. "He is very fond of them and ate a whole one, all but the head."

Early in the Civil War, Buck Barry commanded a company of Texas Mounted Rifles. His men functioned as Rangers in all but name. They were charged with the responsibility of protecting women, children, and old men from Indian attack while almost all of the able-bodied men were away fighting Yankees.

In the fall of 1861 Barry and twenty-five Rangers collided with more than sixty Indians above the Clear Fork of the Brazos. The Indians stampeded the Rangers' pack mules and slashed the packs, scattering the scout's provisions.

A running fight ensued. The Indians escaped, but the contact with the Rangers had forced them to abandon their camp in a hurry.

When the Rangers discovered the deserted Indian camp, they found "a big scaffold of buffalo meat, freshly and finely barbecued," as Frank Wristen later recalled. "It was now very late in the evening, so we preempted the camp and being without provisions gladly availed ourselves of the barbecued buffalo meat."

By the time James B. Gillett enlisted in the Frontier Battalion on June 1, 1875, the State of Texas had begun furnishing food for the Rangers. Such as it was.

As soon as Gillett and several other rookie Rangers completed their oaths of allegiance, his company divided into messes of ten men each. The orderly sergeant then issued ten days' worth of rations to each mess.

"These consisted," Gillett later wrote, "of flour, bacon, coffee, sugar, beans, rice, pepper, salt, and soda. No potatoes, syrup, or lard was furnished, and each man had to supply his own cooking utensils."

The state-issued staples were carried in packs on mules or in the back of a wagon, depending on the terrain of the country the Rangers were scouting.

Bacon was important not only as a source of protein, but as a way to get cooking grease. Since the state did not furnish lard, the Rangers used bacon grease to shorten their bread.

As an old man, Caleb M. Grady of Brownwood looked back fondly on the way the cook in his Frontier Battalion company made bread dough for the Rangers in his company. The recipe he recalled started with a forty-eight-pound bag of flour, which the cook set up on one end and opened on the other. Another Ranger fried bacon for the grease.

Then, Grady wrote:

> They made a hole in the flour in the top of the sack, poured in some water, bacon grease, salt, baking powder, mixed them all together, and soon had enough dough for all. They gave each man a piece about the size of your fist....Each man cut a green stick about three feet long, and the size of your finger, and pulled the dough out like a ribbon, rolled it around the stick, beginning at the end, making it nice and smooth. Then they held it over the hot coals, and it cooked nicely.

The bread, he remembered with obvious pleasure years later, "was as fine a bread as any one would wish." The cook closed the flour sack until the next time.

Though bacon was the usual meat on the Ranger menu, occasionally they dined on state-issued beef. Sometimes a rancher, grateful for protection from Indians or cattle thieves, gave the Rangers a calf.

"Wild game was so plentiful that but little other meat was required," Gillett wrote.

In the fall of 1875 Gillett's company made camp for the winter on the San Saba River, about three miles east of the community of Menardville—later shortened to Menard.

As fall turned to winter, Gillett and two other Rangers set out to acquire the makings for "a real Yule-tide" dinner. Armed with newly purchased .44 caliber Model 1873 Winchesters, Gillett and Ranger Ed Seiker raided a turkey roost on nearby Elm Creek and killed seven big gobblers. On their way back, Seiker dropped a big buck with his new repeating rifle. Another Ranger, presumably armed with a shotgun, returned to camp with an assortment of wild geese and mallard ducks.

Topping off the dinner of wild game with fresh-baked pies and a fruitcake cooked by the captain's wife, Mrs. Dan Roberts, Gillett later recalled "altogether we had the finest Christmas dinner that ever graced the boards of a ranger camp."

Three years later another Ranger found there was more than one way to prepare turkey. On an extended scout from Fort Griffin in Shackleford County to Fort Elliott in the eastern Panhandle, Ranger Captain George Washington Arrington discovered that "the boys had forgotten to put any flour in the pack."

The captain saw a small cabin somewhere on the plains and rode up to it, hoping to borrow enough flour or cornmeal to last at least a day.

"I found a man there," Arrington recalled, "but he said he had neither. I asked him what he lived on, and he showed me several stacks of something that looked like cottonwood chips. They were dried turkey breasts."

The man told the Ranger that was all he and his family had to live on. If the settler offered any of the turkey breast chips to the Rangers, Arrington did not record it in his later recollections.

On another of Arrington's scouts, a daylong rain soaked his company's flour supply. The Rangers were out of meat, as well. They hunted for game, but the best they could come up with was a jackrabbit. Using their knives to cut balls of paste-like flour from the sack, the Rangers cooked a jackrabbit stew. Some raveled bits of flour sack ended up in the stew, but they were easy enough to fish out.

"It was all we had," Arrington wrote. "so we filled up on it."

One time even the jackrabbits seemed to have left the country. Arrington's Rangers made do with prairie dog stew.

On another occasion, while trailing Indians on the upper Colorado River, Arrington's men had dry flour but no meat and no lard for bread.

The captain and one of his men rode off from the rest of the company in search of a buffalo. They saw no buffalo but did note smoke rising in the distance. Thinking he had found Indians, Arrington and the other Ranger rode toward the smoke for a closer look.

The smoke turned out to be coming from the cabin of a lone man whom Arrington took to be a buffalo hunter.

"He had several large cakes of tallow, which had been molded in a washpan," Arrington would write. "We bought a cake of the tallow from him for two dollars, and took it back to camp where the boys made bread. When the chuck call came and we broke open the bread, the smell was so strong we couldn't eat [it]."

The following morning Arrington paid the hunter another call. What, the Ranger demanded to know, had he sold him?

"He said that it was wolf tallow, and that he used the tallow himself in making bread," Arrington recalled.

······ ✪ ······

Former Rangers tended to look back with pleasure on the meals eaten around a campfire, but not always.

Tom White, who served in Company A under Captain John R. Brooks in the early 1900s, remembered that each member of the company took turns doing the cooking. They adhered to a strict rule: Any Ranger who complained about the cooking automatically became the next cook.

A Ranger "eager to turn his job over to someone else," White said, "emptied the salt box into a stew, in order to ensure a complaint."

Once, White claimed, a Ranger who must have been a quick thinker took a swallow of sabotaged stew and nearly gagged.

"My God, that stew is salty!" he roared. "But that's just the way I like it."

White said men in his company were more likely to eat bacon and eggs than beef stew. Since not even the worst cook could ruin such simple fare, it often was on the Ranger's menu three times a day.

"You didn't eat because it tasted good," White continued. "You ate to get your empty belly full."

······ ✪ ······

Skimpy food once helped get the Rangers a pay raise.

In 1929 Governor Dan Moody, his attorney general, and several others went to South Texas on a deer hunt. Ever the astute political player, Captain W. W. "Bill" Sterling assigned several of his Rangers to "act as guides and otherwise assist in making the hunt a success."

About lunchtime on the second day of the hunt, Sterling dropped by the Ranger camp with the governor. When they drove up, the Rangers were sitting around a fire, drinking coffee and eating gingersnaps. One of the Rangers poured coffee for the two visitors.

Seeing no other groceries in camp, Governor Moody asked the men if gingersnaps were all they had to eat.

"They answered in the affirmative," Sterling later wrote, "and when we were leaving, Governor Moody said that he intended to do something about it when he returned to Austin."

That spring the governor signed a bill providing for a Ranger pay raise. The salary of privates was increased from $90 to $150 a month, sergeants from $100 to $175, and captains from $150 to $225. Moody told reporters he was approving the bill because he had seen Rangers whose noon meal was only "black coffee in a tin cup and a few boxes of gingersnaps."

What the governor had not known, Sterling later confessed, was that the Rangers intended to cook fresh meat that night. They ate lightly at noon only because they anticipated a big supper.

Texas Rangers relax with a cup of coffee around the campfire during a search for stolen cattle

Rangers chow down in Palo Duro Canyon State Park in this 1950s DPS photograph. (Author's collection)

······ ⭐ ······

By the 1960s the State of Texas had long since stopped furnishing food for Rangers, at least directly. When traveling on duty, Rangers could claim per diem pay to defray the cost of food and lodging. Often, the costs exceeded the amount the state would pay, but it was better than nothing.

When Hurricane Carla bore down on the Texas coast in September 1961, Company F Captain Clint Peoples ordered Rangers George Roach and Johnny Krumnow to report to Company A in Houston to guard against looting and do anything else that needed to be done.

Roach, a veteran Ranger then stationed in Stephenville, drove to Waco and picked up the younger Krumnow. On their way out of town, Roach told Krumnow they would be needing some supplies.

The two Rangers pooled their money, but Roach did the shopping.

"I was amazed at some of the things he bought," Krumnow later recalled. "Being a rookie I kept quiet, for George was an old-timer and I respected his judgment."

At Houston, Company A Captain Johnny Klevenhagen —whose area included the upper Texas coast—dispatched the two Company F Rangers to Palacios. They left immediately.

By about 2 o'clock that afternoon, Krumnow began thinking about supper. So, apparently, did Roach. The older Ranger pulled out of traffic, stopped the car, and got out.

As Krumnow watched, Roach took a cut of beef from his icebox, laid it on a piece of aluminum foil, and generously sprinkled it with homemade seasoning he had brought with him from Stephenville. That done, he put some sliced potatoes and onions next to the meat. Then he wrapped the foil tightly around the raw food.

Krumnow had no idea how Roach intended to cook that meat. As he pondered the situation, his more experienced partner told him to pop the hood of their car.

Roach lodged the foil package securely near the engine block, slammed the hood down, and said, "Let's go. We'll have supper at seven."

228

That evening, Krumnow recalled, "We had one of the best meals I had for many moons."

Sources

Adams, Verdon R. *Tom White: The Life of a Lawman*. El Paso: Texas Western Press, 1972, p. 17.

Arrington, George Washington. "Organization of Panhandle Counties." Undated, unpublished manuscript. Arrington Papers, Panhandle Plains Historical Museum, Canyon, Texas.

Gillett, James B. *Six Years With the Texas Rangers*. Lincoln: University of Nebraska Press, 1925, 1976, pp. 37, 83-84.

Grady, C. M. "Fifty-eight Years in Texas." *Frontier Times*, June 1934, p. 383.

Greer, James K., ed. *Buck Barry: Texas Ranger and Frontiersman*. Waco: Friends of the Moody Texas Ranger Library, 1978, pp. 133, 137.

Harris, Johnny. *The Authorized Texas Ranger Cookbook*. Hamilton, Texas: Harris Farms Publishing, 1994, p. 102.

Sowell, A. J. *Life of "Big Foot" Wallace: The Great Ranger Captain*. Introduction by Mike Cox. Austin: State House Press, 1989, reprint of 1899 edition, pp. 53-54.

Sterling, William Warren. *Trials and Trails of a Texas Ranger*. Norman: University of Oklahoma Press, 1968, pp. 148-149.

Shootin' from the Lip: The Quotable Ranger

> "The Texas Ranger can ride harder, fight longer,
> lives rougher, and makes less talk about it than
> anybody else that walks on two feet!"
> — 1882 newspaper writer

The stereotypic image of the Texas Ranger is a person who does not have much to say: the quiet, authoritative type.

Despite their taciturn nature, over the years the Rangers have snapped off some good lines, spoken and written, as dead center as a .45 slug aimed in a bad man's direction. And those notable remarks have not always had to do with rangering.

Dan W. Roberts was one of Texas' best-known former Ranger captains. No Indian arrow ever touched him, but Cupid pierced him right in the heart when he met Luvenia Conway, the woman who became his wife. On the occasion of their anniversary twenty-three years later, at the age of fifty-seven in the spring of 1898, he wrote her a love letter.

"Love covers the contingency of every danger on earth," he said. "Treachery will sneak away from its sunshine. It is an anodyne for the sting of poverty, and its citadel is unapproachable to intended evil."

Poetic words from a man who spent nearly a decade of his life handling "intended evil" with a Colt or a Winchester.

By the time Roberts left the Rangers in 1881, there was no more Indian fighting to be done. But the Rangers never seemed to run out of work—or lose their knack for memorable expression.

······ ✪ ······

Ranger Ira Aten, sent to Navarro County in 1888 to deal with barbed-wire fence cutters, wrote from Richland to Captain L. P. Sieker in Austin:

"Nothing will do any good here but a first class killing and I am the little boy that will give it to them if they dont let the fence alone."

Ira Aten
(Author's collection)

······ ✪ ······

From Corporal C. H. Fusselman's report on June 5, 1889, to Adjutant General W. H. King concerning a man he had recently killed in a gunfight:

"I could see that there was no chance for his giving up as he had a bad expression on his face so I fired as he did."

······ ✪ ······

In the early 1900s the town of Alice, not far from the border in Jim Wells County, was the "Cowtown" of South Texas. For a time, it was the busiest cattle shipping point in the United States, thanks largely to the nearby King Ranch. Sometimes as many as a dozen herds dusted up the town, each herd accompanied by ten or twelve trail hands hankering to enjoy the amenities of town life, particularly the watering holes.

The Rangers stationed in Alice tried to be tolerant, but occasionally a drover became seriously overserved and had to be jailed until he sobered up. On one occasion, a cowboy got too drunk for his own good, and Captain J. A. Brooks ordered Ranger Lonnie Livingston to put him in the cross-bar hotel for a while.

As the Ranger approached the cowboy to carry out his captain's order, the cowboy yelled: "Whoopeeee! I'm the worst pill in the box!"

To which Ranger Livingston replied: "You may be the worst pill in the box, but the doctor says take you."

Western artist-writer Frederick Remington came to Texas in 1896 to do a story for *Harper's Magazine* on the Rangers. Someone suggested he talk to John Salmon "Rip" Ford. Remington met the old Ranger at the Menger Hotel in San Antonio and came away with plenty enough material for a good article.

Remington asked Ford if he had ever been charged by a Mexican lancer.

"Oh yes, many times," Ford responded.

Asked what he did in that event, Ford winked and responded:

"I reckoned to be able to hit a man every time with a six-shooter at one hundred and twenty-five yards."

"Then you do not think much of a lance as a weapon?" Remington asked.

"No," Ford replied, "there is but one weapon. The six-shooter when properly handled is the only weapon—mind you sir, I say *properly.*"

Rangers like to tell the story of a captain down on the border whose company was on the trail of bandits. When the Rangers had the outlaws in sight, the captain asked his men to join him in prayer:

"Lord, if you'll just stick around for a few minutes you'll see the golldangdest fight you ever witnessed. And Lord, if you can't see fit to help us, just please don't help them."

Shortly after an assassination attempt on President Theodore Roosevelt in the bitter campaign of 1912, Texas politico and presidential adviser Colonel E. M. House called for former Ranger Captain Bill McDonald to come to Washington and lend a hand in protecting Democratic candidate Woodrow Wilson.

McDonald took the train to the capital and soon was dealing with Wilson's Secret Service contingent. The old Ranger was openly contemptuous of the .38s the federal men packed. The candidate's bodyguards countered that a .38 would kill a person just as dead as the .45 single action Colt McDonald carried.

"Yes," the Ranger replied, "if you give him a week to die in."

Bill McDonald
(Author's collection)

Dan L. McDuffie, a young Ranger who had recently transferred from Captain Light Townsend's Company C in Del Rio to the booming East Texas oilfields, was killed in July 1931 when a drunk shot him. Another former Ranger, Gladewater police chief William A. Dial, then shot and killed the drunk.

On hearing the news, Townsend wrote his friend Dial: "Keep both eyes open all the time.... It is a cinch that if a man stays in this game long enough ... some two-bit bootlegger or some sorry son-of-a-gun equally as bad will bump him off."

Townsend kept his eyes open, but he died while on state business less than a year later in downtown San Antonio—of a heart attack.

W. H. Roberts, a private in his uncle Dan Roberts' Ranger company, later transferred to Company E in West Texas. Not long after joining Captain C. L. Neville's company, in January 1881 W. H. Roberts participated in the last fight between the Rangers and Indians.

"Oh, yes, I killed a couple of Indians," he told a reporter years later. "They got after me, and I ran them to death!"

······ ✪ ······

Ranger Captain A. Y. Allee never had a whole lot to say, but when he did talk people paid attention.

When serious trouble seemed to be brewing in Laredo, the captain dispatched a Ranger with a message for the instigators:

"Tell them people I'm coming down there. Tell them we'll do all the carrying of guns. Tell them we'll do all the enforcing of the law. Tell them we'll do all the fighting. And tell them if there's any killin' done, we'll do it."

At the annual reunion of the Former Texas Rangers Association in San Antonio in 1980, Captain Allee, long since retired, offered an opinion on what it took to be a Ranger in the frontier days:

"All a Ranger needed," the captain said, "was a durn good horse, a pack mule outfitted with a bedroll, a hundred rounds of rifle ammunition and a hundred rounds for a pistol, a little food, and that's about it."

While a reporter was still writing that down, another old Ranger at the reunion added one other item to Allee's checklist:

"And you had to have a little guts to go with it."

When Allee was inducted into the Ranger Hall of Fame in Waco, he was presented an engraved shotgun.

Accepting the weapon with a quizzical grin, the old Ranger remarked:

"I don't know what you're giving me this for. They done took away my hunting license."

······ ✪ ······

Captain Bob Crowder single-handedly—and without violence—put down a riot in 1955 at the Rusk State Hospital for the Criminally Insane.

Crowder later gave a newspaper writer this job description of a Texas Ranger:

"A Ranger is an officer who is able to handle any given situation without definite instructions from his commanding officer or higher authority," Crowder said. "This ability must be proven before a man becomes a Ranger."

Bob Crowder
(Author's collection)

The old "one Ranger, one riot" cliche was the invention of an overimaginative writer in search of a colorful catch phrase. Nearly every writer since then has accepted it as fact. But former Senior Ranger Captain Bill Wilson saw it differently:

"I think we've always been one Ranger short and one riot long."

Bill Wilson
(Author's collection)

····· ⭐ ·····

"Hell, you're proud to be a Texas Ranger," Ranger Glenn Krueger said in 1984, "because, by God, you feel like Texas likes you, or what you do, and you wouldn't want to fail the people of the state."

235

Asked why he had wanted to be a Ranger, retired Captain Eddie L. Oliver replied: "Because I hate a damn thief."

"Forget the stories that you have heard and the movies that you have seen of Texas Rangers who are unkillable and who swagger and make hip shots," Ranger "Dub" Naylor of Headquarters Company said in the 1940s. "But try to remember the Texas Ranger as a quiet, deliberate, gentle type of officer who gazes calmly at trouble and attempts to anticipate the foe's action, and remember that, above all, the Texas Ranger is a great believer in the study of human nature and a graduate of the greatest school in the world—the school of experience. We believe in the Creed of 'Hold your fire until certain that your aim is true and then let go.'"

Retired Ranger Tol Dawson was right on target with his description of longtime Ranger Leo Bishop: "Wherever he went, he took law and order with him."

He also told about two candidates for sheriff in a West Texas town. Both had unsavory reputations. One candidate was a known skirt chaser, the other a big whiskey drinker.

A would-be voter, in a real quandary over who to cast his ballot for, consulted a Ranger who knew both men.

"Well," the Ranger replied diplomatically, "some women need catchin' and some whiskey needs drinkin'."

While the old "one Ranger, one riot" saw is the most common Ranger cliche, a close second is another line of uncertain origin: "No man in the wrong can stand up to a man in the right when he keeps on a comin'." Retired Ranger Dud Barker, who knew the Texas border when horseback Rangers rode the river, offered advice for anyone facing a fight: "If he's wrong, he'll back up."

Two Rangers were looking into possible illegal activities on the part of a county judge in South Texas. The judge got wind of it and invited one of the Rangers to his chambers for a private conversation.

The judge had heard that the Rangers were in town to investigate the county commissioners. "Really," he blurted, "I am the target, am I not?"

"No, you're not the target, judge," Ranger Ramiro Martinez replied. "You're the goddam bull's-eye!"

The Rangers of Company F were in the middle of a company meeting—one of the few times a year they were ever in the same place at the same time—when Captain Bob Mitchell got word of the kidnapping of a little girl. He and all the other Rangers rushed out to begin working the case.

Later, as the Rangers and other officers closed in on the kidnappers, the captain radioed for several of his Rangers to meet him behind an abandoned service station. Ranger Joe Wilie radioed back that he and another Ranger in the car with him were just then being fired on by the kidnappers.

The captain, uncertain if he had heard correctly, asked Wilie if he was sure he was under fire.

"Yes sir," came his reply over the radio, "but we sure would welcome a second opinion."

As Director of the Texas Department of Public Safety, Colonel Dudley M. Thomas is in charge of the Texas Rangers and all other DPS officers and employees. A good-humored optimist, one of his favorite expressions is:

"As long as there's lead in the air, there's still hope."

Dudley M. Thomas
(Author's collection)

237

······ ⭐ ······

Sources

Baskin, Robert E. "Bob Crowder: Ranger." *Dallas Morning News*, September 30, 1956.

Biffle, Kent. *Dallas Morning News*, May 29, 1977.

Dawson, Tol. Interview with the author, May 18, 1997.

"Ex-Ranger, 88, Recalls Thrills of 'Fighting' Days." *Austin Statesman*, April 26, 1950.

Gray, Ted. *Shades of the West: A Cowboy's Memoirs*. Alpine: n.p., n.d., p. 100.

Harris, Johnny. *The Authorized Texas Ranger Cookbook*. Hamilton, Texas: Harris Farms Publishing, 1994, pp. 14, 96, 102.

Redding, Stan. "The Texas Rangers: They got together to honor three of their own at the Ranger Hall of Fame." *Houston Chronicle*, August 19, 1979, p. 25.

Remington, Frederick. "How the Law Got into the Chaparral." *Harper's New Monthly Magazine*, December 1896, pp. 60-65.

Sterling, William Warren. *Trails and Trials of a Texas Ranger*. Norman: University of Oklahoma Press, 1968, pp. 325-326.

Webb, Walter Prescott. *The Texas Rangers: A Century of Frontier Defense*. Boston: Houghton-Mifflin, 1935.

Winingham, Ralph. "Ranger Recalls Career." *San Antonio Express-News*, December 12, 1991.

Zastrow, Steve. "Texas Rangers: Tall Men, Tall Tales." *Corpus Christi Magazine*, February 1984, p. 107.

The Texas Ranger Motel

Slicing diagonally across the state from Texarkana to Presidio is U.S. Highway 67. At its midpoint, the highway passes through a small town in Coleman County called Santa Anna. And off the highway just east of Santa Anna is the Texas Ranger Motel.

Behind the names there's a good story.

Before Texas was crisscrossed with multilane interstate highways, U.S. 67 was a considerably busier roadway. By the end of the twentieth century, the traffic through Santa Anna, along with the town's economy, had noticeably declined. Its 114-year-old weekly newspaper, the *Santa Anna News*, went out of business in early 1999. Several businesses and even the local Western Auto followed suit.

But the Texas Ranger Motel, opened in 1979, remains in operation as Santa Anna's sole lodging place. The only other overnight choices are in Brownwood, twenty miles east, or Coleman, eight miles northwest. Except during hunting season, which starts with opening day for dove on September 1 and continues through deer season up to the last day of quail season in February, there's not much point in calling ahead for a reservation. Any other time of the year, the motel probably will have plenty of rooms available.

The Texas Ranger Motel is not a chain-owned franchise with cookie-cutter rooms operated by some impersonal management company with scores of properties that look no different in El Paso than they do in Houston. This motel is a mom-and-pop operation. Despite its name, the Texas Ranger Motel is not owned by some crusty old ex-Ranger. On the other hand, it's not called the Texas Ranger Motel just because the words "Texas Ranger" have a certain cachet.

The motel sits sidesaddle on the eastern slope of the Santa Anna Mountains. There wouldn't be a Texas Ranger Motel, at least not one in Coleman County, Texas, if it weren't for those mountains and a bunch of old ex-Rangers, particularly Caleb M. Grady.

Grady came to Texas with his family in 1872 from Kentucky. Two years later the Grady bunch moved to Brownwood on the Pecan Bayou, at the time only a community of twenty or so log cabins on the edge of the frontier.

The Santa Anna Mountains predated him a bit, of course. As geologic features go, the flat-topped mesas in the eastern part of the county are nothing exceptional compared with other prominences in Texas and the Southwest. Two miles long and split by a gap, they are not really mountains except in comparison with everything else in Coleman County, which is mostly flat.

The highest point is 2,000 feet above mean sea level, but that would be significant only if the area around it were substantially lower. The "mountains" are only about 300 feet higher than the surrounding landscape. Still, they're as tall as a thirty-story building. Since the landscape for miles in any direction is level, the Santa Anna Mountains constitute the principal landmark in the area. That is what made them important, first to Indians and later to explorers, Texas Rangers, and early settlers. In addition to being a good lookout post, the mountains became a reference point for travelers. Too, with a dependable year-round spring flowing near the base of the eastern peak, the mountains became a stopping place.

How the twin mesas came by their name can only be conjectured, but historian Rupert Richardson believed the features were named after Santa Anna, a Penatuhkah Comanche chief. The landmark is shown on Jacob de Cordova's 1849 Texas map as "Santa Anna's Peak," the first known usage of the name. Twenty years earlier, a map by colonizer Stephen F. Austin identified it merely as "High Peak," a feature north of the Colorado River and west of "Pecan River" (present-day Pecan Bayou in Brown County).

If the mountains were named for the Comanche chief (and Texans were not likely to have named anything after General Antonio de Lopez de Santa Anna), the name is certainly fitting because the mesas stood in the heart of Comanche country. Chief Santa Anna was well known in Texas in the 1840s, having signed treaties with the Republic of Texas, the United States, and the Germans who settled Fredericksburg.

A quarter century later when Caleb Grady first saw the mountains, it was of no particular concern to him who they were named after. Comanche-Texan relations had long since deteriorated past the point of signing treaties. The two cultures were at war and the Texans were winning.

Grady first encountered the Santa Anna Mountains in the winter of 1875, riding west from Brownwood to hunt buffalo. Nearing the mountains, he and his four companions saw a herd of wild horses led by an iron gray stallion, "the most beautiful sight I have ever seen." The young man gave chase. But his horse, good as it was, was no match for the wild stallion.

Looming above the prairie in the distance was the mountain, "silent and beautiful." But, Grady later recalled, it also looked like "a good camping place for the Indians, so we passed on to the south, and camped on Santa Anna Branch."

Grady enlisted that June in Company E of the Frontier Battalion under Captain W. "Jeff" Maltby, a tough old Ranger who soon resigned his command. Grady had first seen the captain and his Rangers the previous fall, when they rode into Brownwood with a dead Indian draped over one of their pack mules. The Indian was exceedingly large, which was why the Rangers bothered to bring him to town. Maltby's gruesome trophy got considerable attention.

"Mexican Joe, who usually hung around the Ranger camp," Grady later remembered, "scalped the Indian, and cut off some of his fingers for souvenirs."

By the time Grady joined Company E, the hostiles had been pushed farther west, beyond the Brownwood-Coleman area. Wanting to keep it that way, the Rangers were constantly on the scout. Their base camp was on Home Creek, at the mouth of Santa Anna Branch, about four miles southwest of the mountains.

The company roster listed forty men, but Grady said no more than ten to fifteen Rangers ever went on a scout at one time. A scout lasted a couple of weeks. As soon as the Rangers returned to camp, another patrol rode out.

Rangers not on scout maintained a twenty-four-hour lookout from the top of the nearby mesa. Twice a day, before daybreak and as dusk approached, two Rangers rode from the camp to the mountain to survey the countryside for campfire smoke or the dust of horsemen, depending on whether they had night or day duty. During the day, mostly all they saw were herds of antelope.

Grady was not the first Ranger to climb the peak for a look-see. John Salmon "Rip" Ford had stopped there in 1858 on his march northwest to take on the Comanches. During the Civil War, a detachment of the 46th Texas Cavalry, rangers in function if not name, camped at the base of the mountain.

"I have a vivid recollection of standing guard near the base of the mountain sixteen years ago," former Ranger Andrew Jackson Sowell wrote in 1886. "At that time instead of hearing the shrill whistle of the locomotive throughout the night we heard the lonesome howl of the prairie wolf. . . . Near the mountain that evening we chased four cougars and succeeded in killing one of them."

Though many Rangers had stood lookout on the eastern end of the Santa Anna Mountains, Grady and his captain, B. S. Foster, were the only ones who left their names there. "On the east end of the East Mountain I carved my initials with the date, 'C. M. G. 1876,' and it can still be read to this day," Grady wrote near the end of his long life.

By 1920 nearly half a century had passed since the Rangers of the Frontier Battalion scouted West Texas for Indians. Realizing that time soon would run out on the old veterans of the battalion, former Ranger W. M. Green organized the Ex-Texas Ranger Association in Weatherford. Whether Grady was at that first meeting of former Rangers is not documented, but by 1924 he was one of the association's officers and remained active in it for most of the rest of his life.

Each summer for the next twenty years the association held a reunion. The location varied from year to year, but it always was in some West Texas community. In 1935 the meeting was in Santa Anna, where Mayor E. D. McDonald declared "Ex-Texas Ranger Week." Of the two hundred former Rangers who had paid one dollar to join the association in 1920, only a dozen or so were able to make the sixteenth reunion.

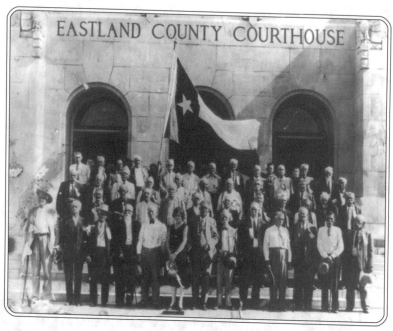

Old Rangers of the Indian-fighting era met annually beginning in 1920. (Author's collection)

The aging leadership of the association figured it was time to decide on a permanent reunion place. Meeting in the Santa Anna High School building, members voted on Santa Anna as a fitting location. Off and on for more than twenty years, the Santa Anna Mountains had been used as a Ranger camping place. As young men, several of the retired Rangers spent solitary days and nights there keeping lookout for Indians. The high ground seemed a logical choice for their annual reunions when they gathered to reminisce about the old days.

The prime movers in the effort to keep the reunion in Santa Anna had been J. J. Gregg, owner of the *Santa Anna News;* Mrs. R. C. Gay, one of Grady's daughters; and Mrs.

John Bannister, whose husband had been a Frontier Battalion Ranger. In 1918, when her husband died in office as sheriff of Coleman County, Emma Bannister had been appointed to serve out his term. She was the first female sheriff in American history.

Aided by donations from the local community, the association bought twenty-five acres on the slope of the eastern mountain for use as a reunion ground. When the old Rangers returned for their next reunion in 1936, local residents donated tow sacks of black-eyed peas, ripe homegrown tomatoes by the tub, frying-sized chickens, and a fat calf worth ten Depression-era dollars. The Santa Anna High School band furnished the musical entertainment and did such a good job that the old Rangers voted them their official band.

Federal funds built the Ranger reunion hall on the side of Santa Anna Mountain in 1935-36. (Author's collection)

Gregg and Mrs. Gay helped get funding from the Federal Works Progress Administration for construction of a frontier-style reunion hall. Built of donated local stone, the two-room facility had a fireplace at each end and a front porch—facing south to catch the breeze—that ran the full length of the structure.

The first reunion at the new building was on August 3, 1937. Retired Ranger Captain John R. Hughes gave the association's official response to Mayor McDonald's welcoming speech. For the next two days, the old Rangers were feted to meals, fiddlers, square dancers, and speechifying.

Realizing that the day drew near when no more old Indian-fighting Rangers would be left, the association voted to create the Ex-Texas Ranger Auxiliary, a body open to all descendants and relatives of former Rangers. After fewer than a dozen old Rangers attended the reunion, the association voted in 1938 to merge with the auxiliary.

One of the more memorable events at one of the Santa Anna Ranger reunions occurred in 1941 when J. Emmor Harston was invited to speak to the old Rangers and their families and friends. Harston, whose father had worked at a trading post on the Comanche reservation near Fort Sill, Oklahoma, had grown up among the Comanches. He had learned to speak their language and had studied their culture.

As Ranger Bannister's daughter Leona Bruce later related the incident, after telling of his life in Oklahoma with the Comanches, Harston "went on to attest to their moral purity and their honesty." The Comanches, he continued, never stole horses and never attacked Texans. Their raids into Texas, he went on, merely were to recover horses stolen from them. Any harm done to Texans was only in self-defense.

The old Rangers had welcomed him cordially to their reunion, but now they sat silently as Harston made it seem as if they had been the aggressors in the Indian wars. "If a very drunk man had turned up in a Ladies' Prohibition Society and praised Bourbon and Scotch," Bruce later wrote, "there would not have been a more astounded audience."

The association had its last reunion at Santa Anna in 1951. Noah Armstrong, ninety-nine years old, was the only Ranger of the Frontier Battalion in attendance. After that, the local Veterans of Foreign Wars post took over the park on the mountainside.

The original acreage purchased by the Ex-Texas Rangers Association was deeded to the Texas Highway Department, which later conveyed the property to the City of Santa Anna. The city sold some of the land, eventually winnowing the park down to 3.96 acres.

The next man to play an important role in the story of the Santa Anna Mountains had never been a Texas Ranger, but Coleman County sheriff H. F. Fenton held a Special Ranger commission from 1960 to 1969. A native of Coleman County, he served in the 142nd Infantry, 36th Division during World War II. After seeing action in Africa, Italy, France, and Germany, he came home a decorated war hero. Among his medals were two Purple Hearts. He ran for sheriff and was elected on November 5, 1946, becoming at the age of twenty-four the youngest sheriff in Texas at the time. He continually returned to office and served until 1961, when he went to work as a Special Ranger for the Texas Sheep and Goat Raisers Association. Fenton went back to work as Coleman County sheriff in 1970 to fill an unexpired term. He ran for office again in 1976, was re-elected twice, and served until his retirement on January 1, 1989.

Sheriff Fenton, who had attended several of the mountainside Ranger reunions, bid on the remaining reunion ground property in 1979 when the City of Santa Anna put it up for sale. City officials accepted his bid, and the sheriff became the new owner of the old Ranger campground. Fenton had the Depression-era reunion building refurbished, adding a second story and converting it into a combination motel office and living area. The motel, with ten double rooms and two singles, was built as a separate structure. In keeping with the historical significance of the site, the sheriff had no trouble coming up with a name for his new business. The Texas Ranger Motel opened for business on May 19, 1979.

Fenton died on April 4, 1990, at the age of sixty-seven, fifteen months after leaving office. His widow, Loretta M. Fenton, still owns the property. Lavell and Juanita Jones have managed the motel since the day it opened.

"Can anyone stay here, or just Texas Rangers?" Juanita Jones remembers a visitor once asking. She assured him that everyone was welcome at the Texas Ranger Motel. Occasionally, though they no longer have to post a lookout for Indians, a Texas Ranger passing through on official duty still spends the night at the base of Santa Anna Mountain. Only now the Rangers get to sleep on a good bed in air-conditioned comfort.

Caleb Grady probably figured the Ranger reunion grounds would remain a park forever. He never would have foreseen a motel on the side of the mountain he loved so much. When he retired from farming, Grady moved back to Brownwood. Though he could no longer see the Santa Anna Mountains every day, they towered over the landscape of his memory.

"That old Santa Anna Mountain is very dear to me," he wrote. "Through all my forty years of residence in Coleman County, I was always in sight of this grand old signal post of my Ranger days...secure in its silent grandeur, beloved by all within sight of it."

Grady never forgot his Ranger days. As he lay dying, with his daughter at his side, he smiled and said, "Look! Can't you see them—the Rangers! There go the boys." In his mind, they were probably chasing mustangs on the slope of the Santa Anna Mountains.

Notes

Grady was born May 8, 1854, in Gradyville, Kentucky. His family moved to Texas in 1872 and two years later came to Brownwood. He spent the rest of his life in Brown and Coleman Counties. After his Ranger service, he married in 1877 and purchased land east of Santa Anna Mountain, which he farmed for forty years. He and his wife had ten children. Grady moved back to Brownwood where he lived the rest of his life. He died there on June 29, 1949, at the age of ninety-five. At the time of his death, he was commander emeritus of the Ex-Texas Ranger Association.

Sources

Bruce, Leona. *Santa Anna's Peak*. Quanah: Nortex Press, 1976, pp. 31, 33, 55-56, 121-124.

Gay, Beatrice Grady. *Into the Setting Sun: A History of Coleman County*. Santa Anna, Texas: n.p., 1936, pp. 167-174.

_____. "Texas Ex-Rangers Hold Reunion at Santa Anna." *Frontier Times*, August 1951, pp. 328-329.

Hunter, Gladys Nevins. *Historically Speaking: Coleman County, Texas*. San Angelo: Anchor Publishing, 1977, pp. 50-51.

Jones, Juanita. Interview with the author, February 7, 1999.

Pelon, Linda. "Were Santa Anna Peaks Named For the Penatuhkah War Chief Santa Anna?" *Texana Living History Newsletter*, May 1994, p. 2, 6.

"Rites For C. M. Grady Held At Brownwood." *Santa Anna News*, July 8, 1949.

Tise, Sammy. *Texas County Sheriffs*. Albuquerque, N.M.: Oakwood Printing, 1989, p. 109.

Hollywood Rangers

Hollywood has been fascinated with the Texas Rangers since the earliest days of the film industry.

Scores of movies with a Ranger as a central character have been produced. In the 1920s alone, filmmakers cranked out forty-one Ranger movies. The trend kept up in the 1930s and 1940s. Twenty-one Ranger movies were produced by PRC Pictures in a span of three years, from 1942 to 1945.

The first movie with the word "Ranger" in its title was *The Ranger's Bride*, a silent flick filmed in 1910. The following year a movie called *Border Ranger* was released. The same man was the star as well as the producer of both films: Gilbert M. "Bronco Billy" Anderson—Max Aronson before he became the first Western film star. That was in 1903, when Anderson played a role in the seminal Western *The Great Train Robbery*. "Bronco Billy" went on to produce some five hundred Western one-reelers.

Soon following in Bronco Billy's bootsteps was Tom Mix, who played a Ranger in several movies. In *Romance on the Rio Grande* (1911), Mix portrayed a Ranger who saved a rancher and his daughter from inebriated Indians, who got their illegal hooch from a Mexican gang. In 1925 Mix played a former Texas Ranger in the movie version of Zane Grey's classic *Riders of the Purple Sage*.

For twenty years Ranger movies were mute, the only sound being the accompaniment of a piano and the hoots, hisses, or cheers of the audience. The first "talkie" dealing with the Texas Rangers was a remake of Zane Grey's *The Lone Star Ranger* shot in 1930, three years after the first-ever full-length picture with sound. Grey's 1915 novel, a book dedicated to the Rangers, had already been done twice as a silent film.

The first radio Ranger was the "Senior Captain" of the genre, the Lone Ranger. He went on the air for the first time in 1933, and he's still in the saddle, at least in terms of his cultural impact. The Lone Ranger was a role model for the

The Lone Ranger became an American icon in the 1930s. (Author's collection)

generation of Americans who went off to fight and win World War II, and later, as a television Ranger, he did similar duty for millions of postwar Baby Boomers.

Two years after the Lone Ranger galloped onto the airwaves and into American popular culture, a cereal company decided to capitalize on Ranger popularity by sponsoring a radio show called *Riding with the Texas Rangers*.

"Created Exclusively for the Southwest," an advertisement for the show explained, *Riding with the Texas Rangers* would be "a series of authentic tales...taken from the States [sic] Archives and [embracing] the richest romance and history of the great Southwest." The show aired on four big Texas radio stations: WFAA in Dallas, WBAP in Fort Worth (which then shared the same frequency with WFAA and switched during the day from studio to studio with the ringing of a cowbell), KPRC in Houston, and WOAI in San Antonio.

The show premiered in a live broadcast from the annual gathering of the Ex-Texas Rangers Association at Santa Anna in the summer of 1935.

Riding with the Texas Rangers did not last long, and it never made it as a nationally broadcast show, but its premise—the dramatization of true Ranger cases—would be revisited fifteen years later.

In 1935 a notable book was transformed into a singularly unnotable Ranger movie when Galveston-born movie mogul King Vidor did a film based on Walter Prescott Webb's *The Texas Rangers: A Century of Frontier Defense*. Vidor's *The Texas*

Rangers starred Fred MacMurray and Jack Oakie as Rangers Jim Hawkins and Wahoo Jones, two men who had metamorphosed from outlaws to lawmen.

The film had its world premiere at the Majestic Theater in Dallas at 8 P.M. on August 21, 1935, capping what had been proclaimed as "Texas Ranger Week" in Texas. Despite all the hoopla, including a guest list who received invitations from Governor James V. Allred, the movie was so pedestrian that even Ranger fan Dr. Webb never got around to seeing it.

Six years after *The Texas Rangers* went over with moviegoers like the proverbial lead balloon, Hollywood assigned contemporary Rangers to deal with a real balloon in *King of the Texas Rangers*. In this 1941 serial from Republic Pictures, the Rangers took on Nazi spies operating from a dirigible floating over the state. The top Ranger was played by former Texas Christian University quarterback "Slingin'" Sammy Baugh.

Sammy Baugh astride his horse in a still from the 1941 movie serial *King of the Texas Rangers*. (Photo courtesy Waco Sports Hall of Fame)

Of scores of black-and-white Ranger movies, one of the more interesting—and better—films was done in 1948. The movie was *The Gallant Legion*, an underrated B-movie starring William "Wild Bill" Elliott as Ranger Gary Conway.

The movie's plot line seemed far-fetched: West Texas is taken over by a separatist who plans to turn that part of the state into his own kingdom. The Rangers are called on to keep Texas whole. Naturally, they succeed.

In the movie, set during Reconstruction, the bad guy was the former head of the reviled State Police. In cahoots with crooked politicians in Austin, this villain plots to become king of West Texas. He bases his case on the 1845 Congressional resolution providing for the annexation of the Republic of Texas, which allows Texas to divide into five states if it chooses.

Anyone seeing the movie prior to 1997 would have thought its premise highly implausible. But on April 27, 1997, Richard McLaren—claiming Texas was an independent Republic and that he was its lawful ambassador—along with several of his followers engaged Texas in a six-day standoff in the Davis Mountains of West Texas. In a case of life imitating art, it was the Texas Rangers, with a lot of help from other law officers, who cut short McLaren's vision of empire. The erstwhile ambassador received a life prison sentence.

NBC began radio broadcasts of *Tales of the Texas Rangers* in 1950 and continued the thirty-minute series for two years. Joel McCrea starred as Ranger Jace Pearson in the dramatic series, which, like the short-lived *Riding with the Texas Rangers*, was touted as being based on real cases from the files of the Texas Rangers. Given the cooperation extended by the Department of Public Safety and the fact that recently retired Ranger Captain Manuel T. "Lone Wolf" Gonzaullas was hired as technical advisor, that claim was true to the extent that anything associated with the entertainment industry can be said to be based on reality.

Parley Baer and Ed Begley often played character roles in the series. The announcer was Hal Gibney. A young Stacy Keach was the producer.

According to Jon D. Swartz and Robert C. Reinehr, authors of *The Handbook of Old-Time Radio*, thirty-six of the episodes are commercially available.

For a time in the early 1950s, dramatic entertainment was available on both broadcast media—radio and television. TV, of course, soon supplanted radio. The first Ranger to ride across the little screen was the granddaddy of them all, the Lone Ranger.

A weekly television version of the *Lone Ranger*, with Clayton Moore as the Lone Ranger and Jay Silverheels as Tonto, went on the air for the first time in 1949. Not only did the show have the distinction of being the first Ranger show on television, it was the first TV western. (Hopalong Cassidy had been on TV, but merely through the broadcasting of short features filmed earlier for use in movie theaters.) The *Lone Ranger* went on for 221 episodes until 1957, outlasting the radio version—which had different actors—by four years.

By the mid-1950s, the Western dominated nighttime television. The peak came in 1958-1959 when forty-eight Westerns were aired each week. Four of the five top-rated shows were Westerns.

In 1955, the same year *Gunsmoke* began its epic twenty-year run, *Tales of the Texas Rangers* was back on the air as a black-and-white television series produced for Screen Gems by Colbert Clark. The radio program had featured contemporary Ranger cases, but the TV version covered the whole history of the Rangers. The same two characters—six-foot four-inch Willard Parker as Jace Pearson and Harry Lauter as Clay Morgan—portrayed nineteenth-century Rangers one week, twentieth-century Rangers the next. This TV time travel, with the same characters fighting Indians or cattle-rustlers one week and hopping into their cars to chase bank robbers the next, was never explained.

Fifty-two episodes of *Tales of the Texas Rangers* were produced. CBS ran the show on Saturday mornings from September 3, 1955, through May 25, 1957. ABC picked up the show and aired reruns through 1959.

No sooner had *Tales of the Texas Rangers* been carried off to TV Land's boot hill than another show pinned on the *cinco peso* in its stead. In the fall of 1957 CBS trotted out *Trackdown*, a half-hour black-and-white oater starring Robert Culp. Like *Tales of the Texas Rangers*, the new series was based on actual cases "from the files of the Texas Rangers." Again, the DPS cooperated fully in the show.

Culp, who played Texas Ranger Hoby Gilman, wrote several of the episodes himself. Four Star Films distributed the series, which was produced by Vincent M. Fennelly.

Actor Robert Culp flanked by Rangers in 1957 in front of the University of Texas Tower in Austin. (Author's collection)

The series was born of one Western and begat yet another. The genesis of *Trackdown* was a May 1957 episode on Dick Powell's *Zane Grey Theater*, "Badge of Honor." An episode on *Trackdown* a year later, "The Bounty Hunter," led to a spin-off series called *Wanted: Dead or Alive*. The bounty hunter in the *Trackdown* episode and also on *Wanted: Dead or Alive* was Josh Randall, played by a young actor named Steve McQueen.

Having at least sired a winner, *Trackdown* bit the dust on September 23, 1959. *Wanted: Dead or Alive* shot to the top of the Nielson ratings, and McQueen went on to greater fame in the movies. So did Robert Culp.

Six years passed before network television went to rangering again. The next television series featuring the Rangers was *Laredo*, an hour-long Western that ran "in living color" each Thursday on NBC from September 16, 1965, to September 8, 1967.

Set in the border town of Laredo in the 1870s, the show focused on the law enforcement efforts of three Rangers—Reese Bennett, Joe Riley, and Chad Cooper—who seemed at times to be as tough on each other as they were on lawbreakers. Beginning with the 1966 season, a fourth Ranger, rookie Erik Hunter (played by Robert Wolders), mustered into the fictional Company B.

For the purposes of this TV show and a comic book that also featured the adventures of these Rangers and their captain, Laredo served as headquarters for the Rangers of Company B, "whose eighteen men comprise the only formal law between the Red River and the Rio Grande."

The series was foaled of another TV show, *The Virginian*, which introduced the three Rangers early in 1965 in an episode called "We've Lost a Train."

Issue Number 1 (the first and last) of the *Laredo* comic book series—which came out in 1966 and cost twelve cents —drew an interesting parallel between the Rangers and the men of another organization with a worldwide reputation: "Not all of the Rangers were men whose earlier careers were open to scrutiny. Some were thieves, some murderers. But within the Rangers (as in the French Foreign Legion), the slate was wiped clean and all were given a fresh start."

One of those men afforded a second chance by the Rangers was Riley, a gunslinger who joined the Rangers hoping to dodge arrest. (The modern Rangers are a bit more exacting in their background investigation of prospective employees). The *Laredo* comic book explained that while Riley has "complete distrust of the world...he has grown attached to his Company and would sacrifice his life for any man in it."

The character Chad Cooper came to the Rangers from the Army, his whole patrol having been wiped out by bandits "armed with the latest U.S. weapons." By joining the Rangers, Cooper figured he could look for gunrunners "legally and with help" and maybe get a little revenge.

The third Ranger, Reese Bennett, had always been a standup lawman. As a youngster of twelve, Bennett looked on in horror as his father was shot to death. Six years later, Bennett got a job as deputy U.S. marshal and tracked down the men who killed his dad. Eventually he left federal work to join the Rangers where his "strong principles and understanding of authority make him a disciplined, dependable Ranger."

The boss of Company B was Captain Parmalee, one of many men whose lives were changed by the Civil War. Somehow, the War Between the States had cost Parmalee "his wife and his fortune." The comic book did not explain whether Parmalee's wife had run off with that fortune and a Yankee, or had met some other fate. No matter, the captain "has no equals and only one superior: the Governor of Texas." Occasionally for old times' sake, Parmalee saddles up and rides out with his men.

Neville Brand, playing Ranger Bennett, got the top billing in the show. As one critic later wrote, Brand portrayed the Ranger "in the mold of Wallace Beery."

Peter Brown, who had previously been on *The Lawman*, portrayed Ranger Cooper. William Smith was Ranger Riley, and Philip Carey was cast as the captain.

"The action was expertly staged, with some fine and exciting combat scenes," the *BFI Companion of the Western* said in assessing the show. The show also offered a "nice line in black humor." Another reference called the show a "light western."

Fifty-six episodes of *Laredo*, produced by Universal Television, were filmed before Rangers Bennett, Cooper, and Riley rode off into TV sunset. Their next stop was a place called Syndication.

"Reruns are shown all over America and finding a whole new audience for the Hi-Jinks and action of the Rangers of Company B," Western televison authority Neil Summers wrote in 1992. "It was a fun show then and continues to be one today."

If *Laredo* offered viewers black humor, a series briefly aired by ABC in 1967 attempted to capitalize on old-fashioned low humor. *Rango*, a half-hour show filmed in color, ran on Friday nights from January 13 to June 25, 1967, before low ratings mercifully gunned it down after the summer reruns. Its theme song alone, sung by Frankie Laine, was probable cause for the use of deadly force: "From San Antone to the Rio Grande, on mountain peaks or desert sand, every outlaw fears the hand of danger from this Texas Ranger. Rango, Rango, Rango."

Set in Gopher Gulch in the 1870s, this Texas Ranger take-off on the popular cavalry-Indian comedy *F Troop* starred comedian Tim Conway, well known for his earlier service in *McHale's Navy*. Conway played a bumbling yet well-intentioned Texas Ranger named Rango. (Rango clearly was some scriptwriter's composite of "Ranger" and "Ringo," the best surname any Western outlaw ever had.) As in the successful spy comedy *Get Smart*, the hapless Ranger Rango always seemed to outsmart his boss. But he got to stick around because his Uncle George was "Commandant of the Rangers."

Rango's faithful companion was his bookish Indian assistant, Pink Cloud, played by Guy Marks. The Ranger in charge was Captain Horton, played by Norman Alden.

Unlike *Andy Griffith Show* deputy Barney Fife, who carried a pistol but only had one bullet, Ranger Rango was not even allowed to pack a piece. Nor would he let anyone else in Gopher Gulch walk around heeled. In fact, that was Rule Number 1 of Ranger Rango's 84 rules, a list drafted on the lawman's premise that "a law-abiding town is a happy town." Rule 84? "No whistling at girls on the street."

Despite Conway's obvious comedic talent, the public did not take to *Rango* like it did to *F Troop*. As one writer later assessed the show, "The jokes in *Rango* were as old as dirt, and if this wasn't bad enough for a comedy series, they were repeated time and time again." Conway's Ranger company was disbanded by the network after seventeen episodes.

After *Rango* left the air, network television still offered twenty Westerns in 1967, but the number began declining each year after. By 1970 only eleven Westerns were being aired, and a decade later the choices were down to three. For more than two decades, the only Rangers getting any air time on national television were the ones swinging baseball bats.

Then came a television miniseries based on a best-selling novel by Larry McMurtry and scripted by Texas screenwriter Bill Wittliff. *Lonesome Dove* the miniseries was almost as long as the novel. First aired on February 5, 1989, it ran for eight hours in four parts. Robert Duvall as ex-Ranger Augustus "Gus" McRae gave even more life to an already lively character while Texan Tommy Lee Jones captured the colder Captain Woodrow Call.

"CBS' faithful version of part-time Houstonian Larry McMurtry's Pulitzer Prize-winning novel is hands-down the best western that TV ever made," wrote *Houston Chronicle* TV editor Ann Hodges. "It may be the best western ever made, period."

A decade later it was still hard to argue against Hodges' assertion. The only thing *Lonesome Dove* failed to do was revive the TV western.

Later in 1989 shooting began in Austin on a made-for-TV movie called *Rip*, a contemporary Ranger story starring two Texans: Kris Kristofferson and singer-songwriter Willie Nelson. The screenplay was written by two former reporters turned fiction writers, Bud Shrake and Gary Cartwright. Originally sold to MGM as a feature film, the project fell through. It got new life when Nelson, who had recently played in an episode of *Miami Vice*, got director Aaron Lipstadt to read it. Lipstadt liked the script and sold it to CBS. Cartwright told a newspaper writer that an executive with the network had described the project as a "male-bonding action movie for the sweeps."

The movie aired in February 1990, during the all-important sweeps rating period used to help stations set their local advertising fees. *Rip* pitted a good guy in a white hat, a Ranger captain, against a longhaired good bad guy, a safecracker. Their bonding came somewhat reluctantly after the Ranger checked the crook out of jail to help him track down a serial killer. The good guy, an authentic-looking Ranger named "Rip" Metcalf, was played by Brownsville native and former Rhodes Scholar Kristofferson. The good bad guy, Billy Roy, was realistically played by Nelson, a musician with a passing familiarity with what the inside of a jail looked like.

Clearly inspired by John Salmon "Rip" Ford, the movie's title was appropriately symbolic. With Ford, the "Rip" stood for "Rest In Peace."

Rip was no *Lonesome Dove*, but critics found it a moderately amusing movie. A sequel, *Another Pair of Aces*, came out in 1992.

Later that year Clint Eastwood decided to film a script by John Lee Hancock called *A Perfect World*. Set in 1963, the screenplay was built on the relationship between escaped convict Butch Haynes and a seven-year-old boy he kidnaps and holds hostage. A tough Texas Ranger captain, forced to cooperate with "an inexperienced but independent" female criminologist, coordinates the search for the not-so-bad con on the lam.

Eastwood cast himself as "grizzled Texas Ranger Red Garnett" and picked Kevin Costner to play the convict. Laura Dern, fresh from her acclaimed role in *Jurassic Park*, played the young criminologist. Filming began in Austin and Central Texas in February 1993 and was completed July 14. The movie had its Texas premiere in Austin on November 22, 1993.

A Perfect World got mixed reviews and by early 1994 had grossed only $30 million. But Eastwood, who visited the DPS headquarters and talked to some real Rangers and others with the agency to get a better feel for his role, came across well as a Ranger captain.

CBS premiered an hour-long drama called *Walker, Texas Ranger* on April 21, 1993. The show, filmed in the Dallas-Fort Worth area and set in Fort Worth, was still going strong in 1999. Chuck Norris played Ranger Cordell Walker. Clarence Gilyard Jr. was Walker's partner, Ranger Jimmy Trivette.

Though the show has a former Texas Ranger as a technical consultant, it is not a 100 percent reflection of the modern Texas Rangers. No real Ranger wears a beard or a black hat, both Walker trademarks. Walker's use of "necessary force" to subdue criminals or save lives in one episode exceeds what any real Ranger might expect in his or her entire career.

But if Saturday night viewers understand that Walker is essentially a televised comic book, they do not seem to care.

Walker, Texas Ranger clearly has become the Lone Ranger of the 1990s. Instead of a mask, Cordel Walker hides part of his face behind a beard. Instead of silver bullets, he expertly uses the martial arts. Instead of a white horse, most of the time he rides in a pickup truck. (He does still use a horse, of course. In one episode, he galloped his horse to catch up with a train.) And instead of Tonto, he has his sidekick Trivette.

There are, however, some differences between *Walker, Texas Ranger* and those "exciting days of yore" when the Lone Ranger reigned on television. Walker's world is far more violent than the Lone Ranger's was. The contemporary plots are more involved. And, thanks to modern technology, *Walker, Texas Ranger*'s production values are higher.

All the Ranger movies, radio programs, and television shows have had an impact on our culture in general and on the Rangers.

Taking popular culture first, screen Rangers have done their share in perpetuating the mythical West. They taught three generations of Americans—and through syndication many more people around the world—a lot of pseudo history.

To what additional extent movies and television—particularly violent Westerns—have affected American culture is an interesting question. But most of the children who grew up watching violent TV westerns did not become violent adults.

The Western, whether the hero is a Ranger or a bounty hunter, is essentially the story of good versus evil, a story line older than the Bible. The formulaic Western, like the Ten Commandments, did not deal in gray areas—its issues were as black and white as the image on the TV screen. The good characters in these horse operas, especially the TV Rangers, gave American youngsters positive role models. Children also learned that the guys in black hats seldom prevail in the long run.

Fran Striker, the creator of the Lone Ranger, went beyond mere script writing to convey a wholesome lesson. He wrote the Lone Ranger Creed:

> I believe that to have a friend, a man must be one. That all men are created equal and that everyone has within himself the power to make this a better world. That God put the firewood there but that every man must gather and light it himself. In being prepared physically, mentally and morally to fight when necessary for that which is right. That a man should make the most of what equipment he has. That 'This government, of the people, by the people and for the people' shall live always. That men should live by the rule of what is best for the greatest number.
>
> That sooner or later...somewhere...somehow... we must settle with the world and make payment for what we have taken. That all things change but truth, and that truth alone, lives on forever. In my Creator, my country, my fellow man.
>
> —The Lone Ranger

The creed, though badly in need of editing, pretty well captured the essence not only of the Lone Ranger's character but also most other folks in white hats.

In the 1950s, when TV Westerns enjoyed their heyday, the perception was that America was one big happy family, just like Ozzie and Harriet and the boys. But America in the 1950s was not without worry. The Cold War at times seemed downright warm. People with apocalyptic visions dug fallout shelters and stocked food and water in the event the Bomb ever fell. So perhaps there was a certain element of escapism in the American passion for Westerns, TV shows reminiscent of simpler times when all a man needed was a good horse, a good gun, and if he was not too much of a loner, a good woman.

Beyond whatever influence Westerns have had on American culture, how has the genre affected the Rangers who wear real guns?

Thanks to pulp fiction and nonfiction books, particularly Albert Bigelow Paine's 1909 biography of Captain Bill McDonald, the Rangers already had a national reputation by the beginning of the movie era. Film, radio, and television have taken that reputation worldwide, internationalizing the Rangers. The Rangers today are almost as familiar as the Royal Canadian Mounted Police or Scotland Yard.

Today's Rangers are well aware of their mythology, and to an extent they capitalize on that reputation. It makes recruiting easy—it's not unusual for 150 to 200 persons to apply for one opening—and it helps them in dealing with the public and with other law enforcement agencies.

Thanks to Hollywood, the Texas Rangers will never outride their myth.

•••••• ✪ ••••••

Sources

Buscombe, Edward, ed. *The BFI Companion to the Western*. New York: Atheneum, 1988, pp. 411, 416, 421.

Eastwood, Clint. Web page, http://www.man-with-no-name.com.

Graham, Don. *Cowboys and Cadillacs: How Hollywood Looks at Texas*. Austin: Texas Monthly Press, 1983.

Holloway, Diane. "Willie, Kris together again in TV movie." *Austin American-Statesman*, October 24, 1989.

MacCambridge, Michael. "Release was 'World'-wind." *Austin American-Statesman*, November 26, 1993.

McNeil, Alex. *Total Television: The Comprehensive Guide to Programming From 1948 to Present*. New York: Penguin Books, 1996, 4th ed., pp. 463, 683, 816, 862.

Moore, Clayton with Frank Thompson. *I Was That Masked Man*. Dallas: Taylor Publishing, 1996.

Summers, Neil. *The Official TV Western Book*. Vienna, W. Va: The Old West Shop, Volume 4, 1992, pp. 53, 71.

Swartz, Jon D. and Robert C. Reinehr. *Handbook of Old-Time Radio: A Comprehensive Guide to Golden Age Radio Listening and Collecting.* Metuchen, N.J.: Scarecrow Press, 1993, pp. 422-423, 571.

Terrace, Vincent. *Television Character and Story Facts: Over 110,000 Details from 1,008 Shows, 1945-1992.* Jefferson, North Carolina: McFarland & Company, Inc., Publishers, 1993, pp. 390-391, 461.

Weinraub, Bernard. " 'Perfect World' Finds Imperfect Reception At the Box Office." The *New York Times*, January 10, 1994.

Texas Ranger Filmography

1910   *The Ranger's Bride*
        Starring: William "Bronco Billy" Anderson
1911   *The Border Ranger*
        Starring: William "Bronco Billy" Anderson
1912   *The Ranger and His Horse*
        Starring: William Duncan
        Studio: Selig
1914   *The Ranger's Romance*
        Starring: Tom Mix
        Studio: Selig
1918   *Heart of the Southwest*
        Director: Frank Powell
        Studio: Goldwyn
1918   *The Ranger*
1919   *The Lone Star Ranger*
        Starring: Charles Clary, William Farnum, Frederick
        Herzog, Lamar Johnstone, Tom London, Louise Lovely, G.
        Raymond Nye, Irene Rich
        Note: First screen adaptation of Zane Grey's novel, a book
        dedicated to the Texas Rangers.
1921   *The Ranger and the Law*
        Starring: Lester Cuneo, Walter I. McCloud, Francelia
        Billington, Clark Comstock
1922   *The Big Ranger*
1922   *The Ranger's Reward*
1923   *The Footlight Ranger*
1923   *King's Creek Law*
1923   *The Lone Star Ranger*
        Starring: Tom Mix
        Note: Second version of Zane Grey's classic.
1925   *The Fighting Ranger*
        Starring: Charles Avery, Slim Cole, Jack Dougherty
1925   *One Shot Ranger*
        Starring: Pete Morrison and Betty Godwin

1925   *Ranger Bill*
        Starring: Dick Carter and Dorothy Woods
1925   *Rider of the Painted Horse*
1925   *Riders of the Purple Sage*
        Starring: Tom Mix
1926   *Ahead of the Law*
1926   *Daredevil's Reward*
1926   *The Fighting Ranger*
1927   *Outlaws of Red River*
        Starring: Tom Mix, Marjorie Daw
        Note: "Gerald Beaumont's Drama of the Fighting Texas
        Rangers."
1927   *Rambling Ranger*
        Starring: Jack Hoxie, Dorothy Gulliver, C.E. Anderson
1928   *Law of the Range*
1928   *The Ranger's Oath*
        Starring: Al Hoxie, L.V. Jefferson, Jack Draper
1929   *Rio Rita*
        Starring: Bebe Daniels, John Boles
        Note: When Ranger Captain James Stewart chases an out-
        law called "The Kinkajou" across the Rio Grande into
        Mexico, he becomes enamored with the lovely Rita. Prob-
        lem is, her brother is the bad guy.
1930   *Last of the Duanes*
        Starring: George O'Brien, Lucile Brown, Myrna Loy
        Studio: Fox
        Note: Based on Zane Grey's novel.
1930   *The Lone Star Ranger*
        Starring: George O'Brien, Sue Carol, Walter McGrail,
        Warren Hymer, Russell Simpson, Roy Stewart
        Studio: Fox
        Note: Third version of Zane Grey's novel, but the first
        version with sound.
1931   *Border Law*
        Starring: Buck Jones, Lupita Tovar, James Mason, Frank
        Rice
        Studio: Columbia
        Note: When outlaw Shag Smith kills a Ranger's brother,
        the Ranger and a colleague quit the force so they can join
        the outlaw's gang in Mexico. Their plan is to lure Smith

and his fellow brigands back to Texas—and Ranger justice.

1931   *The Cisco Kid*
Starring: Warner Baxter, Nora Lane, Edmund Lowe, Chrispin Martin, Willard Robertson, Douglas Haig, Charles Stevens, Conchita Montengro
Studio: Fox
Note: This screenplay was based on "The Caballero's Way," a short story by William Sydney Porter, who used the pen name of O. Henry. See *Texas Ranger Tales*, Volume 1.

1931   *Lasca of the Rio Grande*
Starring: Leo Carrillo, John Mack Brown, Dorothy Burgess
Studio: Universal

1931   *The Texas Ranger*
Starring: Buck Jones, Carmelita Geraghty, Fred Burns, Harry M. Woods, Jim Corey
Studio: Beverly Productions/Columbia
Note: An undercover Ranger is discovered and faces lynching.

1932   *Come on, Danger*
Starring: Tom Keene, Julie Haydon, Roscoe Ates
Studio: RKO-Radio
Note: When the Ranger learns the killer he seeks is a woman, can he bring her in?

1932   *Riders of the Desert*

1932   *Riders of the Purple Sage*
Starring: George O'Brien, Marguerite Churchill, Noah Beery
Studio: Fox
Note: Another Zane Grey classic.

1933   *King of the Arena*
Starring: Ken Maynard, Lucile Browne, John St. Polis
Studio: Universal
Note: Rangers face an outlaw called "Black Death." He shoots chemical bullets that turn victims black in the process of killing them. But in the end, old-fashioned Ranger lead takes care of "Black Death."

1933   *Man of Action*

1933   *The Ranger's Code*
Starring: Bob Steele, Doris Hill, George Hayes, George
Nash, Ernie Adams, Ed Brady, Hal Price, Dick Dickinson,
Frank Ball
Studio: Monogram

1934   *The Dude Ranger*
Starring: George O'Brien, Irene Hervey, Syd Saylor,
LeRoy Mason
Studio: Principal/Fox
Note: Story by Zane Grey.

1934   *The Fighting Ranger*
Starring: Buck Jones, Dorothy Revier, Frank Rice, Bradley
Page, Ward Bond
Studio: Columbia
Note: Bond later starred in the TV Western "Wagon
Train."

1934   *Gun Justice*
Starring: Ken Maynard, Cecilia Parker, Hooper Atchley,
Walter Miller
Studio: Universal

1934   *Miracle Rider*
Starring: Tom Mix, Joan Gale, Charles Middleton, Jason
Robards
Studio: Mascot
Note: This 15-part serial was Tom Mix's last movie. He
was killed in a traffic crash shortly after its filming. See
Texas Ranger Tales, Volume 1.

1935   *Cyclone Ranger*
Starring: Bill Cody, Nena Quartero, Eddie Gribbon
Studio: Spectrum
Note: Even cattle rustlers sometimes try to clean up their
act. But they get in trouble again when they end up at a
ranch where the blind owner thinks one of them killed her
son.

1935   *Rough Riding Ranger*
Starring: Rex Lease, Bobby Nelson, Janet Chandler,
Yakima Canutt
Studio: Merrick/Superior

1936   *Drift Fence*
Starring: Larry "Buster" Crabbe, Katherine DeMille, Tom

Keense
Studio: Paramount
Note: Later re-released as *Texas Desperadoes*.

1936 *The Kid Ranger*
Starring: Bob Steele, Joan Barclay, Earl Dwire, William Farnum, Charles King, Lafe McKee, Frank Ball, Reesty Adams.

1936 *Ride, Ranger, Ride*
Starring: Gene Autry, Smiley Burrnette, The Tennessee Ramblers
Studio: Republic
Note: Ranger goes undercover to escort an Army wagon train laden with ammunition and supplies. Military does not take him seriously until the Comanches attack.

1936 *The Texas Rangers*
Starring: Fred MacMurray, Jack Oakie, Jean Parker, Lloyd Nolan, Edward Ellis, Bennie Bartlett, Elena Martinez, Frank Shannon, George Hayes, Fred Kohler, Hank Bell
Studio: Paramount

1936 *The Unknown Ranger*
Starring: Robert Allen, Martha Tibbets, Hal Taliaferro, Harry Woods, Robert Henry
Studio: Columbia
Note: In the first of a series of Ranger movies starring Allen, he hires on as a cowboy on the Wright ranch to get to the bottom of a major rustling problem. The Ranger discovers the rustler is actually a horse.

1936 *Whistling Bullets*
1937 *Galloping Dynamite*
1937 *Guns of the Pecos*
1937 *The Gun Ranger*
Starring: Bob Steele, Eleanor Stewart, John Merton, Ernie Adams
Studio: Republic
Note: Ranger gets his man but a crooked politician frees the accused murderer. Ranger removes his badge and proceeds to eliminate killers and crooked politicians.

1937 *Law of the Ranger*
Starring: Robert Allen, Elaine Shepard, Hal Taliaferro
Studio: Columbia

Note: Rangers Bob and Wally work undercover to break
up the Nash gang.

1937   *Ranger Courage*
Starring: Robert Allen, Martha Tibbets, Walter Miller
Studio: Columbia
Note: The Rangers are called on to protect a wagon train.

1937   *The Rangers Step In*
Starring: Robert Allen, Eleanor Stewart, Jay Wilsey
Studio: Columbia
Note: The Rangers settle a feud.

1937   *The Reckless Ranger*
Starring: Robert Allen, Louise Small, Jack Perrin
Studio: Columbia

1937   *Rio Grande Ranger*
Starring: Robert Allen, Iris Meredith, Hal Taliaferro
Studio: Columbia

1938   *Code of the Rangers*
Starring: Zeke Clemens, Judith Ford, Kit Guard, Frank La
Rue, Rex Lease, Tim McCoy, Wheeler Oakman, Roger
Williams
Studio: Monogram

1938   *Come On, Rangers!*
Starring: Roy Rogers, Mary Hart, Raymond Hatton, J.
Farrell MacDonald
Studio: Republic
Note: Rangers team up with U.S. Army to combat outlaws.
Among other titles, Rogers sings "I've Learned a Lot about
Women."

1938   *The Little Ranger*

1938   *The Lone Ranger*
Starring: Lee Powell as the Lone Ranger, Chief Thunder-
cloud as Tonto, and the horse "Silver Chief" as "Silver"
Studio: Republic
Note: A 15-chapter serial based on Fran Striker's radio
classic.

1938   *Man's Country*

1938   *Phantom Ranger*
Starring: Tim McCoy, Suzanne Kaaren, John St. Polis,
Karl Hackett
Studio: Monogram

1938   *The Ranger's Roundup*
        Starring: Fred Scott, Al St. John, Christine McIntyre, Earle Hodgins
        Studio: Spectrum

1938   *Renegade Ranger*
        Starring: George O'Brien, Rita Hayworth, Tim Holt, Ray Whitley
        Studio: RKO
        Note: Ranger Jack Steele rides out after Judith Alvarez, lady gang leader battling crooked politicians.

1939   *The Lone Ranger Rides Again*
        Starring: Robert Livingston as the Lone Ranger, Chief Thundercloud as Tonto
        Studio: Republic
        Note: Another 15-chapter Lone Ranger serial.

1939   *The Return of the Cisco Kid*
        Starring: Warner Baxter, Lynn Bari, Cesar Romero, Henry Hull
        Studio: 20th Century Fox
        Note: O. Henry's short story of a gunfight between an outlaw and a Ranger catapulted the outlaw, not the Ranger, into fame.

1940   *Buzzy Rides the Range*

1940   *The Man from Tumbleweeds*
        Starring: Bill Elliott, Dub Taylor, Iris Meredith
        Studio: Columbia

1940   *Northwest Mounted Police*
        Starring: Gary Cooper, Madeleine Carroll, Paulette Goddard, Preston Foster
        Studio: Paramount
        Note: The title correctly implies a Canadian setting, but Gary Cooper plays a Texas Ranger on the trail of a killer. This was Cecile B. de Mille's first color film.

1940   *Rangers of Fortune*
        Starring: Fred MacMurray, Patricia Morison, Albert Dekker
        Studio: Paramount

1940   *The Ranger and the Lady*
        Starring: Roy Rogers, George "Gabby" Hayes, Julie Bishop, Harry Wends, Henry Brandon, Noble Johnson

Studio: Republic

Note: Rogers plays a singing Ranger who comes to the assistance of a lady wagon train boss.

1940   *Rocky Mountain Rangers*

Starring: Robert Livingston, Raymond Hatton, Duncan Renaldo

Studio: Republic

Note: Part of the *Three Mesquiteers* series.

1940   *The Texas Rangers Ride Again*

Starring: John Howard, Ellen Drew, Akin Tamiroff, May Robson, Broderick Crawford, May Robson, Charley Grapewin

Studio: Paramount

Screenplay: William R. Lipman and Horace McCoy

Director: James Hogan

Note: Rangers investigate whereabouts of a large herd of missing cattle. As the promotional copy put it, "daring rescues, shootouts and hoof-pounding chases."

1940   *Two-Fisted Rangers*

Starring: Pat Brady, Bill Cody Jr., Dick Curtis, Kenneth R. MacDonald, Iris Meredith, Bob Nolan, Charles Starrett, Wally Wales

Studio: Columbia

1941   *Dead or Alive*

1941   *Desert Bandit*

Starring: Don Barry, Lynn Merrick, William Haade

Studio: Republic

1941   *Desert Patrol*

1941   *Dynamite Canyon*

Starring: Tom Keene, Evelyn Finley, Slim Andrews

Studio: Monogram

1941   *King of the Texas Rangers*

Starring: Sammy Baugh, Duncan Renaldo, Neil Hamilton, Pauline Moore

Studio: Republic Pictures

Note: Modern Rangers face Nazi spies based in a dirigible above Texas in this 12-chapter serial. Former football star "Slingin'" Sammy Baugh plays Texas Ranger Sergeant Tom King. Get it? King, of the Texas Rangers.

1941   *Last of the Duanes*
Starring: George Montgomery, Lynne Roberts, Eve Arden, Francis Ford
Studio: 20th Century Fox
Note: Screen version of a Zane Grey work.

1941   *Rawhide Rangers*
Starring: Johnny Mack Brown, Fuzzy Knight, Nell O'Day
Studio: Universal

1941   *Riders of the Badlands*
Starring: Charles Starrett, Russell Hayden, Cliff Edwards, Ilene Brewer
Studio: Columbia

1941   *Riders of the Purple Sage*
Note: Screen version of a Zane Grey work.

1941   *Rollin' Home to Texas*

1942   *Bandit Ranger*
Starring: Tim Holt, Cliff Edwards, Joan Barclay, Kenneth Harlan
Studio: RKO

1942   *Come On, Danger!*
Starring: Tim Holt, Frances Neal, Ray Whitley
Studio: RKO
Note: Remake of 1932 movie with same title.

1942   *Down Rio Grande Way*

1942   *Down Texas Way*

1942   *The Lone Star Ranger*
Starring: John Kimbrough, Sheila Ryan, Jonathan Hale, William Farnum
Studio: 20th Century Fox
Note: Another incarnation of Zane Grey's Ranger novel.

1942   *Riders of the Northland*

1943   *Bad Men of Thunder Gap*

1943   *Beyond the Last Frontier*

1943   *Fighting Valley*
Starring: John Elliott, Charles King

1943   *Hail to the Rangers*
Starring: Ernie Adams, Ted Adams, Leota Atcher, Robert Owen Atcher, Lloyd Bridges, Davison Clark, Arthur Hunnicutt, Jack Kirk, Tom London, Charles Starrett,

Norman Willis
Studio: Columbia

1943   *Rangers Take Over*
Starring: James Newill, Dave O'Brien, Guy Wilkerson,
Forrest Taylor, I. Stanford Jolley, Iris Meredith
Studio: PRC

1943   *The Return of the Rangers*
Starring: Richard Alexander, Robert Barron, Henry Hall,
Harry Harvey, I. Stanford Jolley, Charles King, Emmett
Lynn, James Newill, Dave O'Brien, Nell O'Day, Glenn
Strange, Guy Wilkerson
Studio: PRC

1943   *Thundering Trails*
1943   *West of Texas*
Starring: Dave O'Brien, Jim Newill, Guy Wilkerson,
Frances Gladwin
Studio: PRC

1944   *Cyclone Prairie Rangers*
Starring: Charles Starrett, Dub Taylor, Constance Worth,
Jimmy Davis
Studio: Columbia

1944   *Guns of the Law*
1944   *Gunsmoke Mesa*
1944   *Outlaw Roundup*
1944   *Spook Town*
Starring: Dave O'Brien, Jim Newill, Guy Wilkerson, Mady
Lawrence
Studio: PRC

1944   *Trail of Terror*
1944   *Whispering Skull*
Starring: Dave O'Brien, Tex Ritter, Guy Wilkerson, Denny
Burke
Studio: PRC

1945   *Along the Navajo Trail*
Starring: Roy Rogers, George Hayes, Dale Evans, Estelita
Rodriguez
Studio: Republic

1945   *Enemy of the Law*
1945   *Flaming Bullets*
Starring: Tex Ritter, Dave O'Brien, Guy Wilkerson,

Patricia Knox
Studio: PRC

1945   *Frontier Fugitives*
Starring: Dave O'Brien, Tex Ritter, Lorraine Miller, Guy Wilkerson
Studio: PRC

1945   *Lone Texas Ranger*
Starring: Bill Elliott, Bobby Blake, Alice Fleming, Roy Barcroft, Helen Talbot
Studio: Republic

1945   *Marked for Murder*

1945   *Three in the Saddle*
Starring: Dave O'Brien, Tex Ritter, Guy Wilkerson
Studio: PRC

1946   *Roaring Rangers*
Starring: Charles Starrett, Smiley Burnette, Adelle Roberts
Studio: Columbia

1947   *Red Hot Rangers*

1947   *Ridin' Down the Trail*

1948   *Gallant Legion*
Starring: William "Wild Bill" Elliott, Lorna Gray, Joseph Schildkraut, Bruce Cabot, Andy Devine, Jack Holt
Studio: Republic
Note: In this story by John K. Butler and Gerald Geraghty the Rangers save Texas from an evil-minded separatist.

1948   *The Fighting Ranger*
Starring: Johnny Mack Brown, Raymond Hatton, Marshall Reed, Christine Larson, Steve Clark, Milburn Morante
Studio: Monogram

1948   *The Rangers Ride*
Starring: Jimmy Walker, Dub Taylor, Virginia Belmont, Riley Hill
Studio: Monogram

1949   *Ranger of the Cherokee Strip*
Starring: Monte Hale, Paul Hurst, Alice Talton, Roy Barcroft
Studio: Republic

1949   *Riders of the Whistling Pines*
Starring: Gene Autry, Patricia White, Jimmy Lloyd,

Douglass Dumbrille
Studio: Columbia
1949　*South of Rio*
1949　*Streets of Laredo*
Starring: William Holden, MacDonald Carey, William
Bendix, Mona Freeman
Studio: Paramount
Note: A remake of King Vidor's *The Texas Rangers.*
1950　*Border Rangers*
Starring: Don Barry, Robert Lowery, Wally Vernon,
Pamela Blake
Studio: Lippert
1950　*Colorado Ranger*
Starring: Jimmy Ellison, Russell Hayden, Fuzzy Knight
Studio: Lippert
1950　*Guns of Justice*
1950　*Law of the Badlands*
1951　*Prairie Roundup*
1951　*The Texas Rangers: The Lone Wolf Watchdogs of the Lone
Star State*
Starring: George Montgomery, Gale Storm, Jerome
Courtland, Noah Beery Jr., William Bishop, Douglas
Kennedy
Studio: Columbia Pictures
Note: Fictional treatment—very—of the Sam Bass story.
1951　*My Outlaw Brother*
Starring: Mickey Rooney, Robert Stack
Studio: Eagle Lion
1951　*Ridin' the Outlaw Trail*
1952　*Night Stage to Galveston*
Starring: Gene Autry, Pat Buttram, Virginia Huston,
Thurston Hall
Studio: Columbia
Note: Gene Autry plays a singing Ranger.
1953　*Star of Texas*
Starring: Wayne Morris, Paul Fix, Frank Ferguson
Studio: Westwood/Allied Artists
1953　*Winning of the West*
Starring: Gene Autry, Gail Davis, Smiley Burnette
Studio: Columbia

1955 *The Lone Ranger*
Starring: Clayton Moore as the Lone Ranger, Jay Silverheels as Tonto
Studio: Warner Brothers
Note: The Lone Ranger and his faithful Indian companion appear in color for the first time.

1956 *The Searchers*
Starring: John Wayne, Jeffrey Hunter, Vera Miles, Ward Bond
Studio: Warner Brothers
Note: Considered by many to be one of the best Westerns ever.

1958 *The Lone Ranger and the Lost City of Gold*
Starring: Clayton Moore, Jay Silverheels
Studio: United Artists
Note: The Lone Ranger and Tonto solve the mysterious murders of three Indians wearing gold medallions.

1959 *Frontier Rangers*

1960 *Seven Ways from Sundown*
Starring: Audie Murphy, Barry Sullivan
Studio: Universal

1961 *The Last Rebel*

1966 *Lonesome Ranger*

1968 *Three Guns for Texas*
Starring: Neville Brand, Peter Brown, William Smith
Studio: Universal
Note: Television feature film.

1969 *The Great Bank Robbery*
Starring: Zero Mostel, Kim Novak, Clint Walker
Studio: Warner Brothers

1969 *The Over-the-Hill Gang*
Starring: Walter Brennan, Pat O'Brien, Edgar Buchanan
Note: Brennan plays former Texas Ranger Captain Hagues in this made-for-TV movie.

1970 *The Over-the-Hill-Gang Rides Again*
Starring: Walter Brennan, Fred Astaire, Edgar Buchanan
Studio: ABC
Note: Made-for-TV movie sequel to *The Over-the-Hill Gang*.

1974   *The Rangers*
        Starring: James G. Richardson, Colby Chester
        Studio: NBC TV
        Note: Made-for-TV movie.

1974   *The Sugarland Express*
        Starring: Goldie Hawn, Ben Johnson, Michael Sacks,
        William Atherton
        Studio: Universal
        Notes: Based on a true story, the 1969 abduction of a
        Texas Department of Public Safety Highway Patrol
        Trooper. The only Ranger aspect to this movie is that a
        Ranger fires the shot that kills the bad guy.

1976   *The Town That Dreaded Sundown*
        Starring: Ben Johnson, Andrew Prine
        Studio: American-International
        Note: Loosely based on the unsolved 1946 Phantom Mur-
        der case in Texarkana, Texas. See *Texas Ranger Tales*,
        Volume 1.

1981   *The Legend of the Lone Ranger*
        Starring: Klinton Spilsbury as the Lone Ranger, Michael
        Horse as Tonto
        Note: A new generation gets to see the Lone Ranger story
        on the big screen.

1981   *The Texas Rangers*
        Note: Made-for-TV movie.

1982   *The Ballad of Gregorio Cortez*
        Starring: Edward James Olmos, Barry Corbin, E.W.
        Patterson, Moctezuma Esparza
        Director: Robert Young
        Note: Written by Victor Villasenor as an adaptation of *With
        His Pistol in His Hand* by Americo Paredes.

1983   *Lone Wolf McQuade*
        Starring: Chuck Norris
        Note: This movie, in which Norris plays a Ranger profi-
        cient in the martial arts, was the genesis of his television
        series hit *Walker, Texas Ranger*, which premiered in 1993.

1986   *Texas Chainsaw Massacre 2*

1987   *Extreme Prejudice*
        Starring: Nick Nolte

Note: Nolte plays Texas Ranger Jack Benteen in this movie filmed in and around El Paso.

1989   *Lonesome Dove*
Starring: Robert Duvall, Tommy Lee Jones, Angelica Huston
Note: The acclaimed made-for-TV miniseries based on Larry McMurtry's Pulitzer-prize winning novel.

1990   *A Pair of Aces*
Starring: Kris Kristofferson, Willie Nelson
Note: Made-for-TV movie aired on CBS Jan. 14, 1990. Shot in Austin.

1992   *Another Pair of Aces*
Starring: Kris Kristofferson, Rip Torn, Willie Nelson
Note: Kristofferson as Texas Ranger Captain "Rip" Metcalf, Rip Torn as Captain Jack Parsons, and Willie Nelson as Billy Roy

1993   *A Perfect World*
Starring: Kevin Costner, Clint Eastwood, Laura Dern
Studio: Warner Brothers

1994   *One Riot, One Ranger*

1995   *Ranger!*

Sources

Adams, Les and Buck Rainey. *Shoot-Em-Ups: The Complete Reference Guide to Westerns of the Sound Era.* New Rochelle, N.Y.: Arlington House Publishers, 1978.

Baer, D. Richard. *The Film Buff's Checklist of Motion Pictures (1912-1979).* Hollywood, CA: Hollywood Film Archive, 1979.

Graham, Don. *Cowboys and Cadillacs: How Hollywood Looks at Texas.* Austin: Texas Monthly Press, 1983.

The Internet Movie Database, Ltd.

Sublett, Jesse. "Lone on the Range: Texas Lawmen of Lore." www.texasmonthly.com, 1997.

Texas Ranger Reunions

Texas Ranger Battalion 1897-1899

1897   Austin (October 4)
1898   Dallas
1899   San Antonio (November 30)

Ex-Texas Ranger Association 1920-1951

1920	Weatherford (August 10)	1936	Santa Anna/Dallas
1921	Weatherford (August 11-12)	1937	Santa Anna (August 3-5)
1922	Comanche (August 3-4)	1938	Coleman (June 16-18)
1923	Menard (September 6-8)	1939	Santa Anna
1924	Menard (late August)	1940	Santa Anna
1925	Ranger (August 12-14)	1941	Santa Anna (June)
1926	Ranger (August 11-13)	1942	Santa Anna (June 26-27)
1927	Menard	1943	Santa Anna
1928	Colorado City	1944	Santa Anna (August)
1929	San Saba (July 3-5)	1945	Santa Anna
1930	Eastland (August 10)	1946	Santa Anna
1931	San Angelo (July 22-24)	1947	Santa Anna (August 4-5)
1932	(Information lacking)	1948	Santa Anna
1933	Comanche	1949	Santa Anna
1934	Brownwood (July 19-21)	1950	Santa Anna (June 9-10)
1935	Santa Anna	1951	Santa Anna (July 17-18)

Notes

Though the dates for some of the reunions are lacking, they always were held in the summer.

The ex-Rangers may not have met in 1932, which was during the depth of the Depression, but that is only conjecture.

Index

281

Index